TREKKING IN
CHINA

- 50 SELECTED ROUTES -

AUTHOR | **TUBUBANG**

TREKKING IN CHINA

ISBN   978-1-967799-47-3
Library of Congress Control Number   2025918804

First Printing 2025
Maps & Photography
Tububang

Published by
Asian Culture Press, LLC
1942 Broadway,
Suite 314C,
Boulder, CO 80302,
United States.

www.tububang-outdoors.com

Bring a Different China to you!

Real China is not found in the modern,

crowded city attractions,

but in the wild places only trekking can reach.

It demands that we leave our comfort zone,

bravely take that extra step into the mountains and wilds of China,

to feel the rhythm of nature and listen for the whispers of the past.

PREFACE

The China You Haven't Seen

China – this ancient and mysterious land of the East – what is it really like?

People often say that to understand China, you must visit the Forbidden City in Beijing, the Terracotta Warriors in Xi'an, the Bund in Shanghai, the picturesque landscapes of Guilin, the pandas in Sichuan, or the Hongya Cave in Chongqing... Of course, these bustling cities are one side of China. But if you want to see a more authentic and awe-inspiring China, you need to shift your gaze away from the towering skyscrapers and turn instead to the vast mountains and countryside. You'll discover that the true China is hidden in the folds of a 1:50,000 scale map, quietly waiting for every brave explorer to uncover its secrets.

China's vast land of 9.6 million square kilometers is not only the cradle of Chinese civilization, but also a natural outdoor paradise meticulously sculpted by Mother Nature. Every inch of its terrain tells stories of millions of years of dramatic change and enduring legends. From the towering snow-capped peaks of the Roof of the World to the lush tropical rainforests, from the grand and desolate deserts to the winding, picturesque coastlines, from the tranquil depths of primeval forests to the boundless, sweeping grasslands – China encompasses nearly every type of landform found on Earth, and nurtures a stunning diversity of local cultures and traditions. Each night, as the neon lights of Shanghai's Lujiazui sparkle in unison with the flickering butter lamps along Lhasa's Barkhor Street, the dual nature of this nation is revealed: one side racing forward with modern civilization, the other unfolding slowly with the timeless rhythm of its mountains and rivers.

From 2014 to 2025, "Trekking in China" has spent 11 years exploring places unreachable by wheels, measuring the land step by step. As one of the leading outdoor media platforms and clubs in China, we've led more than 50,000 people in various hiking activities. We know where China's most breathtaking landscapes are—and we're eager to share them with more people. That's why this book was created. In it, we've carefully selected 50 of the most representative and captivating trekking routes across China. Each one is the result of countless on-the-ground explorations and meticulous selection by our professional team.

Opening this book is like unfolding three dimensions of China: a matrix of geographical wonders, a cultural amber preserving ancient civilization, and a real China often obscured by internet algorithms. From the towering, snow-covered peaks that touch the clouds, to the lush, vibrant tropical rainforests; from vast, smoke-threaded deserts to endless, green grasslands—China is home to some of the most extreme and awe-inspiring natural landscapes on Earth. This is not just a simple route guide, nor merely a book. Hidden trails erased by navigation apps, ancient rock paintings overlooked by tourist buses, and starry skies dimmed by city neon—all are brought back to life across these 50 Trekking routes.

The towering peaks of the Himalayas pierce the clouds, as if whispering tales of eternal solitude to the heavens. The depth and grandeur of the Yarlung Tsangpo Grand Canyon reveal nature's astonishing craftsmanship. Crossing the Badain Jaran Desert, the undulating sand dunes shimmer with golden light under the sun. Trekking through Tiger Leaping Gorge, the roaring Jinsha River crashes fiercely between steep canyon walls. On the vast Hulunbeir grasslands, endless green meadows stretch to meet the blue sky and drifting white clouds. And in the ancient towns of the South Yangtze River region, the scenery unfolds like a poetic ink painting brought to life—graceful, serene, and timeless. These breathtaking natural landscapes, each with their own unique allure, continue to captivate countless outdoor enthusiasts.

Beyond the breathtaking natural landscapes, these hiking routes also connect to a rich and profound tapestry of history and culture.

On the pilgrimage trails of Ali, you'll encounter devout pilgrims and feel the mystery and solemnity of Tibetan Buddhism. Walking along The Ancient Tea Horse Road, the deep hoofprints embedded in the stone paths speak of past prosperity and hardship—you can almost picture the mule caravans crossing mountains and valleys on their long journeys. Entering the hidden realms of western Hunan, you'll discover ancient stilted houses, mysterious Nuo opera, and the distinctive customs of the Miao people, offering a living glimpse into the memories depicted by writer Shen Congwen. In the Stone City, every rock bears witness to a brilliant fragment of history and the passage of time. Trekking in China is not just a physical journey—it's a ritual of decoding civilization, allowing you to trace the threads of history and experience the enduring legacy of culture with every step.

As a professional team with over eleven years of experience in China's outdoor adventure scene, TrekkinginChina has earned the trust of tens of thousands of hiking enthusiasts through its expertise and high-quality service. We offer more than 150 well-established hiking routes across the globe—including iconic trails within China as well as popular destinations abroad. Each route is carefully planned and designed to ensure a unique and unforgettable experience. Our team of hundreds of professional guides are true experts—deeply familiar with the local environment, culture, and trails. Not only are they highly skilled in outdoor navigation and safety, but they also bring each journey to life by sharing the stories and history along the way, making your hiking adventure all the more vivid and meaningful.

We understand that every hiking enthusiast carries a deep yearning for the unknown and a genuine love for nature. That's why we are committed to combining the thrill of exploration with safe, comfortable, and thoughtful service—so you can leave behind worries about the unknown or the challenges ahead and simply enjoy the pure joy of hiking. Whether you're a seasoned trekker or a first-time adventurer, we tailor each journey to suit your needs and abilities. Our goal is to help you create unforgettable memories as you explore the hidden wonders of the East.

Trekking itself is never easy, especially when trekking through China. Along the way, you may face numerous challenges—battling the scorching sun, braving the wind and rain, walking along long and rugged mountain paths, or camping in remote wilderness. But it is precisely because of these hardships that when you finally witness the breathtaking landscapes ahead, you'll feel that every step was worth it. After all, the true China isn't found in the repetitive city landmarks, but in the wild, untamed areas that can only be reached on foot. It requires us to step out of our comfort zones, to boldly take that "extra step," and venture into China's mountains and forests, to feel the breath of nature and listen to the echoes of history.

We hope that this book, imbued with the landscapes of China, will serve as a key, unlocking a whole new world for you—one where you can discover a different side of China and uncover the beauty and charm of this blue planet.

Finally, it's worth mentioning that this is not a perfect handbook. The book deliberately retains some "imperfections," such as reminders on the Yadin Line about "watching out for altitude sickness," or on the Wusun Ancient Road about "river crossing dangers"... But we insist on keeping these awkward details, because we believe that true adventure is never about eliminating risks; it's about learning to maintain a deep respect for nature.

Now, join us and embark on your own unique adventure in this eastern county! We also hope that one day in the future, we will meet in the mountains and wilderness of China, and that these trekking routes will become beautiful memories of China for you.

Ma Jun
2025.9

CATALOG

Overview

Part 1/Northwest China Region

Part 2/Southwest China Region

Image | ©Majun

overview

Activity Difficulty Assessment Criteria

We have selected five dimensions as evaluation criteria: the highest elevation along the route, the longest daily hiking distance, the maximum daily vertical ascent, trail conditions, and weather conditions. Each dimension is rated on a scale from 1 to 5 points.

1.The Highest Elevation Along the Route
Below 3,000 meters: 1 point
3,000-4,000 meters: 2 points
4,000-5,000 meters: 3 points
5,000-6,000 meters: 4 points
Above 6,000 meters: 5 points

2.The Longest Daily Hiking Distance
Below 10 kilometers: 1 point
10-15 kilometers: 2 points
15-20 kilometers: 3 points
20-25 kilometers: 4 points
Above 25 kilometers: 5 points

3.The Maximum Daily Vertical Ascent
Below 300 meters: 1 point
300-600 meters: 2 points
600-900 meters: 3 points
900-1,200 meters: 4 points
Above 1,200 meters: 5 points

4.Trail Conditions
Gentle paths: 1 point
Safe mountain trails: 2 points
Steep mountain paths: 3 points
Sections with hazards: 4 points
Requires technical equipment: 5 points

5.Weather Conditions
Basically no impact on activity: 1 point
Some impact: 2 points
Significant impact: 3 points
Major impact: 4 points
Decisive impact: 5 points

The final rating is not simply the sum of points but reflects a comprehensive assessment of multiple factors.

Experience Overview of Different Ratings

One-Star Activities
- Minimal hiking, easy activity
- Daily hiking distance not exceed 10 kilometers
- Daily ascent not exceed 500 meters
- Continuous hiking time not exceed 3 hours in one day

Two-Star Activities
- Primarily hiking-based, slightly difficult
- Well-established routes, essentially risk-free
- Suitable for beginners

Three-Star Activities
- Intensive hiking activities, somewhat difficult
- Low risk, no formidable challenge
- Suitable for experienced hikers

Four-Star Activities
- Fairly difficut hiking activities
- Long distance or high elevation
- Risk-involved
- Significantly affected by weather and trail conditions
- Suitable for hikers who enjoy challenging themselves

Five-Star Activities
- Highly difficult and intensive hiking and mountaineering activities
- Severe natural conditions in most cases
- Highly risky
- Considerable uncertainties
- Suitable for hikers with good physical fitness, rich experience, and a love for challenges

All the hiking routes in this book are rated based on the criteria above, with their difficulty levels clearly indicated. Whether you're a beginner hiker or an experienced trekker, you'll find suitable trails here!

We encourage everyone to take it step by step, starting with easier routes, gradually progressing, and eventually hiking across the globe!

PART 1

NORTHWEST
China Region

01. Badain Jaran Desert
[巴丹吉林沙漠, Bādān Jílín Shāmò]

5days
18km

Zhangye
[张掖, Zhāngyè]
Gathering City

8KM
Longest Single-Day Hike

400M
Maximum Daily Elevation Gain

1,611M
Highest Elevation Along the Route

★★★★
Scenic Rating

★★
Difficulty Level

Credit
© All images in this piece
by RK

The Badain Jaran Desert is located in the western part of the Inner Mongolia Autonomous Region, at the southwestern edge of the Inner Mongolian Plateau. It spans across the Ejina Banner (额济纳旗, Éjìnà Qí) and the Alxa Right Banner (阿拉善右旗, Ālāshàn Yòuqí). Covering an area of 49,200 square kilometers, it stretches 270 kilometers from east to west and 240 kilometers from north to south. As the world's third-largest desert and China's second-largest, it is a vast and unique landscape.

Natural Features
The towering sand dunes are a defining feature of the Badain Jaran Desert. Shaped by powerful northwest and southwest winds, these dunes have created many unique sand mountains, typically ranging from 200 to 300 meters in height, with the tallest reaching an impressive 500 meters—making the Badain Jaran Desert home to the world's tallest dunes. Notably, the desert is also characterized by numerous pyramid-shaped dunes, formed when strong winds blowing from different directions. As several powerful air currents of equal strength compete to deposit sand particles in the same location, these magnificent, towering pyramid-shaped dunes emerge.

This region is home to the world's largest singing sand area. As you walk through the Badain Jaran Desert, the sand mountains "sing" in harmony with the wind, creating an eerie, melodic sound. Visitors often feel as though they are stepping back a thousand years in time. In the solitude of this vast desert, one cannot help but recall the mysterious legends that surround the place. Could the treasures left behind by the fleeting Tangut people (党项人, Dǎngxiàng Rén) of the Western Xia Dynasty still lie hidden here? And where, exactly, is the fabled ancient city of Tongjing (古潼京, Gǔ Tóngjīng), mentioned in the popular novel, *The Grave Robbers' Chronicles* (盗墓笔记, Dàomù Bǐji)?

While deserts are often called "forbidden zones for life," the extremely arid Badain Jaran Desert presents the remarkable phenomenon of sand dunes coexisting with lakes. According to Professor Chen Jiansheng (陈建生, Chén Jiànshēng), Director of the Hydrology Research Institute at Hohai University, the annual groundwater recharge in the Badain Jaran Desert amounts to hundreds of millions of cubic meters.

Scientists, both from China and abroad, have proposed various theories about the source of this groundwater. Some suggest it originates from the Qilian Mountains (祁连山, Qílián Shān) through subterranean faults, while others believe it flows from the Yarlung Tsangpo River (雅鲁藏布江, Yǎlǔ Zàngbù Jiāng). Although no definitive conclusion has been reached, this abundant groundwater continues to sustain the vast desert landscape.

Cultural Significance

"Badain Jaran" is a transliteration from Mongolian. The name "Badain" evolved from "Badai" (巴岱, Bādài), which is believed to be named after a person who supposedly lived in the area in ancient times. There are two interpretations of the word "Jaran." One suggests it is derived from the Tibetan word "Zherang" (哲让, Zhéràng), meaning "hell." The other interpretation refers to the number sixty, as people discovered sixty lakes within the region when naming it.

The Badain Jaran Desert is dotted with 114 lakes, which are called "Haizi" (海子, literally "small seas"). Among these lakes hidden deep in desert, one type stands out as particularly rare and unusual—those with distinctively pink (or reddish) waters, referred to as "Rose Lakes" or locally as "Red Haizi" (红海子, Hóng Hǎizi). Under specific conditions, these lakes can display vibrant shades of pink and purple, creating a breathtaking sight, with the most intense pink color emerging only during the height of summer.

The vivid colors of these lakes are believed to be caused by trace elements in the water. For example, lakes with a pink hue have high concentrations of potassium ions, while those with a green tint are rich in magnesium ions. Many of these lakes remain unnamed and are not marked on maps; only local drivers familiar with the area know how to find them..

1 Dagetu
[达格图, Dágétú]

The most popular pink lake in the Badain Jaran Desert, resembling a massive pink "jewel" in the desert landscape.

2 Zhun Jigede
[准吉格德, Zhǔn Jígédé]

The lake with the most magical sights in the Badain Jaran Desert, with its blue and red waters sitting side by side, creating an incredibly beautiful and mystical panorama.

Affected by the concentration of salt and alkaline minerals, water volume, and temperature, the southern part glows with a soft pink hue while the northern part remians a striking blue, earning it the local nickname "Two-colored Lake" (双色湖, Shuāngsè Hú).

3 Zhong Nuoertu
[中诺尔图, Zhōng Nuòěrtú]

The largest lake in the Badain Jaran Desert. Its southern shore is a relatively flat and open expanse, while the remaining three sides—east, north, and west—are surrounded by towering sand dunes that rise over 300 meters high.

This striking contrast between the azure sky, golden sands, tranquil waters, poplar trees, and the resilient needlegrass (芨芨草, Jījī Cǎo, Achnatherum splendens) creates a breathtaking and unique landscape. Because of this, Zhong Nuoertu has earned the poetic title "Jiangnan of the Desert" (沙漠江南, Shāmò Jiāngnán), likening it to the lush and picturesque region south of the Yangtze River, renowned for its beauty and greenery.

Itinerary

Day1 Gather in Zhangye (张掖)

Day2 Zhangye- Alxa Right Banner - Badain Jaran Desert
Driving: 300km, 5 hours
Trekking: 5km, 2 hours

After breakfast, we drive to Alxa Right Banner. Following lunch, we venture into the desert to explore attractions such as Small Jigede (小吉格德, Xiǎo Jígédé), Xianggen Jilin Red Lake (香根吉林红湖, Xiānggēn Jílín Hóng Hú), and other scenic spots.

In the afternoon, we arrive at Zhong Nuoertu, where you can enjoy sand sliding and take in the stunning desert sunset. After the sunset, we will embark on a 5-kilometer hike to our accommodation.

Day3 Badain Jaran - Bilutu Peak - Badain Jaran
Driving: 80km, 1.5 hours
Trekking: 8km, 3 hours

After breakfast, we drive to visit Barun Gelike (巴润格力克, Bārùn Gélìkè), Dabsutu Emerald Lake (达布苏图翡翠湖, Dábùsūtú Fěicuì Hú), Selige Ri (策力格日, Cèlìgé Rì), Zhun Jigede Two-colored Lake, and Dagetu Red Lake.

In the afternoon, we continue our exploration with visits to Zalat (扎拉特, Zhālātè), Fairy Peak (仙女峰, Xiānnǚ Fēng), and Yinde Ritu Sacred Spring (音德日图神泉, Yīndé Rìtú Shénquán). Finally, we will hike to Bilutu Peak (必鲁图峰, Bìlǔtú

Fēng) at 1,611 meters, known as the "Everest of the Desert" (沙漠珠峰, Shāmò Zhūfēng) and the highest peak in any desert worldwide.

Day4 Badain Jaran - Badain Lake
Driving: 70km, 2 hours
Trekking: 5km, 2 hours

We rise early in the morning to climb a sand dune and witness the breathtaking sunrise. After breakfast, we capture the reflection of the Badain Jaran Temple (巴丹吉林庙, Bādān Jílín Miào) before heading to visit Barun Jilin (巴润吉林, Bārùn Jílín), Barun Yike Ri Twin Lakes (巴润伊克日双海子, Bārùn Yīkè Rì Shuāng Hǎizi), Desert Tianchi (大漠天池, Dàmò Tiānchí, "Desert Heavenly Pool"), Saiwusu (赛乌苏, Sàiwūsū), and Singing Sand Mountain (鸣沙山, Míngshā Shān).

In the afternoon, we have free time for sand sliding, camel riding, archery, go-karting, or other recreational activities. After nightfall, we will embark on a 5-kilometer night walk under a starless sky and sit atop the sand dunes to stargaze.

Day5 Badain Lake - Pingshan Grand Canyon - Zhangye
Driving: 300km, 4 hours

After breakfast, we drive to Pingshan Grand Canyon (平山大峡谷, Píngshān Dà Xiágǔ). We will spend about three hours exploring the scenic area before returning to Zhangye.

Important Notes

- Best Season: April to October
- Suitable For: Healthy individuals aged 10 to 65
- Potential Risks: 1. The desert has extreme temperature changes and strong winds.
  2. Protect yourself from the strong sunlight during the day and stay warm at night.
  3. Sand-proof shoe covers and mesh-free hiking shoes are essential.

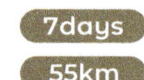

02. Zhagana

[扎尕那, Zhā Gǎnà]

Lanzhou
[兰州, Lánzhōu]
Gathering City

17KM
Longest Single-Day Hike

500M
Maximum Daily Elevation Gain

4,140M
Highest Elevation Along the Route

★★★★⯪
Scenic Rating

★★★★
Difficulty Level

Credit
Image 1 | ©194
Image 2 | ©Zijun

Located in Diebu County (迭部县, Diébù Xiàn) of the Gannan Tibetan Autonomous Prefecture (甘南藏族自治州, Gānnán Zàngzú Zìzhìzhōu) in Gansu Province, Zhagana, meaning "stone box" in Tibetan, is a hidden gem. As early as the 1920s, the famous Austrian-American explorer Joseph Rock discovered this paradise while passing through Diebu County. In his expedition journal, he wrote: "Never in my life have I seen such beautiful scenery. If the author of Genesis had seen the beauty of Zhagana, he would surely have placed the birthplace of Adam and Eve here..." To Joseph Rock, Zhagana was as magnificent and serene as the Western concept of the Garden of Eden.

Cultural Significance

Zhagana has been recognized by the Food and Agriculture Organization of the United Nations as a "Globally Important Agricultural Heritage System." It was ranked fourth in "China's Top Ten Lesser-Known Mountains" by National Geographic of China and listed as "One of the World's 50 Outdoor Paradises" by an renowned American travel magazine. Despite these prestigious titles and accolades, Zhagana remains a hidden gem, attracting only a small number of visitors. Walking through this "utopia" nestled deep in the mountains, you can experience breathtaking natural beauty alongside authentic Tibetan culture.

At that time, Joseph Rock chose to embark on his scientific expedition to Zhagana in Diebu County from Zhagulu Township (卓尼县扎古录乡, Zhuōní Xiàn Zhāgǔlù Xiāng) in Zhuoni County. Today, this route has become a renowned tourist path in the Gannan region, celebrated as "One of China's Most Beautiful 100 Kilometers" and officially named "The Rock's Road" (洛克之路, Luòkè Zhī Lù). Stretching approximately 106 kilometers, the journey offers a stunning display of natural landscapes, including grasslands, canyons, waterfalls, snowcapped mountains, and karst caves, while also immersing travelers in Tibetan Buddhist culture and traditions. The breathtaking scenery and rich cultural heritage have once again brought fame to this route, with Zhagana as its ultimate destination.

After more than two years of research and exploration in the Gannan region, Joseph Rock devoted 46 full pages of National Geographic Magazine to share his observations and experiences, bringing Gannan to global attention for the first time. In the century that followed, countless experts, scholars, backpackers, and adventurers have retraced Joseph Rock's journey, repeatedly traversing what has come to be known as "The Rock's Road."

Natural Features

Zhagana is located on the southern slopes of the Die Mountains (迭山, Dié Shān). Shaped by the Himalayan orogenic movement during the Cenozoic era, the region is characterized by towering, striking peaks and peculiar rock formations. The landscape is dotted with zoomorphic rock formations and eroded features scattered throughout canyons and caves. More than ten peaks rise above 4,000 meters, their intertwined summits soaring into the clouds in bizarre and captivating shapes. Venturing deep into this area feels like stepping into a mysterious, otherworldly realm, reminiscent of the fantastical landscapes of Middle-earth in fantasy films.

Viewed from above, Zhagana appears as a naturally formed "stone city," showcasing nature's extraordinary craftsmanship. Rivers cascade between the mountains, creating spectacular splashes, while a vibrant tapestry of flowers and grasses fills the forests, making you feel as if you're immersed in an ocean of blossoms. Waterfalls hang in the air like flowing white ribbons, crafting scenes as beautiful as poetry or paintings. As you venture into the heart of this stone city, you'll encounter Tibetan villages nestled on the mountain's layered slopes. And their houses interconnected one another. Among them stands some classic Tibetan Buddhist temples, including the Lasang Temple (拉桑寺, Lāsāng Sì), which was built in 1645, during the second year of Emperor Shunzhi's reign in the Qing Dynasty. Prayer flags flutter in the wind throughout the temple, as if quietly narrating the rich human history embedded in the stones.In addition, Zhagana is home to a rich diversity of flora and fauna, with 103 families, 190 genera, and 412 species of higher plants. Among them, one is first-level nationally protected species, 15 are second-level protected species, and six are key protected species in Gansu Province, earning it the nickname "Botanical Museum."

The trees here are diverse and change with the seasons, creating a vibrant, colorful landscape. In autumn, the golden leaves cover the valleys, creating a breathtaking scene. The naturally formed forest also serves as a haven for various wild animals. Zhagana is home to many nationally protected species, such as the snow leopard, golden eagle, and sika deer, offering visitors a chance to experience the beauty of nature in its most primitive and untouched form.

Itinerary

Day1 Gather in Lanzhou (兰州)

Day2 Lanzhou - Zhagana (扎尔那)
Driving: 480km

We rise early in the morning and set off southward, traveling along a route that gradually shifts from the loess landscape, marked by thousands of ravines, to the vibrant emerald green grasslands.

As the scenery transforms, you are gently immersed in the simple yet harmonious beauty of Gannan. In the evening, we stay at a Tibetan guesthouse in Dongwa Village (东哇村, Dōngwā Cūn) in Zhagana.

Day3 Zhagana - Niegan Dawa Sacred Mountain (涅甘达娃神山) - Guanggai Mountain Pass (光盖山垭) - Jiaobu Ke Pass (交布克垭口) - Dongcai Campsite (冬才营地 3,640m)
Trekking: 17km, 9 hours

After breakfast, we depart from Dongwa Village and begin our hike northward along the Rongnao Valley (容闹沟, Róngnào Gōu). Upon entering the canyon, we follow a wide pastoral path. Though it's a dirt road, it is flanked by steep rock walls, with no forks along the way. We continue uphill for about two hours until reaching the foot of Niegan Dawa Sacred Mountain, then proceed to a flat, open area in the canyon to rest and enjoy lunch.

Afterward, we continue along the pastoral path through the Zhagana Stone Forest (扎尔那石林, Zhǎgànà Shílín). As we walk eastward, the elevation gradually rises. After crossing four passes, including Guanggai Mountain and Jiaobu Ke, we descend to the Dongcai Campsite, where we set up camp for the night.

Day4 Dongcai Campsite - Kalake Pass (喀拉克垭口 4,140m) - Unnamed Campsite (无名营地 3,800m)
Trekking: 13km, 500m ascent, 340m descent, 8 hours

Today, we will cross Kalake Pass, the highest point of our journey, and navigate a steep gravel path where we can appreciate the distinctive Danxia landforms, a true test to our physical endurance and experience. After breakfast, we depart from Dongcai Campsite and begin our ascent into Dongcai Canyon. The path ahead mainly follows the mountainside, with little change in elevation, and the terrain is primarily muddy and rocky.

After crossing three passes, each with an elevation between 3,800 and 4,000 meters, we will prepare to conquer Kalake Pass, the highest of them all. From there, we will follow a gravel path

into a region where we can enjoy striking red sandstone Danxia formations. The path continues along weathered gravel roads. After crossing another pass, we will encounter a vast alpine meadow. We will descend through the meadow, and after about half an hour, we will reach Qikena Ridge (七克拿山脊, Qīkènà Shānjí), where we will camp for the night amidst this unique Danxia landscape.

Day5 Unnamed Campsite - "Stool Stone" (大便石) - Anziku Pasture (安子库牧场) - Canyon Entrance Campsite (峡谷口营地 3,200m)
Trekking: 15km, 7 hours

After breakfast, we depart from the campsite and cross the valley with a gentle ascent, before beginning a mainly descending and traversing journey along dirt paths, which are relatively easy to walk on.

As we pass "Stool Stone" (大便石, Dàbiàn Shí), a large rock shaped like a stool, and Naizi Mountain (奶子山, Nǎizi Shān), which features two peaks resembling the shape of breasts, we gradually start to see herders' houses, marking the arrival at Anziku Pasture, a settlement for many local herders.

The picturesque landscape of towering mountains, expansive meadows, and scattered villages evokes the essence of Shangri-La. After a rest at Anziku, we continue through the forests, eventually reaching the meadow at the canyon entrance where we will camp for the night.

Day6 Canyon Entrance Campsite - Guanyin Stone Pass (观音石垭口 3,620m) - Triangle Stone (三角石) - Minxian (岷县)
Driving: 90km, 3 hours
Trekking: 10km, 420m ascent, 4 hours

After completing your morning preparations, we set off and pass through the Tiger's Mouth Canyon (老虎嘴, Lǎohǔ Zuǐ), heading towards the Guanyin Stone Campsite (观音石营地, Guānyīnshí Yíngdì). From there, we begin the final climb of the journey—the Guanyin Stone Pass.

The descent along the ridge is steep, so take your time and proceed with caution. As you descend into the valley, you'll find yourself surrounded by lush forests and streams. Gradually, you will start to encounter herders and the highway. Follow the highway to reach the final destination at Triangle Stone. From there, you can take a vehicle to Minxian County, where you'll check into a hotel for the night.

Day7 Minxian County - Lanzhou
Driving: 270km, 5 hours

Important Notes

● Best Season: June to October

● Suitable For: Healthy individuals aged 18-65 years with hiking and camping experience

● Potential Risks: Crossing steep mountain passes requires extra caution to ensure safety.

1

03. Tengger Desert
[腾格里沙漠, Ténggélǐ Shāmò]

Yinchuan
[银川, Yínchuān]
Gathering City

20KM
Longest Single-Day Hike

250M
Maximum Daily Elevation Gain

1,345M
Highest Elevation Along the Route

★★★
Scenic Rating

★★
Difficulty Level

Credit
Image 1 | ©Kangaroo
Image 2 | ©Huyang

The Tengger Desert is located in the southwestern part of Alxa Left Banner (阿拉善左旗, Ālāshàn Zuǒqí) in Inner Mongolia Autonomous Region, bordering the Gansu Province. It extends beyond the Great Wall in the south, reaches the Helan Mountains (贺兰山, Hèlán Shān) in the east, stretches to the Yalai Mountains (雅赖山, Yǎlài Shān) in the west.

Spanning approximately 240 kilometers from north to south and 160 kilometers from east to west, the desert covers an area of about 43,000 square kilometers, making it China's fourth-largest desert. In Mongolian, the word "Tengger" means "sky," describing this desert as being as high, distant, and vast as the sky.

Natural Features

The desert landscape is a striking mix of sand dunes, lake basins, mountains, and flatlands, with sand dunes being the dominant feature, covering 71% of the area. Of this, mobile dunes make up 64%, mainly consisting of grid-like patterns of 10-20 meters in height. These dunes shift in wave-like formations, driven by the wind toward the Helan Mountains and the Yellow River.

As you enter the Tengger Desert, you'll be greeted by endless sand dunes that resemble frozen waves, stretching across the landscape in varying heights. Against the backdrop of a deep blue sky, the vast sea of sand seems to merge with the horizon. At sunset, the undulating dunes take on a golden hue, resembling waves that are both magnificent and serene—desolate yet majestic.

Although the desert may seem barren, it is far from a "lifeless forbidden zone" where "not a blade of grass grows." The unique climate and geographical conditions support the survival of hundreds of plant species, creating a distinctive "desert forest" landscape. Here, you won't see the stereotypical image of a desert filled with "yellow sand filling the sky," nor the stark barrenness of the Gobi, where nothing grows. Instead, oases are scattered throughout the desert, shimmering with life as they dot and spread across the sands, glistening in the sunlight.

These oases breathe life into the desert, supporting a variety of creatures such as camels, sand lizards, desert foxes, eagles, hedgehogs, beetles, and more. Contrary to common belief, the desert is home to a greater abundance of plant life than we often realize. These plants have developed deep-rooted systems that tap into underground moisture, while their needle-like leaves, coated with waxy surfaces, minimize water evaporation. From the moment their seeds germinate, these plants embody the wisdom and logic of the natural world, holding endless possibilities for development of life.

Every spring and summer, plants such as saxaul (梭梭, Suōsuō), tamarisk (红柳, Hóngliǔ), red wormwood (红艾蒿, Hóng Àihāo), and ephedra (蛇麻黄, Shémáhuáng) thrive with remarkable vigor. During this time, the desert sheds its desolate appearance, bursting with vitality instead. By November, however, the desert transforms into a stark, white world, enduring the harsh cold until the following spring, when the melting snow softens the frozen soil, rejuvenating the landscape and bringing new life to the desert once again.

Cultural Significance

Deep within the Tengger Desert, far from the reach of artificial light pollution and surrounded by year-round drought and sparse clouds, the entire starry sky unfolds in all its glory, visible without the need for any astronomical equipment. The light from stars that originated billions of years ago finally reaches Earth, casting its glow across the vast desert, illuminating both you and me.

Zhaohua Temple (昭化寺, Zhāohuà Sì) is an ancient temple established by the Sixth Dalai Lama, Tsangyang Gyatso (仓央嘉措, Cāngyáng Jiācuò), during his exile in Inner Mongolia. He lived in seclusion here, dedicating himself to the practice and dissemination of the Dharma. After his passing, his remains were kept at Zhaohua for ten years. Built in 1734, the temple has stood for over 300 years, remaining remarkably well-preserved with continuous worship. It is almost unimaginable that, on the edge of the vast Tengger Desert, a Tibetan Buddhist temple would be so deeply connected to a legendary poet and the ever-living Buddha.

2

Itinerary

Day1 Gather in Yinchuan (银川)

Day2 Yinchuan - Zhaohua Temple (昭化寺) - Sacred Spring (神泉) - Camp 1 (1号营地)
Driving: 4 hours | Trekking: 10km, 4 hours

After breakfast, we depart from Yinchuan by bus, passing the Imperial Tombs of the Western Xia Dynasty (西夏王陵, Xīxià Wánglíng) and the Ming Dynasty Great Wall (明长城, Míng Chángchéng). We then cross the Helan Mountains and travel along the Gobi Highway, passing through the Gobi wind turbine zone and pastoral areas, before finally arriving at Zhaohua Temple for a visit.

After lunch, we continue our journey by bus to the starting point of the desert trek, passing the Sacred Spring on our way to Niu Lake (牛湖, Niú Hú). In the evening, we arrive at Mingsha Mountain (鸣沙山, Míngshā Shān), where we set up camp. After dinner, we sit on the sand dunes, waiting as the stars gradually begin to appear.

Day3 Camp 1 - Twin Mountains (双子山) - Fragrant Lake (香湖) - Buddha Affinity Lake (佛缘湖) - Heavenly Pool (天池) - Dragon Ridge (龙脊梁) - Camp 2 (2号营地)
Trekking: 20km, 9 hours

We rise early to witness the breathtaking desert sunrise. After breakfast at camp, we embark on the longest desert trek of the journey. Along the way, we admire the distant views of Twin Mountains, Fragrant Lake, Buddha Affinity Lake, and Heavenly Pool. We then arrive at Camp 2, where we set up for the night.

Day4 Camp 2 - Ovoo (敖包) - Moon Lake (月亮湖) - Sand Driving - Yinchuan
Driving: 4 hours | Trekking: 10km, 3 hours

Today is the last day in the desert. After breakfast, we climb along the magical Dragon Ridge to reach the summit of Ovoo and Thunder Ridge (雷鸣岭, Léimíng Lǐng), view Sacrificial Lake (祭祀湖, Jìsì Hú) from afar, and pass through Reed Lake (芦苇湖, Lúwěi Hú) to arrive at Moon Lake. Then we visit the Shell Museum (贝壳博物馆, Bèiké Bówùguǎn), and after lunch, we take a boat through the reed marshes to the western shore of the lake, enjoying the unique experience of kayaking and swimming in the desert, then take vehicles through the sand dunes to reach the transfer station, where you'll change to a bus returning to Yinchuan city and check into a hotel.

Day5 Yinchuan Departure

Important Notes

- Best Season: April to October
- Suitable For: Healthy individuals aged 10-65 years
- Potential Risks: 1. Desert trails are indistinct, with a risk of getting lost.
  2. Moving alone is forbidden.

04. Ili 72-Kilometer Trek

[伊犁72公里, Yīlí 72 Gōnglǐ]

`9days` `72km`

Yining
[伊宁, Yīníng]
Gathering City

18KM
Longest Single-Day Hike

300M
Maximum Daily Elevation Gain

2,580M
Highest Elevation Along the Route

★ ★ ★
Scenic Rating

★ ★
Difficulty Level

Credit
Image 1/2/4 | ©HuangHuang
Image 3 | ©Harrison

Xinjiang is vast, and discussing its stunning landscapes would likely take three days and nights to cover. However, if I were to recommend just one place, I would without hesitation say: Ili (伊犁, Yīlí).

The Tianshan Mountain Range (天山山系, Tiānshān Shānxì) stretches across central Xinjiang, dividing the region into Southern and Northern Xinjiang, creating two distinctly different climates and landscapes. Within the embrace of the Tianshan Mountains lies a trumpet-shaped valley plain—the Ili River Valley (伊犁河谷, Yīlí Hégǔ).

Natural Features

Ili, home to the largest grasslands in Xinjiang, has been an ideal haven for nomadic peoples since ancient times. The diversity of Ili's grasslands is unparalled, offering not only vastly streching expanses but also highly varied "montane vertical grassland" landscapes. From the valley floors to the mountaintops, it presents a complete spectrum of vegetation zones.

The Ili region offers some of the best outdoor trekking resources in China. You have surely heard the names of these four classic trekking routes: Xiate Ancient Road (夏特古道, Xiàtè Gǔdào), Wusun Ancient Road (乌孙古道, Wūsūn Gǔdào), Mengkete Ancient Road (孟克特古道, Mèngkètè Gǔdào), and the Kalajun Grand Loop (喀拉峻大环线, Kālājùn Dà Huánxiàn). Besides outdoor trekking, the region boasts a wealth of tourism resources, including Kuerdenin Schrenk's Spruce Forest (库尔德宁雪岭云杉, Kù'ěrdéníng Xuělǐng Yúnshān), Tangbula Fairy Lake (唐布拉仙女湖, Táng bùlā Xiānnǚ Hú), Tohulasu Grassland (托乎拉苏草原, Tuō hūlāsū Cǎoyuán), Nalati Grassland (那拉提草原, Nàlātí Cǎoyuán), Sayram Lake (赛里木湖, Sàilǐmù Hú), and Qiaxifeng Scenic Area (恰西风景区, Qiàxī Fēngjǐng Qū). Just hearing these names is enough to ignite any traveler's imagination.

Spring in the Ili River Valley begins in April. As the ice and snow melt, the air is filled with the fragrances of blooming flowers. The best time to visit is from May to August. In May and June, wildflowers bloom in abundance, while from July to August, the sweet scent of fruits and melons fills the air. Who could resist such temptation?

However, Ili is so vast and remote that completing all the classic routes while visiting the must-see attractions would take at least 50 days, with costs that can be quite high—unrealistic for most people. There-fore, we recommend the "Ili 72-Kilometer" trek, which covers the four major grass-lands of Kalajun, Tohulasu, Tangbula, and Zhaosu (昭苏, Zhāosū). This essential route combines the sceneries of grasslands, for-ests, snow-capped mountains, canyons, rivers, lakes, and seas of flowers into one unforgettable experience.

2

Notable Attractions

This 72-kilometer route can be divided into six parts.

1 Xiate Grassland
[夏特草原, Xiàtè Cǎoyuán]

Xiate, also called Xiata (夏塔, Xiàtǎ), both names are used frequently. Xiate Grassland is a classic example of canyon grasslands and is located in southwestern Zhaosu. It combines various landscapes, including Tianshan glaciers, forested canyons, grasslands, and rivers.

With the opening of the Xiate Scenic Area, more and more people are flocking to Xiate in June.

2 Kalajun Grassland
[喀拉峻草原, Kālājùn Cǎoyuán]

Kalajun is currently the most popular summer grassland destination in Xinjiang. It features one of the high-quality alpine grasslands rarely seen in the world, characterized by three-di-mensional undulations that resemble waves, varying in height and layout.

This unique landscape has earned Kalajun the title of "China's Most Beautiful Three-Dimen-sional Grassland Landscape Zone."

3 Tohulasu Grassland
[托乎拉苏草原, Tuōhūlāsū Cǎoyuán]

Tohulasu Grassland is the closest to Yining city. It is a hilly grassland, undulating with diverse landscapes.

In May and June, the Tohulasu Grassland offers captivating views—under the blue skies and white clouds, cattle and sheep graze freely, horses gallop across the land, and the tranquil, untouched grassland scenes captivate visitors. With just a slight shift in perspective, you can capture thousands of unique compositions in your photographs.

4 Qiongkushtai Village
[琼库什台村, Qióngkùshítái Cūn]

Qiongkushtai is actually a village of Kazakh herds, featuring typical valley grassland topography. It is the starting point for both the Kalajun trek and the Wusun Ancient Road.

Here, you can see blue skies, white clouds, silver snow-capped mountains, dark green pine forests, and colorful flower seas on emerald grasslands. Scattered felt-covered tents and wooden cabins display rustic simplicity, resembling a hidden utopia deep within the grasslands.

5 Kuerdenin Grassland
[库尔德宁草原, Kù'ěrdéníng Cǎoyuán]

Kuerdenin is the core area of the Western Tianshan Schrenk's Spruce Natural Reserve and one of Xinjiang's Tianshan World Natural Heritage sites.

Known as "Tianshan's Most Beautiful Green Valley and the Homeland of Schrenk's Spruce," it is home to vast, lush forests of Schrenk's spruce trees, which stretch endlessly, standing tall and majestic, with most reaching heights of 40-60 meters, making it the densest concentration of Schrenk's spruce in the world. From here, you can also catch a glimpse of the distant Kabanbai Peak (喀班巴依峰, Kābānbāyī Fēng), the main peak of the Nalati Mountains and the source of the Kuerdenin River.

6 Tangbula Fairy Lake
[唐布拉仙女湖, Tángbùlā Xiānnǚ Hú]

Tangbula, known as the "Hundred-Mile Gallery," is one of the five most famous grasslands in Ili. The highlight of Tangbula's "Hundred-Mile Gallery" is "Fairy Lake."

The lake's shimmering waters mirror snow-capped mountains, blue skies, and white clouds, creating a scene as serene and pure as a young maiden—truly a fairyland on earth.

3

Itinerary

Day1 Gather in Yining(伊宁)

Day2 Yining - Tianma Drinking River (天马饮河) - Xiata Township/72 Regiment (夏塔乡/72团)
Driving: 160km, 6 hours

Day3 Xiata Township/72 Regiment - Xiata Ancient Road (夏塔古道) - Tekes (Eight Trigrams City) (特克斯八卦城)
Trekking: 16km, 5 hours

After breakfast, we drive to the Xiata Ancient Road and transfer to a shuttle bus that takes us to the hot springs campsite. From there, we begin today's round-trip trek. The trekking distance can vary, but the longest is no more than 16 kilometers. Following the Xiata River (夏塔河, Xiàtǎ Hé) toward Muzhaerte Snow Mountain (木扎尔特雪山, Mùzhā'ěrtè Xuěshān), we pass through canyons, snow-capped mountains, and expansive grasslands. Along the way, adorable marmots occasionally make an appearance.

Day4 Tekes - Kalajun Scenic Area (喀拉峻景区) - East Kalajun Jiasagan Campsite (东喀拉峻加萨干营地)
Trekking: 10km, 3 hours

Today we drive to the Kalajun Scenic Area, visiting Kalajun Lake (喀拉峻湖, Kālājùn Hú), Kuoksu Grand Canyon (阔克苏大峡谷, Kuòkèsū Dà Xiágǔ), Crocodile Bay (鳄鱼湾, È'yú Wān), Kuoksu River's Nine Curves and Eighteen Bends (阔克苏河九曲十八弯, Kuòkèsū Hé Jiǔqū Shíbāwān), as well as East Kalajun's Flower Platform (鲜花台, Xiānhuā Tái), Falcon Platform (猎鹰台, Lièyīng Tái), and Three-level Planation Surface (三级夷平面, Sānjí Yípíngmiàn).

Day5 Jiasagan Campsite - Kurdai River Grand Canyon (库尔代河大峡谷) - Qiongkushtai (琼库什台)
Trekking: 18km, 7 hours

After breakfast, we begin our trek, passing through seas of grassland flowers before descending into the Kurdai River Canyon. We cross the Kurdai River, follow a trail on the western side, and climb over a small pass to reach Qiongkushtai.

Day6 Qiongkushtai - Tekes Eight Trigrams City - Kuerdenin (库尔德宁)
Driving: 200km

After breakfast, we drive to Tekes Eight Trigrams City, enjoying the scenic views along the way. We have lunch in Tekes and spend the afternoon exploring the streets of the City. In the evening, we arrive at Kuerdenin Town and stay for the night.

Day7 Kuerdenin - Small Mohe Valley (小莫合沟) - Kuerdenin Scenic Area - Xinyuan County (新源县)
Trekking: 18km, 7 hours

We drive along the Dajirgelang River (大吉尔格郎河, Dà Jí'ěrgélǎng Hé) upstream to the Great Mohe Valley (大莫合沟, Dà Mòhé Gōu). We ascend to enter the subalpine meadows, which form a natural landscape zone combining grasslands, forests, canyons, and snow-capped mountains.

After traversing through grassland flower seas, we enter the Kuerdenin Canyon for sightseeing.

Day8 Xinyuan County - Tangbula Fairy Lake (唐布拉仙女湖) - Tangbula Honey Bee Small Town (唐布拉蜜蜂小镇)
Trekking: 10km, 3 hours

Following Provincial Road 315, we head to today's trekking starting point. The road, like a sharp blade, cuts through the vast grassland, with cattle and sheep crossing back and forth, gradually mending this "wound" line by line.

In the distance, mountains undulate, fading into a deep green backdrop. Green pines shelter a few white felt tents, while the river meanders alongside the road, cutting through the wind—this is the renowned Tangbula "Hundred-Mile Gallery". From our starting point, we stroll along winding paths and eventually arrive at the shore of Fairy Lake.

Day9 Tangbula - Yining - Urumqi (乌鲁木齐)

After breakfast, we drive back to Yining, arriving by noon. In the afternoon, we visit the Kazanqi Old Town (喀赞其老城, Kāzànqí Lǎo chéng), and in the evening, we take the train back to Urumqi.

Important Notes

- Best Season: May to June, with slight route adjustments in different time periods.
- Suitable For: Healthy individuals aged 8-65 years
- Potential Risks: 1. The weather in Xinjiang can be unpredictable, so be prepared for varying conditions.
  2. Bring water protection and warm clothing, with raincoats being essential.

05. Eastern Xinjiang Trek
[东疆徒步, Dōngjiāng Túbù]

7days
50km

Urumqi
[乌鲁木齐, Wūlǔmùqí]
Gathering City

15KM
Longest Single-Day Hike

200M
Maximum Daily Elevation Gain

554M
Highest Elevation Along the Route

★★★
Scenic Rating

★★
Difficulty Level

Eastern Xinjiang refers to the eastern part of Xinjiang Uygur Autonomous Region, primarily encompassing the two major regions of Turpan (吐鲁番, Tǔlǔfān) and Hami (哈密, Hāmì). It serves as Xinjiang's eastern gateway and an vital portal to inland China. Historically, it was a key crossroads along the ancient Silk Road, playing a central role as a hub where Chinese and world cultures converged.

In contrast to the Ili River Valley mentioned earlier, this region presents a striking difference. The vast plateaus and mountains, which block moisture from almost all directions, combined with its extreme distance from the ocean, make it exceptionally difficult for water vapor to reach the area. As a result, eastern Xinjiang has naturally become the most arid region in China.

Natural Features

If we were to compare the Ili region to a teenage girl, eastern Xinjiang would resemble a rugged, untamed man. The vast deserts and Gobi are the region's most characteristic landscapes, with endless hilly Gobi and dusty yellow deserts that exude both wildness and mystery. Despite its harsh conditions, exploration of this land has never ceased. For over a century, explorers and archaeologists have flocked to this area, bringing about numerous significant archaeological and exploration routes.

This region boasts a variety of world-class landscapes: the Dahai Road Yardang Landform Group (大海道雅丹地貌群, Dàhǎi dào Yǎdān Dìmào Qún), which is the largest yardang landform area in the world; Jiaohe Ancient City (交河故城, Jiāohé Gù chéng), home to the best-preserved earthen castle on Earth; Flaming Mountain (火焰山, Huǒyàn Shān), one of the hottest places on the planet; and Kumtag Desert (库木塔格沙漠, Kùmùtǎgé Shāmò), the closest desert to the urban area globally.

Through the "50-Kilometer Eastern Xinjiang Trek," we can fully immerse ourselves in the magnificence of this region and explore the extreme beauty of the desert.

Notable Attractions

1 Dahai Road
[大海道, Dàhǎidào]

Dahai Road was once a shortcut on the Silk Road from Dunhuang to, Hami, Turpan and Urumqi in ancient times. First established during the Han Dynasty, it spanned over 500 kilometers, mostly through uninhabited regions. Due to its extremely treacherous conditions, the road gradually faded from memory after the Tang Dynasty.

Today, Dahai Road is home to the world's largest and most developed yardang landforms in terms of geological morphology. Here, visitors can experience the essence of yardang landscapes, where water and wind erosion have sculpted a stunning array of formations. In this extraordinary place, your imagination can run wild—layered pastries, castles, warships, aliens, dragon heads... whatever you dare to envision, it will come to life in the remarkable scenery.

As early as the Late Cretaceous period, this place was a vast ocean. After long periods of plate movement, uplift, collision, and other geological activities, the seawater gradually receded, marine sediments transformed into terrestrial sediments, and coupled with year-round strong winds of level 7-8, the Dahai Road yardang landform group was ultimately formed. Every piece of sand and stone beneath your feet may have existed for tens of millions of years.

The Gasun Gobi (噶顺戈壁, Gāshùn Gēbì), traversed by Dahai Road, is as vast as the sea. This earned it the name "Great Sand Sea" during the Tang Dynasty, which also inspired the name of Dahai Road (literally meaning "Great Sea Road"). Although there is no actual sea along Dahai Road, traveling across it in an off-road vehicle gives you the sensation of being at sea due to the bumpy terrain. Along the journey, while letting your imagination soar, you'll often find yourself searching for hidden treasures—many agates and strange stones lie buried here.

Like many arid gobi regions in China, Dahai Road is often described as resembling the surface of Mars. To enhance visitors' comfort and entertainment, a Mars Base has actually been built here. It is the only supply station in the uninhabited area of Dahai Road, and we will stay in this "hotel" surrounded by yardang landforms, enjoying the stars and the "sea," and experiencing an extreme "journey to Mars."

4

2 Jiaohe Ancient City
[交河故城, Jiāohé Gùchéng]

Located in the Turpan Basin at the foot of Flaming Mountain and surrounded by river valleys on both sides, Jiaohe Ancient City was named "Jiaohe" (meaning "intersecting rivers") because the river water split and flowed around the city. It is currently the world's largest, oldest, and best-preserved ancient city built with rammed earth architecture. Additionally, it is the most complete site from the Han Dynasty. Jiaohe is also one of the few well-preserved examples for studying ancient cities and has been hailed as the "world's most perfect ruins."

Throughout the long river of history, Jiaohe was once an important town on the Silk Road and the most prosperous city in the Western Regions. From the Northern Wei Dynasty to the early Tang Dynasty, it served as the Jiaohe Commandery under the Kingdom of Gaochang. Later, during the Zhenguan period of the Tang Dynasty, after the Kingdom of Gaochang was conquered, the Anxi Protectorate—the highest military and political institution in the Western Regions at the time—was established here.

Today, Jiaohe Ancient City stands as a desolate ruin, yet amidst the crumbling walls, the city's distinct layout remains evident. The various divisions—residential areas, government offices, storage zones, temples, and burial grounds—are still clearly defined. From a distance, the city resembles a fortress with multiple layers of defense, making it both easy to protect and difficult to conquer. With such strategic advantages, Jiaohe was destined to become a coveted location, fiercely contested by military forces.

3 Flaming Mountain
[火焰山, Huǒyàn Shān]

In the classic novel "Journey to the West," when the master and his three disciples embarked their journey to obtain Buddhist scriptures, they had to pass by the Flaming Mountain.

However, the place was infamous for its harsh conditions: "the Flaming Mountain is covered by eight hundred miles of flames, with not a blade of grass growing around it. " Therefore, they had to borrow the banana leaf fan from the Iron Fan Princess to extinguish the raging fire. In reality, Flaming Mountain truly exists, except that the fire has been replaced by red mountain rocks and rolling heat waves under the sunshine.

Flaming Mountain is located far from the ocean, situated in a low-lying basin where the foehn effect—caused by descending and warming air currents—results in some of the hottest temperatures in China. In the summer, the surface temperature can exceed fifty degrees Celsius. An egg buried in the sandy soil can be fully cooked in less than thirty minutes, and the area once recorded an extraordinary high temperature of 89.2°C.

Flaming Mountain is home to five stunning valleys, among which the Tuyugou Grand Canyon (吐峪沟大峡谷, Tǔyùgōu Dà Xiágǔ) stands out as the longest, widest, and most magnificent. Stretching approximately 8 kilometers in length with an average width of 1 kilometer, this majestic canyon cuts through Flaming Mountain from north to south, showcasing the essence of the region's landscape. At the canyon's exit lies Mazar Village (麻扎村, Mázhā Cūn), an ancient settlement that has stood for over 2,600 years.

4 Mazar Village
[麻扎村, Mázhā Cūn]

The full name of Tuyugou Mazar Village is "Mazar Ardi Village" (麻扎·阿勒迪村, Mázhā Ā'lèdí Cūn), meaning "holy place" or "tomb of the saint." Mazar Village is small and is an ancient village where Buddhist culture and Islamic culture merge. It is also China's largest Islamic holy site, known as the "Eastern Mecca."

Mazar Village preserves the most primitive rammed earth buildings and traditional Uyghur customs, earning the title of "China's First Earth Manor." While most of the village's residents have now relocated, the yellow earth houses remain, arranged in an orderly manner to form a continuous stretch. Many of these buildings feature numerous holes, which were once used for drying grapes, apricots, and mulberries.

5

5 Kumtag Desert
[库木塔格沙漠, Kùmùtǎgé Shāmò]

The Kumtag Desert (库木塔格沙漠, Kùmùtǎgé Shāmò) is one of China's eight major deserts and forms part of the vast Taklamakan Desert. It borders the Altun Mountains to the south, stretches toward the Beishan Mountains to the north, adjoins the Xihu Wetland and Dunhuang Oasis to the east, and lies near the Lop Nor Basin to the northwest.

The name "Kumtag" means "sand mountain" in Uyghur. Remarkably, it is the only desert in the world directly connected to a city, with just

a river separating the oasis from the arid sands. On one side, the endless yellow expanse of the desert stretches as far as the eye can see, while on the other side lies a lush, green oasis where human life thrives.

The sharp contrast between the vibrant green of the oasis and the vast yellow of the desert creates a striking and unforgettable sight, highlighting once more how Eastern Xinjiang perfectly embodies the concept of "extreme" in its most awe-inspiring form.

6

Itinerary

Day1 Gather in Urumqi (乌鲁木齐)

Day2 Urumqi - Jiaohe Ancient City (交河故城) - Turpan (吐鲁番)
Driving: 240km, 4 hours
Trekking: 10km, 3 hours

We will drive to Turpan, taking in the stunning scenery along the way. Upon arrival, our journey will begin with a trek through the historic Jiaohe Ancient City, where farmlands and orchards stretch along the route.

Finally, we will ascend to the city's elevated ruins, offering us the chance to appreciate the grandeur of this thousand-year-old city from various perspectives.

Day3 Turpan - Crossing Flaming Mountain (火焰山) - Tuyugou Grand Canyon (吐峪沟大峡谷) - Mazar Village (麻扎村) - Shanshan (鄯善)
Driving: 110km, 2.5 hours
Trekking: 15km, 5 hours

Flaming Mountain stretches 100 kilometers from east to west. For our trek, we will focus on the main peak section, covering a 15-kilometer route that begins in Mutou Valley (木头沟, Mùtou Gōu) to the east. We will ascend to the ridge line, where to the north lie the majestic Eastern Tianshan Mountains and Lianmuxin Town (连木沁镇, Liánmùqìn Zhèn) on the northern slopes of Flaming Mountain.

To the south, the vast Turpan Basin stretches out. On clear days, the distant ruins of Gaochang Ancient City (高昌故城, Gāochāng Gùchéng) can be seen. Afterward, we will return to the Shanshan County via the northern section of the Tuyugou Grand Canyon.

Day4 Shanshan County - Mirage (海市蜃楼) - Kumtag Desert Trek - Shanshan
Driving: 80km, 2 hours
Trekking: 13km, 4 hours

We will undertake a 13-kilometer U-shaped trek through the heart of the Kumtag Desert, climbing sand mountains, walking along dragon ridges, and "running wild" in the desert to fully experience a genuine desert trek.

Day5 Shanshan - Liaodun (了墩) - Dahai Road (大海道) - Mars Base (火星基地)
Driving: 260km, 5 hours

We will drive to Hami's Dahai Road, home to China's most spectacular yardang landform group. This stretch is part of Xinjiang's renowned "Hundred Mile Wind Zone."

Upon reaching Liaodun, we will transfer to an off-road vehicle to venture into the Dahai Road scenic area, where we'll capture the stunning yardang landforms at sunset.

Day6 Mars Base - Dahai Road - Hami (哈密)
Driving: 260km, 5 hours
Trekking: 12km, 4 hours

We will trek 12 kilometers around the Mars Base, immersed in the stunning landscape of yardang landforms.

Day7 Hami Departure

Important Notes
- Best Season: October to April of the following year
- Suitable For: Healthy individuals aged 8-65 years
- Potential Risks: Large temperature differences between day and night, high ground surface temperature during the day, and changeable climate.

06. Kanas Trek
[喀纳斯徒步, Kānàsī Túbù]

Altay
[阿勒泰, Ālètài]
Gathering City

24KM
Longest Single-Day Hike

300M
Maximum Daily Elevation Gain

1,955M
Highest Elevation Along the Route

★★★★★
Scenic Rating

★★⯪
Difficulty Level

Credit
Image 1/3 | ©Majun
Image 2 | ©Huyang

Where is Kanas? Kanas is located in the far northern part of China, at the "tail of the rooster" on the map, even farther north than Altay City. It marks the starting point of National Highway G219. This area is characterized by its cold temperate and alpine climate, with lush vegetation in the summer and a uniquely breathtaking autumn landscape.

Natural Features

The lush and dense taiga forest is a distinctive feature of this region. These northern coniferous forests, found in the cold temperate zone, are primarily composed of spruce, fir, and larch. When walking along the pristine western shore of the Three Bays (三湾, Sān Wān), one can clearly experience the unique topographical features of the taiga. In addition to the Christmas tree-like conifers, the forest floor is blanketed with layers of shrubs, herbs, and tundra vegetation, all teeming with life.

The most spectacular feature is the brilliant display of autumn colors—an exquisite blend of red, orange, and yellow. From mid-September to early October, the forests lining both shores of the Three Bays undergo a stunning transformation, shifting from lemon yellow to vibrant red-yellow contrasts, and finally to a rich orange-yellow hue. In just half a month, the changing colors make the passage of time visibly apparent.

Kanas is situated at the crossroads of China, Kazakhstan, Russia, and Mongolia, making it a truly unique border region. Baihaba Village (白哈巴村, Báihābā Cūn), located on the China-Kazakhstan border, is known as the "Top Village of Northwest China." The river that separates it from Kazakhstan is called the "Haba River" (哈巴河, Hābā Hé).

Baihaba Village (白哈巴村, Báihābā Cūn) is the smallest settlement of the Tuva ethnic group (图瓦族, Túwǎ Zú) in China, yet it is the one that most harmoniously lives with nature. The Tuva people here primarily travel on horseback and sustain their lives through nomadic herding. Sheep and cattle roam freely through the streets, almost as if they are the true residents of the village. Their relaxed pace often draws groups of tourists, making one wonder how these visitors appear in their eyes. Although most traditional houses in Baihaba have been changed to guesthouses, the wooden cabin style, constructed from locally sourced materials, has remained

unchanged throughout history. Using birch trees as the primary material and moss as a supplement, these cabins offer warmth in winter and coolness in summer, and can be quickly built.

Can you believe that the water flowing through Kanas eventually travels thousands of miles to merge with the Arctic Ocean? The Kanas River originates in the Altay Mountains, flows through Kanas Lake, and then joins the Hemu River (禾木河, Hémù Hé) to the south to form the Burqin River (布尔津河, Bù'ěrjīn Hé). The Burqin River then merges with the Irtysh River (额尔齐斯河, É'ěrqísī Hé) at Burqin (布尔津, Bù'ěrjīn). The Irtysh River continues its journey from southeast to northwest into Kazakhstan, passing through Lake Zaysan (斋桑泊, Zhāisāng Pō), entering the West Siberian Plain, and eventually joining the Ob River (鄂毕河, Èbì Hé) at Mansi (曼西斯克, Mànxīsīkè) in Russia. Finally, it flows into the Arctic Ocean.

This river, the only one in China that flows into the Arctic Ocean, forms the famous Three Bays downstream of Kanas Lake: Fairy Bay (神仙湾, Shénxiān Wān), Moon Bay (月亮湾, Yuèliàng Wān), and Dragon Bay (卧龙湾, Wòlóng Wān). When talking

3

about the Three Bays, we must mention their gem-like "transparent blue," which rivals the lakes of the Tibetan Plateau. The source of this striking blue color lies in the extraordinary clarity of the water in the Three Bays. This river valley was originally shaped by glacial erosion, creating a U-shaped valley with ancient glacial deposits but little sediment. Combined with the clear skies of the Kanas region, the water in Kanas Lake reflects the blue sky, creating the brilliantly blue hues that characterize the Three Bays.

If you look closely, you'll notice that the water here shifts between blue and green. This is due to the rich minerals in the tributary rivers, along with factors such as temperature changes, varying viewing angles, and differences in vegetation along the riverbanks and lakeshores. These elements cause the Three Bays and Kanas Lake to "change colors," which has earned Kanas Lake the nickname "Color-Changing Lake."

Of course, the splendor of the Three Bays extends far beyond the water. As their names suggest, each bay possesses its own unique characteristics. Fairy Bay, located in a low-lying area, is shrouded in clouds and mist every day. The birch forests on both shores appear and disappear with the rising water vapor, creating an ethereal, otherworldly atmosphere. When the sun rises and sunlight pierces through the mist, Fairy Bay transforms into a natural stage, with its curtains drawn open.

Moon Bay is a place you'll fall in love with at first sight. Compared with other bays, the water here has a more vibrant green hue. With its winding curves, Moon Bay resembles a delicate and graceful young lady. In contrast to the majestic grandeur of the entire Kanas region, it feels more exquisite and charming.

Dragon Bay is considered the climax of the Three Bays journey, with its beautiful scenery concentrated in the middle of the river. The water flowing over small sand dunes in the riverbed resembles a reclining dragon. Combined with the dense forests on both shores, it spontaneously evokes the saying: "A mountain need not be high, but is spiritual if inhabited by immortals; water need not be deep, but is spiritual if inhabited by dragons."

Itinerary

Day1 Gather in Altay (阿勒泰)

Day2 Altay - Burqin/Habahe County (布尔津/哈巴河县) - Baihaba Village (白哈巴村)
Driving: 240km, 4 hours
Trekking: 4km, 2 hours

After breakfast, we drive to Burqin/Habahe County to obtain a border pass. After lunch, we continue our journey to Baihaba Village, where you can explore the village and, weather permitting, photograph the sunset.

Day3 Baihaba Village - Kanas (喀纳斯)
Trekking: 24km, 8 hours

Today, we'll rise early to capture the sunrise over Baihaba Village. After breakfast, we depart from Baihaba and begin our trek from west to east towards Kanas.

The journey starts with a short, steep slope, followed by a gradual ascent. We'll cross a small pass (elevation 1,874 meters), skirt around a small marsh, and soon the Fish-Viewing Platform (观鱼台, Guānyú Tái) atop Kalakaite Mountain (喀拉凯特山, Kālākǎitè Shān) will come into view on the left, signaling that Kanas Village is not far off. Today marks the first day of trekking, which involves a relatively long distance and requires a certain level of intensity, so it's important to be mentally prepared.

Day4 Kanas Leisure Day Tour
Trekking: 10km

We will explore attractions at your leisure, including the Fish-Viewing Platform, lakeshore, pier, lake mouth, Turuk Rock Paintings (吐鲁克岩画, Tǔlǔkè Yánhuà), old village, and other scenic spots.

Day5 Kanas - Three Bays Trek - Jiadengyu (贾登峪)
Trekking: 14km, 6 hours

We rise early to catch the first shuttle bus to Fairy Bay, where we'll photograph the morning mist. Afterward, we'll trek to Moon Bay and Dragon Bay before taking the shuttle bus to Jiadengyu. Today promises to be a fulfilling day filled with spectacular scenery.

Day6 Jiadengyu - Bieke Ranch (别克山庄)
Trekking: 22km, 8 hours

Today, we will pass several gentle uphill and downhill sections, mainly following a farm track. You can also venture onto small forest paths nearby, wandering through the magnificent canyons of the Altay Mountains—where yellow birch trees, red European aspens, dark brown larches, and evergreen Siberian spruces or firs stand tall. Along the way, the rushing Kanas River will accompany us.

Day7 Bieke Ranch - Hemu (禾木)
Trekking: 6km, 2 hours

After breakfast, we trek along the Hemu River to Hemu Village. After checking in, you can explore Hemu Village, where scenery and tourists abound everywhere.

Day8 Hemu - Altay
Trekking: 4km, 2 hours

We rise early to watch the sunrise over Hemu from the viewing platform. Afterward, we will take the shuttle bus to the main entrance of the Kanas Scenic Area, and then switch to a vehicle returning to Altay. It is recommended to book flights departing after 7 PM.

Important Notes

- Best Season: September to October
- Suitable For: Healthy individuals aged 10-65 years
- Potential Risks: 1. The weather of Xinjiang is unpredictable, with autumn temperatures being lower than other places and a high likelihood of snow.
    2. Be sure to keep warm and protect yourself from the cold, with raincoats being essential.
- Border Pass: A border pass is required to visit Baihaba Village.

1

07. Kalajun Glassland Trek

[喀拉峻草原徒步, kālājùn cǎoyuántúbù]

7days
97km

Yining
[伊宁, Yíníng]
Gathering City

21KM
Longest Single-Day Hike

740M
Maximum Daily Elevation Gain

2,920M
Highest Elevation Along the Route

★★★★★
Scenic Rating

★★★☆
Difficulty Level

Many people say that without visiting Xinjiang, one cannot truly grasp the vastness of China; and without visiting Ili, one cannot fully appreciate the beauty of Xinjiang. Among Ili's many breathtaking landscapes, the 100-kilometer trekking route connecting Kalajun to Kuerdenin (库尔德宁, Kù'ěrdéníng) is celebrated by seasoned travel enthusiasts as "the most beautiful trekking and photography route in China's Tianshan Mountains.

Natural Features

Located in the Ili River Valley of Xinjiang, Kalajun breaks the monotony often associated with the samilar colors and landscapes of ordinary grasslands, offering a stunning beauty of mountain grassland. It can confidently be said that Kalajun redefines the very concept of the beauty of China's grasslands.

In terms of culture, Kalajun boasts ancient villages, tombs, grassland stone figures, and other cultural heritage, revealing the cultural development over thousands of years. In terms of landscape, Kalajun features undulating terrain, with grasslands, snow-capped mountains, ice peaks, forests, rivers, canyons, and hot springs, creating a diverse and dynamic topography. In terms of color, Kalajun brings together a vibrant array of natural hues, including multicolored meadows, to snow-caped peaks, azure skies, green forests, and beyond.

Every year, from May to June, the Kalajun Grassland bursts into a vibrant sea of colorful flowers, undulating like an ocean. Schrenk's spruce, dense-leaf poplars, and a mix of coniferous and broad-leaved trees blend seamlessly with the grassland, creating a stunning, multicolored tapestry.

The flowers in Kalajun bloom in a distinct pattern. In early spring, yellow lilies and tulips are the first to blossom, transforming the grassland into a golden-yellow carpet. Next come the rose-purple primroses and blue forget-me-nots. From early to midsummer, the grassland becomes even more vibrant, as if all the flowers have bloomed at once, competing for attention across the vast expanse. Among them are globeflowers, anemones, thyme, blue gentians, raincoat plants, willowherbs, gentians, bellflowers, edelweiss, and many more. These blossoms passionately intertwine, spreading endlessly toward the horizon. These wildflowers can bloom for up to one or two months, transforming the grassland into a vibrant, multicolored flower garden, earning Kalajun its reputation as a "five-colored sea of flowers." Experts from the United Nations even visited to investigate, recognizing it as one of the "world's top ten alpine meadow grasslands."

Additionally, here you will find China's most beautiful speckled forest. Around the Tianshan Snow Ranges, the forests and grasslands intertwine at varying elevations, creating a unique beauty of shifting landscapes. Locals have given it an intriguing name—"speckled forest." Influenced by the microclimate of the Tianshan Mountains, lush primeval forests thrive on both the northern and southern sides of Kalajun, with Schrenk's spruces lining the base of the snow-capped Tianshan peaks.

The verdant forests and meadows stretch across diverse terrains, presenting a stunning, colorfully patterned landscape that truly deserves the title of "China's most beautiful speckled forest."

2

3

Day1 Gather in Yining (伊宁)

Day2 Yining - Tekes County (Eight Trigrams City) (特克斯县八卦城) - **Flower Platform** (鲜花台 2,000m)
Driving: 200km, 4 hours
Trekking: 4km, 2 hours

After breakfast in Yining, we drive to the Eight Trigrams City—Tekes County. The city features a radial, circular layout, with streets arranged like a maze, all interconnected.

Enjoy a delicious lunch of local specialties in the city. Afterward, we drive to the Kalajun Bulake (布拉克, Bùlākè) ticket station, where we transfer to a shuttle bus to reach the Flower Platform, marking the start of our trek. Looking around, you'll be captivated by a scene of flowers, grasslands, blue skies, white clouds, yurts, herders, snow-capped mountains, and grazing cattle and sheep.

Wildflowers dot the emerald grassland, filling the air with the fresh scent of grass and the fragrance of blossoms. Surrounded by this stunning flower meadow, you'll feel your body and mind relax completely. We will camp for the night at the Flower Platform campsite.

Day3 Flower Platform Campsite - East Kalajun Campsite (东喀拉峻营地 2,650m)
Trekking: 20km, 7 hours

After breakfast, we take a leisurely stroll through one of the most beautiful grasslands on Earth, surrounded by breathtaking natural scenery. Heading east, we encounter deeply carved valleys, lush vegetation, and majestic snow-capped mountains. The velvet-soft pastures and naturally formed gullies add a dynamic beauty to this expansive landscape. We will camp for the night at the East Kalajun campsite.

Day4 East Kalajun Campsite - Kezilesi Pass (克孜勒斯达坂 2,920m) - **Tarim Valley Campsite** (塔里木河谷营地 1,430m)
Trekking: 21km, 8 hours

After breakfast, we continue heading east. Today, you'll experience the most magnificent, grand, and untouched scenery of the entire journey. Though distant from the main scenic area, East Kalajun has preserved its pristine landscapes.

As you walk through the stunning five-colored meadows, you'll be left in awe! The journey begins with a gentle uphill slope, and after crossing the Kezilesi Pass at an elevation of 2,920 meters, it's all downhill, ultimately reaching the Tarim Valley Campsite at 1,430 meters.

Day5 Tarim Valley Campsite - Qiaxi Campsite (恰西营地)
Trekking: 19km, 7 hours

Our journey today begins with a series of rolling grass slopes, dotted with the homes of herders who have lived in this tranquil landscape for generations, evoking a sense of peaceful pastoral life.

We then continue through the Qiaxi Grassland National Forest Park, where the terrain is mostly flat or gently sloping downhill, offering a different kind of charm compared to the three-dimensional grassland vistas we've experienced in the past few days.

Ili, often referred to as the "Jiangnan Beyond the Great Wall" (a reference to the picturesque region south of the Yangtze River), is renowned for its natural beauty, and Qiaxi is considered the most stunning part of this area. The Qiaxi Grassland is at its most serene and captivating during the spring and summer seasons, when its beauty is truly at its peak.

4

Day6 Qiaxi Campsite - Mohu'er Campsite (莫乎尔营地 1,750m)
Trekking: 18km, 7 hours

After breakfast, we'll journey from the Qiaxi Grassland toward the Mohu'er Grassland. Here, the mountains rise and fold into one another, while the river waters in the valleys flow gently, sparkling in the sunlight. The lush vegetation creates a vibrant, serene atmosphere, with the smoke from cooking fires blending with the light mist among the trees.

The yurts of herders appear and vanish, scattered across the landscape—majestic yet captivating. This poetic scenery is the very essence of a pastoral idyll! Today, we will have the privilege to admire the Tianshan Mountain ranges up close, an experience that only those who have been there can truly appreciate.

Day7 Mohu'er Campsite - Kuerdenin (库尔德宁 1,650m) - Yining
Trekking: 15km, 5 hours
Driving: 200km, 3 hours

Today marks the final day of our trek, yet we will be treated to the most breathtaking views. While the famous Kalajun Grassland is well-known, Kuerdenin remains a hidden gem, largely unknown to the outside world. In 2013, Tianshan was inscribed as a World Heritage Site, with Kuerdenin recognized as a key part of the Tianshan Heritage Site, representing the quintessential Tianshan coniferous forests.

Kuerdenin is home to a rich variety of landscapes, including alpine meadows, subalpine meadows, pristine spruce forests, mixed coniferous and broad-leaved forests, wild fruit forests, meadows, and grasslands. Afterward, we will gradually make our way to the Kuerdenin Scenic Area and then drive back to Yining.

Important Notes

- Best Season: May to June
- Suitable For: Healthy individuals aged 18-65 years with hiking and camping experience
- Potential Risks: The weather of grasslands is changeable in summer, so be sure to keep warm and protect yourself from the cold.

08. Xiata North Line
[夏特北线, Xiàtè Běixiàn]

- 7days
- 67km

Yining
[伊宁, Yīníng]
Gathering City

17KM
Longest Single-Day Hike

1,100M
Maximum Daily Elevation Gain

3,760M
Highest Elevation Along the Route

★★★★★
Scenic Rating

★★★★
Difficulty Level

For many outdoor enthusiasts, the Wusun Trek (乌孙, Wūsūn) has long been regarded as the premier trekking route in Xinjiang. However, for those who have ventured along the Xiata North Line, Wusun now holds second place. As the saying goes: while the Xiata Grand North Line boasts features that Wusun may lack, such as glaciers and snow-capped mountains, what Wusun offers is equally remarkable when compared to the Xiata Grand North Line. Moreover, the Jade Lake (玉湖, Yù Hú) in Zhaosu (昭苏, Zhāosū) is often considered the equal of the famed Heaven Lake (天堂湖, Tiāntáng Hú).

Natural Features

Jade Lake is also known as the "Color-Changing Lake." Throughout the four seasons, due to different lighting conditions, the lake water displays different colors. In May, as the ice and snow melt, the lake water appears grayish-blue; in June, as vegetation grows, the lake water turns azure; in July and August, due to the upstream inflow and the influence of rainfall, Jade Lake shows alternating milky white and dark green, resembling a landscape painting; in September and October, the autumn colors are splendid, and the lake water colors are at their most intense—viewed from above, it resembles a lake-blue jade belt inlaid in the valley, no less stunning than Wusun's Heaven Lake. While not difficult to reach, it remains a niche destination as a scenic spot. Only seasoned travelers and trekking enthusiasts have the previlige to witness the beauty of Jade Lake.

Another highlight of the Xiata North Line is the opportunity to experience glaciers up close, without the dangers of climbing them. Located in the Tomur Peak (托木尔峰, Tuō mù'ěr Fēng) area of the Southern Tianshan Mountains, the vast Muzhaerte Glacier (木扎尔特冰川, Mùzhā'ěrtè Bīngchuān) covers 1,500 square kilometers, making up one-sixth of the total glacier area in the Tianshan range. Due to its remote location, it has preserved its pristine, snow-white beauty. Here, you can experience all four seasons in a single day, transitioning from the lush green fields of spring to the snowy plains of winter. The ancient glacier appears almost within reach, and the imposing, towering snow mountains loom directly before you, their peaks rising into the clouds with a sense of unyielding grandeur. The cold, ethereal light at the mountain tops seems to captivate the soul.

Zhang Chengzhi (张承志, Zhāng Chéngzhì), a writer, wrote in his essay "Love of Xiatai" (《夏台之恋》, Xiàtái zhī Liàn): "You should believe me that the blue pines and white snow along the Xiatai line, over a hundred kilometers along the northern foothills of the Tianshan Mountains, are indeed the most beautiful place on this planet." The "Xiatai" mentioned here is what we call Xiata.

The Xiata Grand North Line features the most complete vertical landscape zones of the Tianshan Mountains, including snow mountains, glaciers, forests, grasslands, canyons, wetlands, lakes, rivers, and more. In all of Xinjiang, it's unlikely you'll find another place that combines snow mountains, glaciers, forests, and grasslands in such a unified landscape as Xiata.

During spring and summer, tender green pasture occupies the entire grassland canyon, dotted with dark green Schrenk's spruce. Large patches of globeflowers, wild lilies, tulips, and wild roses all bloom in competition. The azure glacial river, like the finishing touch in a painting, outlines a paradise on earth.

As autumn winds blow, the meadows eagerly take on a golden hue. The distant snow-capped mountains and the nearby yellow-green mountains complement each other, naturally forming an exquisite oil painting. Rather than calling it heaven, perhaps describing it as the Garden of Eden is more fitting—a land of bliss that only a select few have had the fortune to set foot upon.

This place possesses the beauty of Wusun, yet with far fewer glacial rivers. It boasts a pristine white glacier, purer than that of Bogda, but without the treacherous crevasses and hidden rivers. The grandeur of its snow-capped mountains surpasses that of Langta (狼塔, Lángtǎ), yet there is no need to cross countless passes, nor is there the looming threat of altitude sickness (the highest point being Toglasu Pass at 3,760 meters).

In short, the Xiata Grand North Line gathers the essence of all Xinjiang's trekking routes, while avoiding their challenges and hardships. It is clearly a gift from heaven to ordinary people, or perhaps even nature itself is unwilling to conceal Xiata's beauty, eager for more to witness it firsthand! With such a precious gift at hand, what reason could you possibly have to refuse?

Itinerary

Day1 Gather in Yining (伊宁)

Day2 Yining - Zhaosu Gezhouba Jade Lake Scenic Area (昭苏葛洲坝玉湖景区) - Aheyazi Valley(阿合牙孜沟) - Kongguer Bulake River Valley Campsite(空古尔布拉克河谷营地 2,600m)
Trekking: 11km, 500m ascent, 5 hours

We will begin trekking from Zhaosu Jade Lake, a magical lake hidden in the heart of the Tianshan glaciers. The winding lake water extends into the distance. In the afternoon, we will arrive at the Kongguer Bulake River Valley Campsite.

Day3 Kongguer Bulake River Valley Campsite - Adenbulake Pass (阿登布拉克达坂 3,700m) - Adenbulake Campsite (阿登布拉克营地 3,000m)
Trekking: 15km, 1,100m ascent, 700m descent, 8 hours

Departing from the Kongguer Bulake Campsite, we will cross the Adenbulake Pass and arrive at the Adenbulake Campsite. Today's journey will be challenging, but all the hardships will be well worth it when you stand atop the pass, taking in the breathtaking scenery below.

Day4 Adenbulake Campsite - Talede Bulake Pass (塔勒得布拉克达坂 3,760m) - Xiata Cabin Campsite (夏特小木屋营地 2,800m)
Trekking: 14km, 850m ascent, 960m descent, 7 hours

From the Adenbulake Campsite, we will trek to the Talede Bulake Pass, then continue on to the Xiata Cabin Campsite. At the Xiata Cabin Campsite, we will spend an unforgettable night, gazing at the starry sky and immersing ourselves in the tranquility and harmony of nature.

Day5 Xiata Cabin Campsite - Xiata Su River Valley (夏特苏河谷) - Unnamed Campsite (无名营地 3,300m)
Trekking: 12km, 500m ascent, 5 hours

From the Xiata Cabin Campsite, we will trek to the Xiata Su River Valley and the Unnamed Campsite. Today, we will ford the cold waters of the Xiata River, feeling the coldness of glacial meltwater.

Day6 Unnamed Campsite - Toglasu Pass (托格腊苏达坂 3,760m) - Dundugole River Valley (敦都郭勒河谷地 2,800m)
Trekking: 15km, 600m ascent, 960m descent, 7 hours

From the Unnamed Campsite, we trek to the Toglasu Pass, then continue on to the Dundugole River Valley Campsite.

Day7 Dundugole River Valley Campsite - Yining
Driving: 260km, 3 hours

Important Notes

- Best Season: June to October
- Suitable For: Healthy individuals aged 18-65 years with at least two days of trekking and camping experience
- Potential Risks: 1. The highest pass stands at 3,760 meters.
  2. Those sensitive to high altitudes may experience discomfort and should move slowly to avoid severe altitude sickness.
  3. The daily trekking distances are relatively long, so good physical fitness is essential.
  4. Be sure to rest adequately to ensure a safe and enjoyable journey.

1

09. Wusun Ancient Road

9days
109km

[乌孙古道, Wūsūn Gǔdào]

Yining
[伊宁, Yīníng]
Gathering City

22KM
Longest Single-Day Hike

1,240M
Maximum Daily Elevation Gain

3,830M
Highest Elevation Along the Route

★★★★★
Scenic Rating

★★★★
Difficulty Level

Credit
Image 1 | ©Baoyu
Image 2 | ©194
Image 3 | ©Majun
Image 4 | ©Harrison

Among the many classic trekking routes in Xinjiang, if the Xiata Ancient Road (夏特古道, Xiàtè Gǔdào) is renowned for its fame, Langta (狼塔, Lángtǎ) for its sheer difficulty, and the Bogda Circuit (环博格达, Huán Bógédá) for its sacredness, then the Wusun Ancient Road uniquely blends breathtaking beauty with fame, hardship, and spiritual significance. The beauty of the Wusun Ancient Road is both delicate and rugged, elegant yet barren—a harmony where tenderness and resilience intertwine.

Cultural Significance

Two thousand years ago, a graceful beauty once traveled this ancient road, making her way to the royal palace of Kucha (龟兹, Qiūcí). In those days, transportation was slow, and the King of Kucha fell deeply in love with Dishi (弟史, Dìshǐ), the daughter of Princess Jieyou (解忧公主, Jiěyōu Gōngzhǔ). For love, the King of Kucha crossed the Tianshan Mountains, trekking through its valleys and ridges, traversing countless mountains and rivers, and passing by the crystal-clear Heaven Lake (天堂湖, Tiāntáng Hú) high in the mountains.

Thus, he forged a legendary path of love—the Wusun Ancient Road.

Princess Dishi also traveled this road to join the King of Kucha in marriage. Their powerful love not only made Kucha the Han Dynasty's most trusted neighbor among the 36 states of the Western Regions, but also helped to solidify the Han Dynasty's dominance in the region.

Spanning over 100 kilometers across the northern and southern Tianshan Mountains, this magnificent road connects the Junggar Basin (准噶尔盆地, Zhǔngá'ěr Péndì) in the north with the Tarim Oasis (塔里木绿洲, Tǎlǐmù Lǜzhōu) in the south, controlling the crucial passage through the Tianshan range. Many outdoor enthusiasts who have ventured along it call it the most beautiful ancient road in Xinjiang.

Natural Features
The route traverses a variety of landscapes, including grasslands, dense forests, snow-capped mountains, glaciers, and lakes, with the scenery constantly changing at every turn, leaving one in awe. Its beauty is both diverse and extreme—grand yet exquisite, profound yet delicate—offering not only challenges but also breathtaking views that tempt the senses. Along the way, deep river valleys and turbulent rapids require visitors fording the water numerous times.

Whether crossing wooden bridges or wading through rivers, travelers must exercise caution to avoid falling into the water. In some areas, the current is rapid, and falling in could lead to serious hazards. When wading, travelers should keep their clothes dry and ensure that the clothing and sleeping bags in their backpacks are properly waterproofed. If a traveler falls into the water, hypothermia can set in quickly, so it's essential to know the correct methods for treating hypothermia.

This kind of long-distance trek with certain risks must be undertaken with careful consideration of one's physical condition and shall not be approached recklessly.

2

Notable Attractions

1 Heaven Lake
[天堂湖, Tiāntáng Hú]

Heaven Lake, hidden deep within the Wusun Ancient Road, is a vast lake rarely found in Xinjiang. Its surface remains calm, like a giant mirror reflecting the azure sky and snow-capped mountains. The ever-changing clouds, climate, and seasons cause the lake to shift in color, displaying hues of blue, green, and white.

At times, the lake's water transforms into a spectrum of colors in just a single day—azure, bright blue, pale green, and dark green. Whenever a breeze ripples its surface, the lake shifts between moments of brilliance and misty stillness, exuding an air of mystery. Heaven Lake truly lives up to its name; only by experiencing it firsthand can one truly appreciate its unmatched beauty!

2 Tianshan Forest
[天山森林, Tiānshān Sēnlín]

Unlike the vibrant "hundred flowers blooming" landscapes of eastern China, the Tianshan forest is dominated almost entirely by a single type of tree - Schrenk's spruce (雪岭云杉, Xuě lǐng Yúnshān).

These majestic trees stand tall and straight, like swords piercing the sky, extending from the southern range of the Tianshan Mountains to Hami. Spanning over 1,800 kilometers from east to west, they create a vast, unbroken sea of green.

3 Alpine Meadow
[高山草甸, Gāoshān Cǎodiàn]

The Wusun Ancient Road is renowned for Heaven Lake, but its true beauty lies in the rich diversity of its landscapes. Along this ancient path, the alpine meadows, rising over 3,000 meters above sea level, unfold like the graceful curves of a beautiful woman. Here, flowers bloom and wither, spring gives way to autumn, and the cycle of seasons repeats year after year.

From June to August, as the rainy season arrives and the snow melts, the meadows, nourished by sufficient water, grow even more vigorously. The soft green grass forms a rolling carpet, as if ruffled by the wind, dotted with colorful flowers. This is also the time when the Wusun Ancient Road is at its most stunning.

4 Akebulake Pass
[阿克布拉克达坂, Ākèbùlākè Dábǎn]

The highest point along this route reaches an elevation of 3,820 meters. Akebulake Pass is a seasonal snow-capped peak, with snow melting during the summer and autumn months. In contrast to the light green grasslands and dark green forests, the landform of the pass is characterized by gray gravel slopes.

The rough gravel road makes the journey more challenging, requiring extra caution to avoid falls. However, the pass offers an expansive view, allowing travelers to take in a breathtaking panoramic vista of the Tianshan Mountain range—truly magnificent.

3

Itinerary

Day1 Gather in Yining (伊宁)

Day2 Yining - Tekes (特克斯) - Qiongkushtai (琼库什台 2,000m) - Qiongkushtai River Valley Campsite (琼库什台河谷营地 2,500m)
Driving: 220km, 5 hours
Trekking: 10km, 500m ascent, 4 hours

We drive through Tekes County (Eight Trigrams City), arriving at the trekking starting point in Qiongkushtai Village around noon. From there, we follow the Qiongkushtai River upstream, entering dense pine forests and traveling along clear horse paths for about 7 kilometers.

We then cross a wooden bridge that leads us to a pasture, continuing along a grassy path that gradually ascends to an open riverside meadow—the Qiongkushtai River Valley Campsite.

Day3 Qiongkushtai River Valley Campsite - Qiong Pass (琼达坂 3,740m) - Kunosai Campsite (库诺萨依营地 3,300m)
Trekking: 17km, 1,240m ascent, 440m descent, 8 hours

We continue gradually ascending along the river valley. Upon reaching the confluence of two rivers, we turn toward to the valley on the right side and climb along a riverside stone path for about 3 kilometers. We then find a suitable location to cross the river and continue upward, reaching a gravel beach.

After ascending approximately 200 meters of gravel, we cross the Qiong Pass at an elevation of 3,740 meters. From there, we descend for about 3 kilometers to reach today's campsite, Kunosai, located at an elevation of 3,300 meters.

Day4 Kunosai Campsite - Kuoksu River Campsite (阔克苏河营地 2,000m)
Trekking: 15km, 1,300m ascent, 7 hours

We begin by descending along the valley and meadows, experiencing a significant drop in elevation; knee braces are recommended for this section. Along the way, we cross over a dozen small rivers.

After walking approximately 10 kilometers, we reach the Kuoksu River. We then turn right and continue downstream along the Kuoksu River Valley for 5 kilometers, finally reaching the campsite near the cable bridge. Nearby, there is a grocery store run by local herders, yet it is open intermittently.

Day5 Kuoksu Campsite - Heaven Lake (天堂湖 3,050m)
Trekking: 18km, 1,050m ascent, 8 hours

Crossing the cable bridge was once the most thrilling part of the entire journey, but in recent years, an iron bridge has been constructed. After crossing the river, we enter the forest, where we must cross the river seven times within the woods. We then begin a gradual ascent, occasionally crossing meadows and other times passing through forests.

In the afternoon, after crossing a small pass, we continue gently forward for 3 kilometers to reach Heaven Lake, located at an elevation of 3,050 meters, where we set up camp.

Day6 Free Day at Heaven Lake
Heaven Lake is the major scenic highlight of our

journey, surrounded by snow-capped mountains and tranquil waters, truly a paradise on earth. From the campsite, you can appreciate the view of Xinjiang's most beautiful alpine lake.

You can also hike around the lake to take in the scenery and explore different perspectives of Heaven Lake. Sitting by its shores, sipping coffee, listening to your favorite music, and watching the sunrise, sunset, and starry sky—this is a feast of mountains and lakes, a unique present that belongs solely to you.

Day7 Heaven Lake - Akebulake Pass (阿克布拉克达坂 3,830m) - Upper Bozikerige River Valley Campsite (博孜克日格河谷上营地 3,000m)
Trekking: 15km, 780m ascent, 830m descent, 7 hours

We proceed along the boardwalk by Heaven Lake, passing through the famous "Tiger's Mouth" (老虎口, Lǎohǔ Kǒu), a popular photo spot. After leaving the lakeside, we begin the climb up Akebulake Pass. The slope is very steep, and snow is frequently encountered along the way.

The surface layer of snow melts during the day and freezes at night, making the ascent particularly challenging. Once we cross the pass, the descent begins. After dropping more than 800 meters in elevation, we reach the Bozikerige River Valley, where we set up camp at 3,000 meters by the riverside.

Day8 Upper Bozikerige River Valley Campsite - Lower Bozikerige River Valley Campsite (博孜克日格河谷下营地 2,180m)
Trekking: 22km, 820m ascent, 8 hours

We continue descending along the Bozikerige River Valley, where the real challenge begins: crossing the river. As we walk along the riverbank, we must cross the river dozens of times.

The vegetation becomes increasingly sparse, gradually creating a sense of desolation. Eventually, we set up camp in a forested area by the river.

Day9 Lower Bozikerige River Valley Campsite - Heiying Mountain Pass (黑英山山口 1,940m) - Kuqa (库车)
Trekking: 12km, 240m descent, 4 hours

We continue crossing the river more than 20 times, following the broad river valley downstream. In the afternoon, we reach Heiying Mountain Pass, marking the end of the trek. From there, we drive to Kuqa and conclude our journey.

Important Notes

● Best Season: June to October
● Suitable For: Healthy individuals aged 18-65 years with experience in long-distance trekking and camping
● Potential Risks: 1. The river is swift in summer and icy cold in autumn. Exercise caution when crossing, usually with the assistance of a guide or companions.

2. Be extra cautious when crossing Daban Pass, and watch out for falling rocks.

3. In June and October, you may encounter blizzards, and the path near the may be icy, requiring the use of crampons.

4. Around the National Day holiday, the temperature may drop as low as -15°C, so be sure to take precautions for cold weather and stay warm.

10. Langta C+V Trek
[狼塔C+V, Lángtǎ C+V]

12days
183km

Urumqi
[乌鲁木齐, Wūlǔmùqí]
Gathering City

21KM
Longest Single-Day Hike

1,070M
Maximum Daily Elevation Gain

4,010M
Highest Elevation Along the Route

★★★★
Scenic Rating

★★★★★
Difficulty Level

Credit
© All images in this piece
by Snail

For many Chinese trekking enthusiasts, Xinjiang's Langta is more than just a geographical landmark, but holds spiritual significance. They aspire to one day stand atop the Tianshan Mountains, scale the tower peaks guarded by wolves, and complete a trekking route steeped in over 2,000 years of nomadic heritage. For outdoor adventurers, life is incomplete without traversing Langta C+V.

Cultural Significance

Historically, various ethnic groups in the Western Regions, centered around the Tianshan Mountains—such as Loulan (楼兰, Lóulán), Yuezhi (月氏, Yuèzhī), Wusun (乌孙, Wūsūn), and Kucha (龟兹, Qiūcí)—either clashed or coexisted, flourished or faded away, collectively weaving a rich and complex chapter of history.

Today, there are three classic routes that traverse the Tianshan Mountains: Xiata, Wusun, and Langta. The Xiata Ancient Road is renowed for its historical significance, with relics of the ancient Silk Road still visible along the way. The Wusun Ancient Road is celebrated for its unparalled natural scenery, with the stunning vistas of Heaven Lake inspiring a deep desire to visit. The Langta Route, however, is defined by the thrill of wilderness trekking, challenging adventurers to discover the true meaning of "perseverance" as they cross one pass after another.

In the past, when transportation infrastructure was underdeveloped, this route served as a vital shortcut through the Hutubi area, providing access to Barentai (巴伦台, Bālúntái), an important town in southern Xinjiang. Despite the numerous dangers along the way, frontier soldiers and Kazakh herders would risk the crossing each summer. However, after 1949, with the gradual establishment of highways and railways connecting northern and southern Xinjiang, many ancient routes were abandoned. Over time, these routes transformed into pilgrimage paths for adventurers seeking extreme challenges.

In 2003, under the leadership of renowned Xinjiang mountaineer Wang Tienan (王铁男, Wáng Tiěnán), the first Langta expedition team successfully completed the crossing after nine days and nights of grueling trekking, thereby establishing the Langta C Route. The route's unique historical, cultural, ecological, and mountaineering significance quickly captured the attention of China's outdoor community, marking the beginning of an era of Langta exploration and research.

To date, there are six crossing routes: A, B, C, D, V, and C+V. Among them, Route A is the least difficult, while the C+V route is the most challenging routes in China and also the most popular one in recent years.

The Lonta C+V trek spans approximately 200 kilometers and encompasses nearly every type of terrain and risk typically found in extreme outdoor routes, including snow-capped mountains, deep canyons, boulder fields, glacial rapids, cliffside plank roads, and wild animals. Along the way, the carcasses of ibex and the skulls of wild boars serve as silent reminders that animals are the true rulers of this land, and we are merely visitors.

Notable Attractions

1 Alpine Pastures
[高山牧场, Gāoshān Mùchǎng]

Langta, meaning "tower mountain guarded by wolves," refers to Heyuanfeng (河源峰, Héyuán Fēng), the highest peak in the region, and is also considered a sacred site by Kazakh herders.

This remote area, seldom visited by humans, is home to vast alpine meadows, making it an ideal highland pasture. In the 1970s, Hutubi County specifically carved out herding paths to facilitate grazing.

2 Six Magnificent Passes
[六个壮美达坂, Liù gè zhuàngměi Dábǎn]

As the longest, most arduous, and most dangerous trekking route crossing the northern Tianshan Mountains, Langta C+V route spans about 200 kilometers of uninhabited wilderness, crossing six passes with an average elevation exceeding 3,500 meters.

These are, in sequence: Baiyangou Pass (白杨沟达坂, Báiyángōu Dábǎn 3,850m), Kulaateng Pass (库拉阿特腾达坂, Kùlā'ātéténg Dábǎn 3,550m), Montekaizeng Pass (蒙特开增达坂, Méngtèkāi zēng Dábǎn 3,950m), Kanagaite Pass (喀纳尕依特达坂, Kānàgá'yītè Dábǎn 3,760m), Ulabutu Pass (乌拉布图达坂, Wūlābùtú Dábǎn 4,010m), and Tianger Pass (天格尔达坂, Tiāngé'ěr Dábǎn 3,750m).

3 Glacial Rivers
[冰河, bīng hé]

Mountaineers who have traversed this route often describe it as "crossing rivers endlessly," and this is no exaggeration. Although water levels fluctuate with the seasons, the currents are usually fast, and the water remains ice-cold. Without proper protective measures, the risk of being swept away is significant.

In certain areas, the water flow is so swift that falling in could have serious consequences. When crossing rivers, it's crucial to avoid getting your clothes wet, and all clothing and sleeping bags in your backpack should be properly waterproofed. It's advisable to use ropes for added safety and to be well-prepared with the correct techniques to handle hypothermia. Never underestimate the danger of any river crossing.

4 Tiger's Mouth
[老虎口, Lǎohǔkǒu]

This is the most perilous section of the entire journey. It is a narrow path, with a cliff on one side and a precipice on the other, beneath which flows a swift river.

The path is barely wide enough for a single person. If it happens to rain, crossing Tiger's Mouth becomes even more dangerous. Every step must be taken with the utmost caution, as slipping could easily send you plunging over the edge.

Itinerary

Day1 Gather in Urumqi (乌鲁木齐)

Day2 Urumqi - Hutubi County (呼图壁县) - Baiyanggou Coal Mine (白杨沟煤矿 2,070m) - Baiyanggou Campsite (白杨沟营地, 2,780m)
Driving: 180km, 3 hours
Trekking: 15km, 710m ascent, 6 hours

In the early morning, we depart from Urumqi by vehicle, arriving at the starting point of the trek, Baiyanggou Coal Mine, by noon. This area is nestled among mountains with lush vegetation.

We head west along the Baiyanggou River Valley, which gradually widens as the trees become sparser. This marks the Kalamoyinake (喀拉莫依纳克, Kālāmòyīnàkè) Alpine Pasture, located below Baiyangou Pass. Along the way, traces of ancient glacial retreat can be seen, along with high glacial moraines formed by past glacial movement. We set up camp in Baiyanggou for the night.

Day3 Baiyanggou Campsite - Baiyanggou Pass (白杨沟达坂 3,850m) - Five Star Campsite (五星营地 2,730m)
Trekking: 18km, 1070m ascent, 7 hours

We continue ascending along Baiyanggou.

After about two hours, we reach the glacier area. The glacial moraines, raised by past glacial movement, resemble towering steps that block the path ahead. We bypass these massive moraines and ascend along the glacier's edge to cross Baiyanggou Pass at an elevation of 3,850 meters.

From the top of the pass, we can see the iconic Heyuanfeng peak of Langta, with Route B to the left and Route C to the right. Beyond this, a saddle-shaped ridge becomes visible. We follow the horse path leading up to the plank road, then continue along the plank road, passing above the Taipuxikema (台普希克马, Táipǔxīkèmǎ) River Valley, officially entering Langta. We set up camp at the Five Star Campsite for the night.

Day4 Five Star Campsite - Taipuxikema River Valley (台普希克马河谷 2,400m) - Sky Plank Road - One Tree Campsite (一棵树营地 2,550m)
Trekking: 18km, 500m ascent, 7 hours

We descend to the Taipuxikema River Valley, located at an elevation of 2,400 meters, entering the core area of Langta. The Taipuxikema River is a major tributary of the upper Hutubi River. The river valley is narrow and deep, with rapid water flow and dense forests on both sides, remaining in its pristine state.

Today, we will pass through the legendary plank road, which is carved into the vertical cliff and is only 30-40 centimeters wide—just enough for a horse without a load to barely pass through. We then follow the Taipuxikema River Valley upstream for about 8 kilometers. As the valley bottom gradually widens, we continue walking for about an hour until we reach the Taipuxikema River. After crossing the river, we will reach the One Tree Campsite.

Day5 One Tree Campsite - Kulaateteng Pass (库拉阿特腾达坂 3,550m) - Ertelantan River (尔特兰塔河) - Wolf Restaurant Campsite (狼餐厅营地 2,880m)
Trekking: 19km, 1,000m ascent, 1,050m descent, 9 hours

We begin the day by traveling from the campsite to Kulaateteng Pass, which sits at an elevation of 3,550 meters. Although the straight-line distance is less than 4 kilometers, the vertical elevation gain is a challenging 1,000 meters. After crossing the pass, we descend for 6 kilometers to the primitive forest at the valley bottom, located at 2,500 meters elevation.

The waters from Lantekaizeng Glacier (兰特开增冰川, Lántèkāizēng Bīngchuān) and Montekaizeng Glacier (蒙特开增冰川, Méngtèkāizēng Bīngchuān) converge here, forming numerous tributaries. Today, we will need to cross the river frequently—about ten times.

Afterward, we pass through the Langta summer pasture, continue upstream along the Ertelantan River, and camp at the Wolf Restaurant below Montekaizeng Pass.

Day6 Wolf Restaurant Campsite - Montekaizeng Pass (蒙特开增达坂 3,950m) - Kanagaite Pass (喀拉尕依特达坂 3,760m) - Hargatenguole Valley Campsite (哈尔嘎腾郭勒沟营地 3,400m)
Trekking: 16km, 1,070m ascent, 550m descent, 8 hours

We follow the herding path to cross Montekaizeng Pass at an elevation of 3,950 meters and Kanagaite Pass at 3,760 meters.

Afterward, we descend into Hargatenguole Valley. At this point, we leave Changji and enter the Bayingolin Mongol Autonomous Prefecture (巴州, Bāzhōu). The two sides of the pass are governed by different autonomous prefectures, each with distinct religious beliefs and customs. The northern slope is primarily inhabited by Kazakh herders who follow Islam, while the southern slope is mainly home to Mongolian herders who practice Buddhism.

The climate also varies between the two sides: the northern Hutubi region is more humid, while the southern Hejing County (和静县, Héjìng Xiàn) is drier. We set up camp in Hargatenguole Valley for the night.

Day7 Hargatenguole Valley Campsite - Ulan Pass (乌兰达坂 3,380m) - Hunza Campsite (浑扎营地 2,900m)
Trekking: 16km, 6 hours

We proceed along Hargatenguole Valley, crossing Ulan Pass at an elevation of 3,380 meters. Along the way, we wade through a canyon section and cross the river multiple times on both banks.

After passing through the canyon, we begin the Langta V Route and eventually reach the Hunza Campsite.

Day8 Hunza Campsite - Xiare Pass (夏热达坂 3,150m) - Green Lake Campsite (绿湖营地 3,380m)
Trekking: 21km, 480m ascent, 8 hours

We cross Xiare Pass, known as the "Golden Pasture," gradually ascending until we reach Green Lake. Green Lake is an alpine lake, hidden deep within the Tianshan Mountains, renowned for its mysterious beauty.

Day9 Green Lake Campsite - Ulabutu Pass (乌拉布图达坂 4,010m) - Santun River Campsite (三屯河营地 2,350m)
Trekking: 15km, 630m ascent, 1660m descent, 7 hours

We cross the highest pass of the journey—Ulabutu Pass. From Green Lake Campsite to the top of the pass, it's only a 600-meter ascent, but the path is exceptionally challenging. After crossing the pass, the elevation drops rapidly by 1,660 meters to the main channel of the Santun River. We then find a flat spot to set up camp.

Day10 Santun River Campsite - Tianger Pass Front Campsite (天格尔达坂前营地 2,950m)
Trekking: 12km, 400m ascent, 1,100m descent, 7 hours

We follow the main channel of the Santun River upstream, a relatively easy stretch. Along the way, we can admire the river's beauty, flowing like a young maiden, and imagine ourselves as gold miners at an abandoned gold mine, uncovering hidden treasures.Afterward, we set up camp below Tianger Pass. Today, we will need to cross the river 5-6 times.

Day11 Tianger Pass Front Campsite - Tianger Pass (天格尔达坂 3,750m) - Qiaolenggel Pass Front Campsite (乔楞格尔达坂前营地 2,350m)
Trekking: 15km, 800m ascent, 1400m descent, 8 hours

We cross the third pass of the V Route—Tianger Pass, the most difficult pass of the journey. Most of the path is covered in gravel, making it exceptionally challenging. The final 300 meters are particularly steep, almost vertical.

After crossing the pass, we head north again. As the elevation decreases, Schrenk's spruce trees of the Tianshan Mountains become more abundant. Eventually, we reach the Qiaolenggel Pass Front Campsite.

Day12 Qiaolenggel Pass Front Campsite - Qiaolenggel Pass (乔楞格尔达坂 2,500m) - Agricultural University Forest Farm (农大林场 1,800m) - Urumqi
Trekking: 15km, 150m ascent, 700m descent, 6 hours
Driving: 150km, 2 hours

We cross Qiaolenggel Pass, located less than 200 meters from the campsite, and enjoy an easy journey to the endpoint at the Agricultural University Forest Farm.

The valley at the Agricultural University Forest Farm is uniquely magnificent and steep, offering distinctive scenery. After arriving at the forest farm, we drive back to Urumqi.

Important Notes

- Best Season: September to October
- Suitable For: Healthy individuals aged 18-65 years with highland long-distance trekking and camping experience
- Potential Risks: 1. Tiger Mouth is the most dangerous section of the entire route, with a cliff on one side and a precipice on the other, barely wide enough for only one person. Extreme caution is essential, especially in rainy weather, when the risk of slipping and falling off the cliff is significantly increased.

    2. Crossing river is also one of the highest risks of Langta. Water levels vary throughout the four seasons, but the current is extremely rapid and cold in most cases. All team members must cross rivers under the protection of the guide and assistants. Meanwhile, you should also master the correct methods for rescuing someone experiencing hypothermia.

    3. Weather changes can be unpredictable, with a high probability of encountering blizzards. Temperatures may drop below freezing at night, reaching as low as -30℃ at the coldest.

1

11. Xinjiang K2 Base Camp Trek

21days
338km

[新疆K2大本营徒步, Xīnjiāng K2 Dàběnyíng Túbù]

Kashgar
[喀什, Kāshí]
Gathering City

30KM
Longest Single-Day Hike

900M
Maximum Daily Elevation Gain

4,818M
Highest Elevation Along the Route

★★★★★
Scenic Rating

★★★★⯪
Difficulty Level

The Karakoram (喀拉昆仑, Kālā Kūnlún) is a majestic mountain range that stretches northwest to southeast, forming a natural boundary between Tibet and Kashmir. With an average elevation exceeding 6,000 meters, it ranks as the second-highest mountain range in the world, surpassed only by the Himalayas. The range is home to four peaks soaring over 8,000 meters and more than 20 peaks exceeding 7,000 meters. Notably, it boasts the most extensive and longest glaciers outside the polar regions. The Karakoram spans the borders of China, Pakistan, Tajikistan, Afghanistan, and India. Its remote location, complex political landscape, sparse human presence, and breathtaking beauty together define the unique character of this extraordinary region.

Mount Qogir (乔戈里峰, Qiáogēlǐ Fēng), known as K2, stands at an impressive 8,611 meters. It is the principal peak of the Karakoram Range and the second-highest mountain in the world. The northern face of K2 lies within Chinese territory, while the southern side is part of Pakistan. Widely regarded as the most difficult 8,000-meter peak to summit, K2 is notorious for its extreme challenges. Its sharp, rugged profile seems as though it has been hewn by knives and axes, with granites bearing the scars of relentless weather. The pyramid-shaped summit, with its distinctly sharp edges, rises dramatically from the earth, and the immense vertical drop of its slopes makes it a striking and awe-inspiring presence amidst a sea of snow-capped peaks.

Notably, the mountain is divided by ridges that stretch from east to west, creating two entirely distinct worlds on either side of the mountain between China and Pakistan. On the southern side, moisture carried from the distant Indian Ocean transforms into snow, which accumulates year-round, and covers the slopes from the summit all the way down to the glacial valleys, stretching dozens of kilometers below. In contrast, the northern side presents a starkly different landscape. Here, dark rock layers are exposed, with sheer cliffs revealing intricate rock textures, and ice crevasses crisscross the terrain.

One side is draped in snow, while the other is dominated by sheer cliffs, yet approaching K2 from either direction demands an arduous journey. This makes it one of the most inaccessible peaks in the world. To date, only a few hundred individuals have had the rare privilege of attempting to approach it from the Chinese side.

Natural Features

The Keleqin River Valley (克勒青河谷, Kèlèqīng Hégǔ), a crucial passage to Mount Qogir from China, lies between the Karakoram and Aghil Ranges (阿吉里山脉, Ājílǐ Shānmài), truly at the heart of the Karakoram. In this breathtaking region, Mount Qogir, Broad Peak (布洛阿特峰, Bùluò'ātè Fēng), Gasherbrum I (加舒尔布鲁木I峰, Jiāshū'ěrbùlùmù I Fēng), and Gasherbrum II stand in a majestic sequence, their towering peaks rising alongside vast canyons.

The area is home to a high concentration of glaciers, including the Yinsugaiti Glacier (

音苏盖提冰川, Yīnsūgàitī Bīngchuān), China's longest glacier, along with nearly 10 other large glaciers stretching more than 18 kilometers. Lacking lush vegetation and vibrant wildlife, the region exudes a stark desolation, where its extreme beauty and grandeur create an imposing "keep out" atmosphere.

K2 is located near Kashmir, a politically sensitive area, so it also takes complex application procedures for entry permit. Before reaching the valley, we must cross the Aghile Pass (阿格勒达坂, Āgélè Dábǎn) at 4,818 meters elevation. Beyond the pass, there is virtually no human presence for over a hundred kilometers, only primitive and remote wilderness... These factors contribute to the extremely small number of people who have entered this valley, with even fewer having had the chance to experience the "savage giant peak" up close.

As one of China's premier trekking routes, the K2 Base Camp Trek offers more views of 8,000-meter snow-capped peaks than the east slope of Mount Everest, more magnificent glaciers than the Shishapangma Circuit, a longer distance than the Langta C+V Trek, and a greater number of days than the Loya Great Circuit. This is a true wilderness, with only a few hundred visitors. Along the entire journey, trekkers must rely on their own strength and camels—either pushing on to the mountaineering base camp at the heart of the route or returning the way they came with regret. There is no third option.

If you're an outdoor enthusiast who loves snow-capped mountains, glaciers, and starry skies, and if you're ready to challenge yourself, unafraid of glacial rapids and rugged glaciers, then the K2 Trek awaits you. Completing it will leave you with a deep sense of accomplishment and pride!

Notable Attractions

1 Kulule Village
[苦鲁勒村, Kǔlǔlè Cūn]

A remote Kyrgyz village, it is the closest village to Mount Qogir and an important starting point for the journey.

Here, the team is assembled and supplies are loaded by camel caravan before officially trekking into the uninhabited wilderness.

2 Singhi Kangri
[特拉木坎力冰川, Tèlāmùkǎnlì Bīngchuān]

It is acclaimed as one of the six most beautiful glaciers in China. Located beneath Singhi Kangri (特拉木坎力峰, Tèlāmùkǎnlì Fēng 7,441m) in the Karakoram Range, the glacier is over 28 kilometers long, with its terminus at 4,520 meters elevation and its snowline at 5,390 meters. The glacier's net ice storage volume is 26.774 cubic kilometers, making it a veritable "solid water tower."

Its total coverage area reaches 37,835 square kilometers, accounting for 37% of the mountainous area in its region, with a coverage of 23% within Chinese territory, making it the mountain area with the highest glacier coverage in western China.

3 Kashgar Ancient City
[喀什古城, Kāshí Gǔchéng]

Kashgar is the gathering point for this trekking route. This ancient city, having withstood over 2,000 years, stands as one of the most historically significant and culturally rich cities along the ancient Silk Road.

Today, it has become a tourist attraction, but is still a residential area for Uyghur people, maintaining traditional Uyghur ethnic customs, handicrafts, and specialty foods. After completing the trek, you should consider taking the time to explore the city and try its unique dishes.

4 Gaotai Residences
[高台民居, Gāotái Mínjū]

Located on the highest cliff in Kashgar's Ancient City, the Gaotai Residences have stood for over two thousand years. Legend has it that the famous Han Dynasty generals Ban Chao (班超, Bān Chāo) and Geng Gong (耿恭, Gěng Gōng) once passed through here.

The residences are situated on rugged terrain with a dense population and a maze of interconnected alleyways, many of which house century-old buildings.

The Uyghur residents are known for their hospitality, and visitors should respect local customs.

Itinerary

4

Day1 Gather in Kashgar (喀什)

Day2 Kashgar - Yecheng (叶城) - Kulule Village (苦鲁勒村 3,500m)
Driving: 550km, 14 hours

We depart by vehicle. As we enter the mountain region in the latter half of the trip, the terrain becomes steeper, and the valleys deeper and more precipitous. Special caution is required when crossing the Akazi Pass (阿卡孜达坂, Ākǎzī Dábǎn) at an elevation of 3,221 meters and the Seliyak Pass (赛力亚克达坂, Sàilìyàkè Dábǎn) at 4,920 meters, where the road is narrow, winding, and slippery.

Afterward, we turn right at the Mazar Military Station and continue along the branch road for 42 kilometers to reach the Yilike Checkpoint. From there, we will proceed to Kulule Village, the starting point of the trek. This remote Kyrgyz village, located closest to Mount Qogir, serves as an important gateway for the journey to the mountain.

Day3 Kulule Village - Two Forks Campsite (两叉营地 3,772m)
Trekking: 17km, 7 hours

Today, we officially begin our trek toward K2 from Kulule Village, located at an elevation of 3,500 meters. The journey starts on a relatively wide dirt road. After about 10 kilometers, we descend into the valley, passing scattered sheepfolds along the way.

After hiking 17 kilometers, we arrive at the Two Forks Campsite, situated at the confluence of two valleys. The terrain here is flat, and abundant water sources make it an ideal place to rest.

Day4 Two Forks Campsite - Sheepfold No. 1 (1号羊圈) - Sheepfold No. 2 (2号羊圈 4,279m)
Trekking: 13km, 500m ascent, 7 hours

We depart from the campsite and gradually ascend to Sheepfold No. 2 at 4,279 meters elevation. This is the winter pasture of Yilike Village and an ideal resting place before crossing the Aghile Pass.reaching the Tarim Valley Campsite at 1,430 meters.

Day5 Sheepfold No. 2 - Aghile Pass (阿格勒达坂 4,818m) - Tamarisk Flat No. 1 (1号红柳滩 3,940m)
Trekking: 20km, 540m ascent, 880m descent, 9 hours

Today, we face a challenging trek. Departing from Sheepfold No. 2, we gradually ascend in elevation. After about 2.5 hours, we reach an alpine lake at 4,800 meters, not far from the Aghile Pass. From the pass, we are greeted with a breathtaking view of the steep, towering Karakoram mountains to the south. We then descend more than 800 meters into the Keleqin River Valley.

This point marks a divide: turning left leads to Gasherbrum, while turning right leads to Qogir. Both sides feature campsites named Tamarisk Flat, which can be confusing. Today, we will stay at Tamarisk Flat No. 1 campsite, located in the direction of Gasherbrum.

Day6 Tamarisk Flat No. 1 - Tamarisk Flat No. 2 (2号红柳滩 4,038m)
Trekking: 6km, 2 hours

After crossing a pass yesterday, both the team members and the camel caravan are exhausted. Today, we will only trek to Tamarisk Flat No. 2 campsite, situated at an elevation of 4,038 meters, for a well-deserved rest. There is a hot spring near the campsite, providing us with an opportunity to bathe and do laundry.

Day7 Tamarisk Flat No. 2 - Gasherbrum Base Camp (迦舒布鲁姆大本营 4,231m)
Trekking: 24km, 8 hours

Today, our journey is relatively long but quite gentle, requiring us to cross multiple rivers—sometimes by riding camels, other times by jumping across. Today we will stay at the Gasherbrum Base Camp for the night. Weather permitting, the Gasherbrum mountain range will be visible.

Day8 Gasherbrum Base Camp - Small Prairie (小草原 4,340m)
Trekking: 16km, 6 hours

Today's journey is not long, but it will be filled with breathtaking sights. Four 8,000-meter snow-capped peaks are all within view, and the terminus of the Gasherbrum Glacier reaches the Keleqin River Valley, so close you can almost touch it. At this moment, you'll realize that all the challenges of the journey have been more than worth it. Tonight, we will camp at the Small Prairie campsite, located at an elevation of 4,340 meters.

Day9 Small Prairie - Singhi Kangri (特拉木坎力冰川 4,525m)
Trekking: 22km, 8 hours

Today's hike covers a relatively long distance and involves challenging terrain. We will rise up early to reach the Singhi Kangri as early as possible. To save time and energy, you can leave unnecessary supplies at the Small Prairie campsite and ride camels with lighter loads.

We will camp for the night by a small lake at the foot of the Singhi Kangri, located at 4,545 meters. The ice tower forest of Singhi Kangri is truly spectacular, and you can venture into it for photography and exploration. This will undoubtedly be an unforgettable and extreme experience.

Day10 Singhi Kangri - Small Prairie (4,340m)

From the campsite, you'll have a stunning view of Gasherbrum I and Gasherbrum II. You can wake up early to witness the sunrise over these majestic peaks or climb a nearby slope to capture the entire ice tower forest in your photographs.

Afterward, we will return to the Small Prairie campsite.

Day11 Small Prairie - Gasherbrum Base Camp
Trekking: 19km, 7 hours

Although this is a return journey, the snow mountains and glaciers along the way are breathtaking, making it worthwhile.

Day12 Gasherbrum Base Camp - Tamarisk Flat No. 2 (4,038m)
Trekking: 17km, 6 hours

The hot springs at 4,038 meters elevation, near Tamarisk Flat No. 2, are still a favorite among everyone. After several days of trekking through snow-capped mountains and glaciers, everyone is in need of rest and relaxation.

Day13 Tamarisk Flat No. 2 - Tamarisk Flat No. 1 (3,966m)
Trekking: 13km, 5 hours

Today, our journey is not long, but it marks an important turning point. We will shift from the Gasherbrum direction to the K2 direction, passing through two sections of "No. 1 Tamarisk Flats." From Tamarisk Flat No. 2, we will hike about 6 kilometers to reach Tamarisk Flat No. 1 on the Gasherbrum side. From there, we cross the valley and continue northwest to Tamarisk Flat No. 1 on the K2 side, located on the opposite bank.

This Tamarisk Flat No. 1 campsite is a lovely spot, situated at 3,966 meters, with a nearby water source so clear that you can see numerous small fish swimming in it.

Day14 Tamarisk Flat No. 1 - Tamarisk Flat No. 2 - Tamarisk Flat No. 3 - Tamarisk Flat No. 4 (3,800m)
Trekking: 22km, 7 hours

We will walk along the Tamarisk Flats, from No. 1 to No. 4. Tamarisk Flat No. 4 is located at the end of "Saddle Mountain," near "Flying Peak." Ahead lies the delta where the Keleqin River Valley meets the Yinsugaiti River.

In the delta, a mountain has been carved by the two rivers, disconnecting it from the surrounding riverbanks, which has led people to call it "Flying Peak."

Day15 Tamarisk Flat No. 4 - Yin Red Flat (音红滩 3,900m)
Trekking: 11km, 4 hours

Departing from Tamarisk Flat No. 4, we cross a nearby small hill and are soon greeted by the sight of the Yinsugaiti River Valley. We continue along the left side of the valley toward Yin Red Flat. As we round a bend, K2 suddenly appears, standing tall on the horizon in the distance. Yin Red Flat is vast and expansive.

In the summer, the Yin Red Flat Base Camp is covered in green grass, with fresh spring water where cold-water fish thrive. While K2 is not visible from the base camp, the terrain here is flat and open, with ample water and grass, making it an ideal resting spot for trekkers and the camel caravan.

Day16 Yin Red Flat - Italian Camp (意大利营地 4,650m) - Yin Red Flat
Trekking: 30km, 750m ascent/descent, 12 hours

Today will be the most challenging day of our trek. The hiking distance is long, the elevation gain is significant, and the trail conditions are difficult. It is recommended to start before 6 am. After about two hours of hiking, we will reach the terminus of the Qogir Glacier tongue, where K2 becomes visible in the distance. Many teams stop here, with some choosing to camp at the glacier tongue campsite (4,130 meters) to witness both the sunrise and sunset over K2.

After leaving the glacier tongue campsite, we will continue along the right side of the glacier slope for about 10 kilometers to reach the Italian Camp, established by the Italian mountaineering team in 1983, marked by a stone-piled windbreak wall.

On the return journey, extra caution is required, especially when passing through hazardous landslide areas where the trail is unclear. Be sure to pay close attention to trail markers as you walk.

Day17 Yin Red Flat - Tamarisk Flat No. 4 - Tamarisk Flat No. 3 - Tamarisk Flat No. 2
Trekking: 22km, 7 hours

Today's leg presents a slight challenge. However, the camel team will find the going relatively easier after resting yesterday and with progressively lighter loads. Trekkers who feel physically weaker may opt to ride on camels.

Day18 Tamarisk Flat No. 2 - Tamarisk Flat No. 1
Trekking: 11km, 3 hours

Today is considered the final rest day before the challenging days ahead. The past two days involved long, high-intensity treks, and tomorrow we will face the crossing of the Aghile Pass once again.

Day19 Tamarisk Flat No. 1 - Aghile Pass - Sheepfold No. 2 - Sheepfold No. 1
Trekking: 23km, 900m ascent, 600m descent, 9 hours

Another tough day of trekking lies ahead. Crossing the 4,818-meter Aghile Pass remains a challenge, even though altitude sickness is no longer a concern for the team after 16 consecutive days of trekking.

Day20 Sheepfold No. 1 - "Single-file Pass" (一线天) - Two Forks Campsite - Kulule Village
Trekking: 30km, 9 hours

Although today's journey is the longest, it is relatively easier due to the continuous downhill path.

If arrangements are made in advance with the vehicle team, they can meet you at the valley exit, saving you 10 kilometers of walking.

Day21 Kulule Village - Mazar (麻扎) - Yecheng - Kashgar
Driving: 540km, 12 hours

Important Notes
- Best Season: March to May, October to November
- Suitable For: Healthy individuals aged 18-65 years with highland long-distance trekking and camping experience
- Potential Risks: 1. Ultra-long distance trekking requires excellent physical fitness from all team members.
  2. The Keleqin River Valley requires numerous river crossings. In summer, the water flows swiftly and the current is strong, making crossing difficult, even when riding camels.

Image | ©Liangshuang

PART 2

SOUTHWEST

China Region

12. Dangling Trek
[党岭徒步, Dǎnglǐng Túbù]

6days

29km

Chengdu
[成都, Chéngdū]
Gathering City

17KM
Longest Single-Day Hike

900M
Maximum Daily Elevation Gain

4,300M
Highest Elevation Along the Route

★★★★
Scenic Rating

★★★★⯪
Difficulty Level

Credit
© All images in this piece
  by HuangHuang

The term "Dangling" often appears on the travel lists of outdoor enthusiasts. It sounds familiar, yet few can explain what it exactly refers to when asked.

Does it refer to Dangling Village (党岭村, Dǎnglǐng Cūn)? Situated about 70 kilometers northwest of Danba County, this hidden village is nestled in a remote mountain basin called "Dangling." Legend has it that in the early Yuan Dynasty, when Mongol cavalry crushed the once-powerful Western Xia Kingdom, the Dangxiang and Qiang peoples fled south, passing through Danba and continuing onward to the Daofu-Luhuo region. Some Dangxiang people settled in the village, and the name "Mountain Ridge of the Dangxiang People" has been passed down through generations for over a millennium.

Does it refer to Dangling Snow Mountain (党岭雪山, Dǎnglǐng Xuěshān)? In the northern section of the Daxue Mountain Range of the Greater Hengduan Mountains, Dangling Snow Mountain stretches from northwest to southeast. Its main peak, "Xiaqiangla" (夏羌拉, Xiàqiānglā), stands at 5,470 meters and is a sacred pilgrimage site for local Tibetans. Around it, 28 snow-capped peaks over 5,000 meters high form a magnificent panorama of clustered-summits and interconnected snow-covered mountains.

Does it refer to Dangling Nature Reserve? It is a hidden gem nestled among the mountains on the border between Danba and

Daofu, cradled by sacred peaks and adorned with alpine lakes. In summer, the reserve bursts into a vibrant array of blooming flowers, while autumn transforms it into a mesmerizing tapestry of colorful forests. Its beauty is a year-round spectacle. The reserve is home to waters that rival the crystal-clear lakes of Jiuzhaigou, snow-capped mountains that echo the majesty of Yubeng, alpine lakes as stunning as those in Daocheng Yading, and forests with hues as striking as those in Miyaluo. Entering Dangling feels like stepping into a living landscape painting.

Natural Features

The Dangling we're discussing today refers to the area centered around Dangling Village, stretching from Tiantang Valley (天堂谷, Tiāntáng Gǔ) in the east to Xiaqiangla Peak in the west. With an average elevation nearing 4,000 meters, this breathtaking landscape is home to countless snow-capped mountains, sacred lakes, and wild hot springs. While the area may seem understated at first glance, once you enter, there will inevitably be moments in which the scenery takes your breath away.

Throughout the year, the most enchanting seasons in Dangling are the transition from spring to summer and mid-October. The former period sees wild rhododendrons blooming magnificently across the mountains. Starting from mid-May each year, Dangling ushers in the rainy season, which nurtures a spring full of vibrant flowers. Among them, rhododendrons bloom with unmatched intensity, blanketing the valley in a sea of pink and purple. As the blossoms compete for attention, the entire landscape transforms into a living masterpiece, and walking through it feels like stepping into a painting.

The latter period features layered colorful forests adorning the mountains and wilderness. Around Frost's Descent (a Chinese solar term), the forests below the snow line don their autumn finery. The journey from Tiantang Valley to Dangling Village begins to "suprise" visitors with color: fiery red maple leaves, golden fir branches, and evergreen pines intertwined densely, complemented by the deep blue sky and snow-capped mountain peaks. This scene, like an oil painting from a master's brush, seems almost too vivid to be real. Shifting your gaze to the lakeshores, where water and sky blend into one, a bright yellow announces the arrival of autumn, displaying "the beauty of autumn leaves" at its peak.

Besides the extremely breathtaking sceneries, trekking in Dangling also offers unique experiences.

Within 5 kilometers south of Dangling Village, there are three wild hot springs created by geothermal activity. The nearest one is called "Murichaqu" (木日插曲, Mùrì Chāqǔ), meaning "Gunpowder Bathhouse," with water temperatures ranging from 34°C to 37°C. A few hundred meters further, you will reach a large meadow and find "Bukachaqu" (布卡插曲, Bùkǎ Chāqǔ), which has the smallest spring eye but the highest temperature, peaking at 75°C–hot enough to boil eggs. The surrounding land and rocks have been calcified over time, and the hot spring is marked with Tibetan script on stone tablets, symbolizing ancient people's devout prayers to the hot springs. Continuing onward, you'll find Hot Spring No. 3, which has the most comfortale bathing temperature and is large enough to accommodate more than 5 people bathing at the same time.

With the faint scent of sulfur in the air, the warm waters gently soothe your meridians, washing away the fatigue from your trek. Completely immersed in the vastness of these mountains and waters, you can't help but feel a deep sense of gratitude for nature's extraordinary gifts.

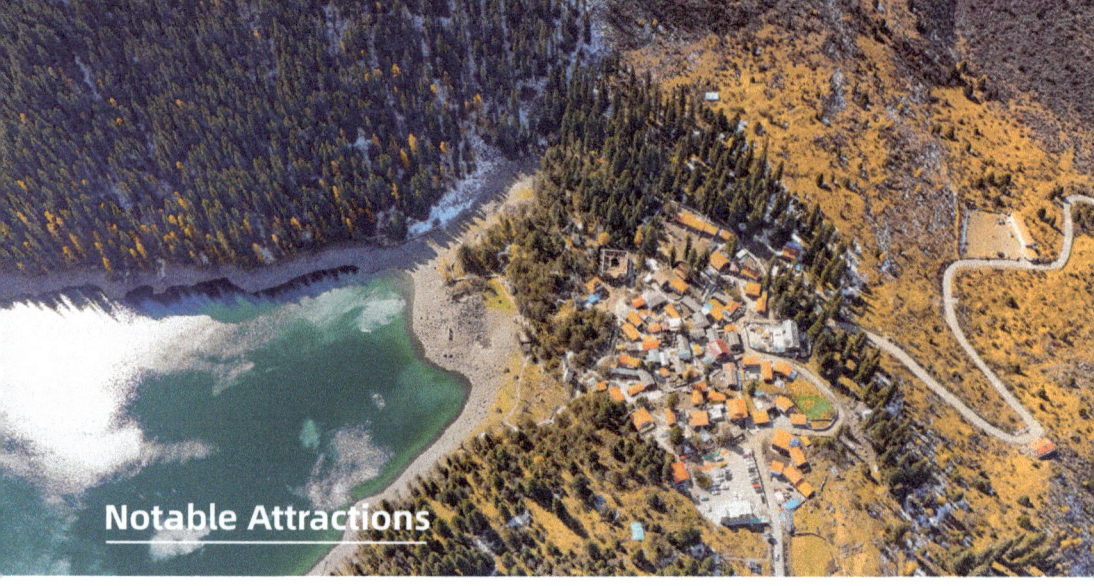

Notable Attractions

1 Xiaqiangla
[夏羌拉, Xiàqiānglā]

The main peak of Dangling Snow Mountain, known by its Tibetan name meaning "Beautiful Goddess Mountain," has long been revered by Tibetan worshippers. It is surrounded by 28 snow-capped peaks towering over 5,000 meters, forming an awe-inspiring cluster.

Among the most prominent are Xiaqiangnie'a (夏羌涅阿, Xiàqiāngniè'ā), Xiaqiangla, and Peak 5240, which stretch from left to right like a mighty screen, standing between heaven and earth. These peaks not only separate Daofu from Dangling but also serve as guardians of the land, watching over the villages and creatures below.

2 Jiayila Lake
[甲依拉措, Jiǎyīlā Cuò]

Also known as "Jiaoyima Lake" (叫一马措, Jiàoyīmǎ Cuò), this lake sits at an elevation of about 4,100 meters. When viewed from above, its shape resembles the face of a horse, which gives it its unique name. Still largely undeveloped, it lies in Qimei Village, Yuke Township in northern Daofu, close to Danba's Dangling, and can be more easily accessed by hiking from Ka'erza Village.

Its waters maintain an otherworldly milky white color year-round, reminiscent of a "milk sea." Unlike Yading's Milk Lake, this alpine lake is surrounded not only by towering pure white snow mountains but also by vast stretches of lush forests, adding a distinct charm to its already breathtaking beauty.

3 Gourd Lake
[葫芦海, Húlú Hǎi]

Named for its distinctive gourd-like shape, it has quietly rested at the bottom of the valleys for thousands of years. The pebbles at the lake's edge extend layer by layer to its depths, shifting in color from green to blue.

As the light changes, the lake perfectly mirrors the surrounding snow-capped mountains and dense forests, creating a serene and captivating reflection.

4 Zhuoyong Lake
[卓雍措, Zhuóyōng Cuò]

This is the largest lake with the highest elevation in the Dangling area. From here, you can enjoy a sweeping panorama of snow mountains in the Dangling region of the Hengduan Range. This is also the best angle to appreciate Gourd Lake.

5 Mosika Village
[莫斯卡村, Mòsīkǎ Cūn]

Located on a high plateau pasture about 60 kilometers from Dangling Village, the village sits at an elevation of 4,300 meters and is built in the form of a mandala. Revered by Buddhists as the "Mandala in the Sacred Land," it is believed to be a place where Buddhas and Bodhisattvas reside.

The village's temples house many stone carvings of the Tibetan hero King Gesar, giving the village a solemn and mysterious atmosphere.

Itinerary

Day1 Gather in Chengdu (成都)

Day2 Chengdu - Four Sisters Mountain (四姑娘山) - Danba Tibetan Village (丹巴藏寨 2,200m)
Driving: 70km, 2 hours
Trekking: 12km, 5 hours

After breakfast, we head out together via the Chengdu-Guanxian Expressway, traveling toward Balang Mountain (巴郎山, Bālángshān).

We'll reach Four Sisters Mountain Town by noon for lunch, then continue our journey, following the Xiaojin River (小金川, Xiǎojīn Chuān) downstream to the Middle Road Tibetan Villages of Danba, nestled beneath the majestic Mount Moerduo (墨尔多神山, Mò'ěrduō Shénshān). Here, we'll immerse ourselves in the unique cultural richness of the Jiarong Tibetan area.

Day3 Danba Tibetan Village - Ka'erza (卡尔杂) - Jiayila Lake (4,000m) - Dangling Village (3,400m)
Driving: 70km, 2 hours
Trekking: 12km, 5 hours

From Danba Tibetan Village, we set off toward Jiayila Lake. We begin by driving for about 40 minutes to reach the trailhead, then embark on a 3-hour hike to the lakeside.

The lake's water maintains a milky white color year-round, earning it the local name "Milk Lake." Due to its remote location, very few tourists venture here, making it a peaceful and untouched gem.

Day4 Dangling Village - Airplane Meadow (飞机坪) - Gourd Lake (4,100m) - Zhuoyong Lake (4,300m) - Dangling Village
Trekking: 17km, 7 hours

Today, we embark on a hike deep into the Hengduan Mountains. Following the winding path of the Kelou River Valley (柯鲁河谷, Kēlǔ Hégǔ) upward, we arrive at the stunning Gourd Lake.

True to its name, the lake resembles a gourd and is made up of two parts—one large and one small. Continuing forward, we'll catch sight of Small Gourd Lake. After climbing about 200 meters from Small Gourd Lake, we reach the perfect vantage point: to the east, a panoramic view of Gourd Lake, and to the west, Zhuoyong Lake, nestled beneath the Three Sacred Mountains. Its waters, made even more sacred by the surrounding glaciers, create an awe-inspiring scene.

Day5 Dangling Village - Mosika (莫斯卡) - Danba County Town (2,000m)
Driving: 145km, 4 hours

Mosika is a pristine Tibetan village, steeped in legend as the place where the heroic King Gesar once fought and lived. It stands as a pure land, carefully nurtured by the hands of kind-hearted people, creating a harmonious coexistence between humans and nature.

Mosika is also renowned for its unique social calling card: the fearless marmots, who appear suddenly, exuding a wild charm that captures the spirit of the place.

Day6 Danba County Town - Luding (泸定) - Chengdu
Driving: 310km, 7 hours

Important Notes

- Best Season: May to November
- Suitable For: Healthy individuals aged 12-65 years
- Potential Risks: Risk of altitude sickness.

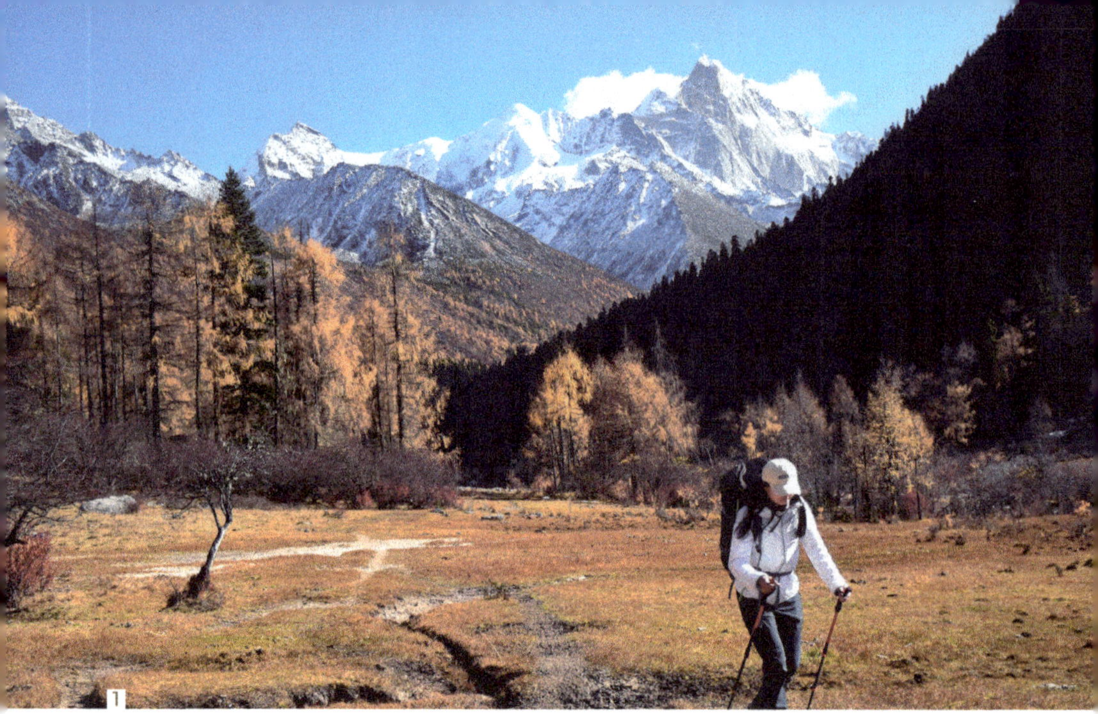

1

13. Changchuanbi Trek

[长穿毕, Cháng Chuān Bì]

5days

44km

Chengdu
[成都, Chéngdū]
Gathering City

21KM
Longest Single-Day Hike

760M
Maximum Daily Elevation Gain

4,660M
Highest Elevation Along the Route

★★★★
Scenic Rating

★★★½
Difficulty Level

Starting from Chengdu, a famous city in southwestern China, it takes about a 4-hour drive west to reach the Western Sichuan Plateau. Here, the earth has pushed up four snow-capped peaks that are named after "maidens" but renowned for their "masculine and towering" stature–this is the Four Sisters Mountain (四姑娘山, Sìgūniáng Shān), known as the "Queen of Sichuan Mountains." This is a dream destination for outdoor enthusiasts and a paradise for photographers who never tire of capturing stunning shots.

Hidden in the outdoor sanctuary of Four Sisters Mountain is one of China's "Top Ten Classic Trekking Routes" that outdoor adventurers shouldn't miss–the Changchuanbi Trek.

Natural Features

This trek begins in Changping Valley (长坪沟, Chángpíng Gōu), located at the western foot of Four Sisters Mountain in Xiaojin County, and extends northeast. It crosses a pass at 4,668 meters in elevation before entering Bipengou Valley (毕棚沟, Bìpéng Gōu) in Li County, situated at the northern foot of Four Sisters Mountain. The trek takes 3 days, covering approximately 34 kilometers, and travels beneath many of western Sichuan's famous snow mountains. Along the way, towering mountains and deep

Credit
Image 1 | ©Banban
Image 2/3 | ©Harrison

valleys intertwine, clear springs merge into rushing streams, snow-capped peaks contrast with red rocks, and the ground is carpeted with moss and pine needles. The elevation difference of over 1,500 meters creates diverse alpine landscapes, including snow-capped mountains, glaciers, forests, meadows, waterfalls, and alpine lakes, attracting countless hiking enthusiasts every year.

The most difficult and dangerous part of the Changchuanbi traverse is the section with loose rocks and steep slopes. Here, you climb from the 3,800-meter camp to the 4,668-meter pass. From finding your way with headlamps to seeing the first light of dawn; from starlight and moonlight to sunrise and the sky filled with clouds... Until the moment you stand at the pass and gaze into the distance, seeing vast seas of clouds spreading across the entire valley, white mists drifting with an ethereal quality surrounding the mountains on both sides. The massive mountains are either covered in snow or gleaming with a cold silver-blue radiance in the sunlight. A sense of grandeur emerges as you realize the world lies at your feet. At this moment, any doubts about why "Changchuanbi" ranks among China's "Top Ten Classic Trekking Routes" suddenly become clear.

After crossing the pass of Chaziwei Valley (叉子沟尾垭口, Chāzi Gōu Wěi Yágǒu), you officially leave the Four Sisters Mountain area and enter Bipengou Valley in Li County, experiencing a different scenary. This is a giant panda habitat and also the core area of the Miyaluo (米亚罗, Mǐyàluó) colorful forests.

While intense summer heat engulfs the cities, Bipengou Valley remains refreshingly pleasant. In summer, the mountains are covered in verdant green with flourishing trees; in autumn, the red maples blaze like fire as the forests change color. It deservedly earns the praise from those who have seen it as "Little Switzerland of Western Sichuan."

Notable Attractions

1 Changping Valley
[长坪沟, Chángpíng Gōu]

Located in the Four Sisters Mountain scenic area, it is the place where the original ecology and ethnic customs of the Four Sisters Mountain region are most concentrated. The deep river valley is filled with rare redwood forests, dense sea buckthorn trees laden with red berries in autumn, and glistening Spanish moss, together forming a vibrant plant kingdom.

By mid-October, when autumn winds sweep through, the forest is completely transformed into a colorful tapestry, truly embodying the saying "walking within a painting."

Itinerary

Day1 Gather in Chengdu (成都)

Day2 Chengdu - Yingxiu Town(映秀镇) – Wolong (卧龙) - Four Sisters Mountain Town (3,150m)
Driving: 190km, 4 hours

After breakfast, we depart from Chengdu by vehicle, passing through Yingxiu town and Wolong, crossing over Balang Mountain (巴郎山, Bālángshān).

We'll take a rest at Maobiliang viewing platform (猫鼻梁观景台, Māobí Liáng Guānjǐng Tái) and take photos before arriving at Four Sisters Mountain Town.

Day3 Four Sisters Mountain Town - Lamasery (喇嘛寺 3,400m) - Dead Tree Beach (枯树滩) - Muluozi Campsite (木骡子营地 3,760m)
Trekking: 12km, 360m ascent, 6 hours

After breakfast, we take a sightseeing shuttle into Changping Valley, and officially begin our three-day trekking journey. Changping Valley stretches 29 kilometers, with Four Sisters Mountain situated on its right side. Within the Changping Valley scenic area, there are ancient cypress paths, a lamasery, dry lake beds, and waterfalls dozens of meters high, as well as unique rock formations.

In summer, mountain flowers bloom alongside rapeseed flowers; in autumn, red birch trees compete in beauty with red maples. We'll camp at Muluozi camp site at the foot of Yaomei Peak (幺妹峰, Yāomèi Fēng) of Four Sisters Mountain.

Day4 Muluozi Campsite - Shuida Dam (水打坝) - Turtle Rock (乌龟石) - Chazi Valley End Campsite (叉子沟尾营地 3,900m)
Trekking: 11km, 240m ascent, 6 hours

Today, our schedule is relatively relaxed, allowing us to enjoy ourselves as we hike.

After breakfast, we depart from the Muluozi campsite and begin a gentle trek towards the end of Changping Valley, passing through Shuida Dam, Turtle Rock, and Yangmantai (羊满台, Yángmǎn Tái) before reaching the Chaziwei Valley Campsite.

Day5 Chazi Valley End Campsite - Pass (4,660m) - Shanghaizi Reception Station (上海子接待站) - Li County (理县) - Chengdu
Trekking: 21km, 760m ascent, 10 hours
Driving: 250km, 4 hours

We set out around 3 AM and cross the pass. The section at the beginning is very steep and requires extra caution. The slope becomes slightly gentler later on, and after passing a large platform, the pass comes into view.

After crossing the pass, we descend all the way to the Three Trees Campsite (三棵树营地, Sānkē Shù Yíngdi) inside Bipengou Valley. From there, we follow the main road of the Bipengou scenic area, enjoying stunning scenery all the way until we reach the rest station, marking the end of our trek.

We then take an electric cart to Shanghaizi Reception Station, followed by a scenic shuttle to the entrance of Bipengou Valley, before driving back to Chengdu.

Important Notes

- Best Season: June to November
- Suitable For: Healthy individuals aged 16-65 years
- Potential Risks: The pass is steep, and the downhill sections can be slippery and dangerous. Please exercise extra caution!

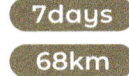

14. Qizang Valley
[七藏沟, Qīzàng Gōu]

7days

68km

Chengdu
[成都, Chéngdū]
Gathering City

16KM
Longest Single-Day Hike

650M
Maximum Daily Elevation Gain

4,250M
Highest Elevation Along the Route

★★★
Scenic Rating

★★★
Difficulty Level

Credit
© All images in this piece by Jason

Qizang Valley is located in northwestern Sichuan Province, in the southeastern mountainous region of the Songpan Grassland. To its north lies Jiuzhaigou (九寨沟, Jiǔzhài Gōu), and to its south is Huanglong (黄龙, Huánglóng). Together, they form a breathtakingly beautiful natural scenic area under subtropical climate control, encompassing mountains, alpine lakes, primeval forests, and alpine meadows. The wilderness and tranquility are the greatest charms of Qizang Valley. Its pristine natural beauty is a perfect match for the tastes of outdoor hiking enthusiasts.

The name "Qizang Valley" allegedly came from seven mountain valleys hidden in this area, formed by melting snow. However, there are actually more than seven valleys in this region, such as Kaka Valley (卡卡沟, Kǎkǎ Gōu), Aweng Valley (阿翁沟, Ā'wēng Gōu), Sandaoping (三道坪, Sāndào Píng), Gami Valley (尔米沟, Gǎmǐ Gōu), Hongxing Valley (红星沟, Hóngxīng Gōu), White Bear Valley (白熊沟, Báixióng Gōu), and Wanglang Valley (王朗沟, Wángl_áng Gōu). The hiking route in Qizang Valley essentially involves traversing these valleys.

Natural Features

The most distinctive feature of Qizang Valley is its numerous concentrated highland pearls—"haizi" (海子, Hǎizi), or alpine lakes, represented by Long Lake (长海子, Chánghǎizi), Grass Lake (草海, Cǎohǎi), and Red Star Lake (红星海子, Hóngxīng Hǎizi). The scenery along the route reveals no trace of human development. Walking through this untouched highland mountain area, the sense of accomplishment from crossing mountain passes, combined with the sight of near and distant snow-capped peaks looming ahead, evokes an unparalleled sense of awe. The rippling lakes along the way are particularly spectacular under the azure sky.

If Jiuzhaigou is a must-visit tourist destination in Sichuan, then Qizang Valley is a must-hike outdoor route in the region. Unlike the popular, bustling tourist spots, it has less foot traffic and fewer controversies, leaving behind only stunning landscapes. It's like a hidden gem that only true outdoor enthusiasts would discover. There's no need to feel pity for its lack of attention, nor should one regret that its fame doesn't match its beauty. Its tranquility and distance from the bustling crowds are important components of its charm. What we come here to experience is its wild untouched nature and its raw, unpolished beauty.

Notable Attractions

1 Long Lake
[长海子, Chánghǎizi]

Long Lake is known as the "Eye of the Ghost," surrounded by high mountains. After crossing the mountain pass, it suddenly appears before your eyes, leaving people in awe.

2 Red Star Lake
[红星海, Hóngxīng Hǎi]

Red Star Lake is a sacred site for the locals. The lake's surface forms an asymmetrical five-pointed star, surrounded by serene forests and snow-capped mountains.

Its shimmering blue waters captivate all who behold it. Red Star Lake is to Qizang Valley what Heaven Lake is to the Wusun Ancient Path—it is the soul of this route.

3 Fish Lake
[鱼海子, Yú Hǎizi]

Fish Lake is a marsh lake formed by accumulated creek water, beautiful yet unassuming. It is about 100 meters wide and 1,000 meters long.

Due to the lush water plants, this place is home to the "Min River Cold Water Fish," which can grow up to 18 cm in length and are extremely rare and precious.

Itinerary

Day1 Gather in Chengdu (成都)

Day2 Chengdu - Wenchuan (汶川) - Songpan County(松潘) - Chuanzhusi Town (川主寺 3,200m)
Driving: 340km, 7 hours

We travel upstream along the Min River valley, passing through Wenchuan, the epicenter of the May 12, 2008 earthquake. Along the way, we can see the enormous destruction brought by the Wenchuan earthquake, as well as revitalized mountain villages rebuilt from the disaster.

Afterward, we arrive at Songpan county and then stay at Chuanzhusi town for overnight accommodation.

Day3 Chuanzhusi - Kaka Valley Entrance - Cattle Shed (牛棚子) - Long Lake (3,700m)
Trekking: 16km, 7 hours

After breakfast, we drive to the entrance of Kaka Valley and begin our hike. As we venture further in, we encounter narrow ravines surrounded by towering peaks, steep cliffs, flowing sand, and flying rocks, making careful progress essential. In the afternoon, we reach the Long Lake campsite.

Day4 Long Lake - Long Lake Pass (4,200m) - Fish Lake (3,300m)
Trekking: 14km, 500m ascent, 900 m descent, 7 hours

Today, we will cross Long Lake Pass, a challenging stretch due to the high altitude.

Once we reach the pass, we'll be rewarded with a breathtaking view of Red Star Rock. Afterward, we enter Aweng Valley. The downhill path proves difficult to navigate, with a section of shifting sand and loose rocks that can be quite treacherous. In the evening, we reach Fish Lake and set up camp for the night.

Day5 Fish Lake Campsite - Grass Lake - Red Star Lake Pass (3,900m) - Red Star Lake Lower Campsite (3,600m)
Trekking: 10km, 600m ascent, 5 hours

We hike toward Red Star Lake, passing through steep mountains and sparse forests along the way. Midway, we traverse a flat mountain depression—a dried-up lake now covered in grass, aptly named "Grass Lake." Continuing upward, we ascend the 3,900-meter Red Star Lake Pass. The slope is about 45 degrees, with a vertical climb of 400 meters.

After crossing the pass, a short 200-meter walk brings us to Red Star Lake. Surrounded by rugged, rocky peaks, the lake stretches wide and calm, its waters a deep azure blue. After taking in the beauty of Red Star Lake, we continue to the Lower Red Star Lake Campsite and set up camp for the night.

Day6 Red Star Lake Lower Campsite - Jade Lake Pass (4,250m) - Jade Twin Lakes - Tazi Valley Campsite (3,400m)
Trekking: 16km, 650m ascent, 8 hours

After breakfast, we depart from the campsite and begin our ascent along Tazi Valley. By noon, we reach the 4,250-meter Jade Lake Pass.

Once we cross the pass, the Jade Twin Lakes (翡翠双海子, Fěicuì Shuāng Hǎizi) come into view. We continue onward to the Small Jade Lake (翡翠小海子, Fěicuì Xiǎo Hǎizi) and then begin a steady descent. The towering trees here are all over a hundred years old. After passing through the ancient primeval forest, we reach today's campsite in Tazi Valley.

Day7 Tazi Valley Campsite - Changgou Village (长沟村) - Chuanzhuzi - Chengdu
Trekking: 12km, 4 hours
Driving: 340km, 7 hours

Today's itinerary is relatively relaxed. After breakfast, we'll depart from the campsite and begin our journey, circling around the mountain.

Upon crossing the 3,700-meter pass, we'll be rewarded with a panoramic view of the entire Chuanzhusi town. Continuing downhill along the trail, we'll make our way to Changgou Village. From there, we'll drive back to Chengdu.

Important Notes

- Best Season: June to October
- Suitable For: Healthy individuals aged 12-65 years
- Potential Risks: Risk of altitude sickness; the gravel slope at the mountain pass is slippery.

15. Genyen C Route

[格聂C线, Géniè C Xiàn]

Chengdu
[成都, Chéngdū]
Gathering City

22KM
Longest Single-Day Hike

800M
Maximum Daily Elevation Gain

4,980M
Highest Elevation Along the Route

★★★★★
Scenic Rating

★★★★
Difficulty Level

Genyen is situated in the southwestern part of Litang County, within Ganzi Prefecture in Sichuan Province. It borders Batang to the west, connects to Daocheng to the south, and is traversed by National Highway 318 along its northern edge. The name "Genyen" translates to "lay Buddhist practitioner" in Tibetan. Genyen is one of the many scenic spots in the Tibet-Sichuan region, with a reputation that is as serene and understated as its name suggests.

Believe it or not, this region is blessed with abundant natural beauty and rich historical significance. Its stunning landscapes, combined with a deep cultural heritage, have woven a timeless paradise that has endured through the centuries. The blend of nature and history here creates an irreplaceable treasure, shaped by the passage of time.

Natural Features

In a narrower sense, Genyen specifically refers to the highest peak of the Shaluli Mountain Range in the Great Hengduan Mountains of western Sichuan, standing at 6,204 meters above sea level. It is the only peak in the region that exceeds 6,000 meters. Revered as a sacred mountain by Tibetans, it is considered the thirteenth female deity among the 24 sacred mountains of Tibetan Buddhism, known as Mount Genyen (格聂神山, Génièr Shénshān).

In terms of its mountain profile, Genyen Sacred Mountain may not be as strikingly distinctive as some of its counterparts. It lacks the towering grandeur of Mount Gongga, the majestic beauty of the Three Sacred Mountains of Yading, and the delicate uniqueness of Four Sisters Mountain. From a distance, it appears rounded like a steamed bun. Its summit is blanketed in snow year-round, while below, distinct layers of primeval forests, shrub- covered grasslands, river channels winding through bay areas, and marshy meadows unfold. The northern slope is characterized by exposed bedrock scattered with boulders, while the southern slope is adorned with cascading glaciers and towering ice formations. The eastern slope is dotted with glacial lakes, and the western slope boasts lush river valleys, where herds of cattle and horses roam. Though it may not be strikingly beautiful in the traditional sense, Genyen Sacred Mountain exudes a quiet, understated charm, rich in natural diversity and unique allure.

In a broader sense, "Genyen" refers to a cluster of snow-capped mountains in the shape of a lotus, with Mount Genyen at its core. This area is commonly known as the Genyen Mountain Range, most of which lies within Litang County, with a portion extending into Batang County. This region is scattered with over 20 peaks rising above 5,000 meters. Beneath the snow-capped mountains and glaciers, it is home to expansive grasslands, meandering rivers, alpine lakes, and a variety of unique geological formations and cultural relics.

Cultural Significance

In foreign books and Buddhist classics, Genyen is also called Gongbo Gongga or Gongga Xiangbo, serving as a famous place for ascetic practices. Historically, this place was once a center of immense glory. At its peak, it was home to over 20 monasteries representing various sects of Tibetan Buddhism, with countless monks and a continuous flow of pilgrims. Today, the ancient and quiet Laoleng Monastery (老冷古寺, Lǎolěng Gǔsì) still stands at the foot of Mount Genyen—legend has it that it was founded in 1164 by the first Karmapa, and is the oldest Kagyu (White Sect) temple in the region.

In 1877, the famous explorer William Gill arrived on the Litang Plateau and saw Mount Genyen. He wrote in his diary, "Words can hardly capture the majesty of this towering mountain. Here, any traveler can come to understand the deep reverence Tibetans hold for it and why they call it a sacred mountain."

Genyen is at its most beautiful during the summer months of July and August, when the land is blanketed with a vibrant tapestry of yellow, blue, white, and purple flowers, stretching endlessly like a "sea." The term "sea of flowers" is not an exaggeration in Genyen. Walking through the summer grasslands here, it's impossible not to be captivated by the sight of these blooms. Amid the vast meadows, your heart swells with a sense of longing for love and freedom, and a profound appreciation for the flowers themselves. As you pass through the small forest at the beginning of the trek, undulating alpine meadows emerge, adorned with a variety of small flowers. There's no need to obsess over whether the flowers at your feet are gentians or primroses—their nameless beauty, beneath the snow-capped peaks, is simply a reflection of their pure nature.

On the journey to cross the 4,980-meter pass, you may come across the densest cluster of King's Crown (*Tǎhuáng) you've ever seen. The river valley area between the scree slopes on either side of the pass is teeming with this unique flower. True to its name, the King's Crown blooms only once in its lifetime. Its tall, straight stems are adorned with layers of pale yellow bracts, and it blooms in July and August on alpine rock beaches and wetlands above 4,000 meters. From a distance, the flowers resemble magnificent golden pagodas—elegant, noble, and striking. Walking through this sea of flowers, with your body enveloped in their sweet fragrance, is the most heartfelt gift that Genyen offers to those who journey from afar.

Beyond the snow mountains and sea of flowers, the landforms along the way are extremely diverse, including snow-capped mountains, glaciers, alpine meadows, winding river valleys, marshes and shrubs, unique landscapes, groups of alpine lakes, vast grasslands...This hiking route covers almost all the main scenic spots in the Genyen mountain area. If you want to hike in western Sichuan and see the most stunning scenery in the region in one trip, then Genyen is highly recommended!

Itinerary

2

Day1 Gather in Chengdu (成都)

Day2 Chengdu - Kangding (康定) - Litang (理塘 4,000m)
Driving: 550km, 10 hours

We will depart early and take the Chengdu -Ya'an Expressway to reach Ya'an (雨城雅安, Yǔchéng Yǎ'ān), the "City of Rain." From there, we continue on the Ya'an-Kangding Expressway, passing through the Erlang Mountain Tunnel to arrive in Kangding City.

Afterward, we will climb over Zheduo Mountain (折多山, Zhéduō Shān), the first pass of Kham, and make a brief stop at Zheduo Mountain Pass (elevation 4,298 meters) for rest and photos before continuing westward.

We will pass through Xinduqiao (新都桥, Xīndūqiáo), reach Yajiang (雅江, Yǎjiāng), the hometown of matsutake mushrooms, cross Gaoersi Mountain (高尔寺山, Gāo'ěrsì Shān), Jianziwanshan Mountain (剪子弯山, Jiǎnziwān Shān), and Kazila Mountain (卡子拉山, Kǎzilā Shān), and arrive in the town of Litang County by evening.

Day3 Litang - Blacksmith Mountain Pass (铁匠山垭口 4,770m) - Lama Pass (喇嘛垭) - Ranrika Village (然日卡村 3,750m)
Driving: 1.5 hours
Trekking: 7km, 900m ascent, 4 hours

The morning is free for activities. You can visit Renkang Ancient Street (仁康古街, Rénkāng Gǔjiē), Changqingchun Korsi Temple (长青春科尔寺, Chángqīngchūn Kē'ěrsì), and the Thousand Households Tibetan Village (千户藏寨, Qiānhù Zàngzhài).

After lunch, we will drive to cross Blacksmith Mountain Pass, where you can enjoy a distant view of the Genyen mountain range and admire the giant rocks, strange stones, and nearby beautiful alpine lakes of Blacksmith Mountain. We will then descend into the valley to reach Lama Pass. Afterward, we will cross Laze Pass (拉则垭口, Lāzé Yágǒu), where you can see three massive snow-capped peaks rising on the horizon. From left to right, you will spot Genyen, Xiaozha (肖扎, Xiāozhā), Cameron (喀麦隆, Kāmàilóng), and other sacred mountains.

Descending further into the valley, we will reach our destination for the day–Ranrika Village. Here, you can enjoy the breathtaking views of the snow mountains and relax in the wild hot springs, soaking in the warmth while taking in the stunning scenery.

Day4 Ranrika Village - Eye of Genyen (格聂之眼) - Offering Sanghoma Platform (煨桑台) - Lengda Campsite (冷达营地 3,800m)
Trekking: 17km, 7 hours

After breakfast, we will climb a small slope to reach the Eye of Genyen, experiencing its mysterious allure, often described as "the eyes of the earth." From here, we can closely observe Genyen, Xiaozha, and other snow- capped peaks, as well as the sea of flowers below. After leaving the Eye of Genyen, we will head towards the main peak of Genyen Snow Mountain, walking across open grasslands, surrounded by lush meadows and vibrant flowers.

In the afternoon, we will arrive at an observation platform on the southeastern slope of Genyen, where you can not only enjoy the stunning views of Genyen Snow Mountain but also take in the beauty of Xiaozha Valley. We will then descend for about 2 hours to reach the Lengda Campsite.

Day5 Lengda Campsite - New Lenggu Monastery (新冷古寺) - Hangda Campsite (夯达营地 3,800m)
Trekking: 13km, 6 hours

Today, we will rise early to capture the sunrise over Mount Genyen. After breakfast, we will visit New Lenggu Monastery to explore three rare treasures: the doe's antlers, the reversed conch shell, and the "Heart of Genyen."

After leaving the monastery, we will begin climbing the slopes, first passing through a primeval forest and then reaching an alpine meadow, covered with wildflowers and offering a stunning view of the crystal-clear sacred Mount Genyen in the distance. We will then follow the scenic route along the southern slope of Genyen, arriving at Hangda Campsite, located at the foot of the southern slope in the afternoon.

This campsite is very close to Mount Genyen, giving you the opportunity to closely observe the snow-capped peaks and glaciers right from your tent.

Day6 Hangda Campsite - Daodao Valley (岛岛河谷) - Reti Campsite (热梯营地 4,180m)
Trekking: 18km, 9 hours

After breakfast, we will leave Hangda Campsite, first climbing to the ridge, followed by a horizontal traverse—a physically demanding challenge. The area is covered with meadows and various wildflowers, and throughout the journey, you will have a constant view of Mount Genyen, with the stunning scenery making it easy to forget any physical fatigue.

In the afternoon, after passing through the final canyon—Daodao Valley—you will catch sight of tonight's campsite. We will cross the ridge beside Daodao Valley, descend past a river, and walk a few more kilometers deeper into the valley to reach Reti Campsite, located in the middle of Reti Valley. This is the last campsite where you can still see Mount Genyen.

Day7 Reti Campsite - Yele Valley (耶勒沟) - Mountain Pass (4,980m) - Gemu Village (格木村 3,820m)
Trekking: 22km, 800m ascent, 1160m descent, 10 hours

Today is the most physically demanding day of the hike. After breakfast early in the morning, we will begin our climb from the campsite, reaching the 4,980-meter pass in about 5 hours.

At the pass, we take a final look at Mount Genyen, as it will no longer be visible once we cross over the pass. After the pass, we will descend all the way, following the Lapu Valley (拉普沟, Lāpǔ Gōu) down to Bangduo Valley (邦多河谷, Bāngduō Hégǔ), and continue onward to Gemu Village.

Day8 Gemu Village - Hagala Pass (哈嘎拉垭口 4,790m) - Anjiu Village (安久村 4,200m) - Litang
Trekking: 18km, 6 hours
Driving: 80km, 2 hours

Today, you will cross the final pass of the journey, but the overall elevation gain is not significant. In the morning, we will drive from Gemu Village to Hagala Pass, then hike for about 5 hours from the pass to reach Anjiu Village.

In the afternoon, we will wade across a wide river. After crossing the cold river, we will find a natural hot spring where we can soak our feet. We will then follow Hari Valley (哈日沟, Hārì Gōu) to Anjiu Village, a nomadic settlement on the Maoya Great Grassland (毛垭大草原, Máoyá Dà Cǎoyuán).

The hike concludes here, and we will take local vehicles across the Maoya Great Grassland to Litang County town.

Day9 Litang - Kangding - Chengdu
Driving: 550km, 10 hours

Important Notes

- ● Best Season: June to October
- ● Suitable For: Healthy individuals aged 18-65 years with high-altitude long-distance trekking and camping experience
- ● Potential Risks: 1. High-altitude trekking, be aware of altitude sickness;
  2. The Genyen area experiences frequent rainfall in the summer, so be sure to bring waterproof gear.

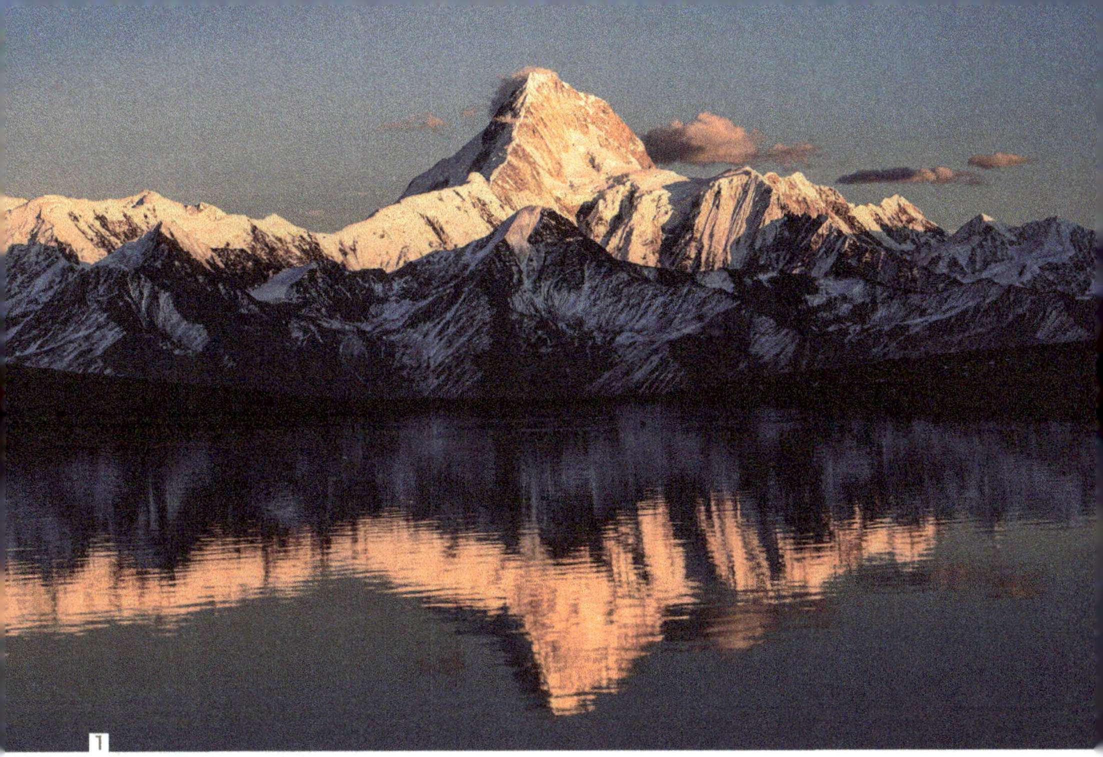

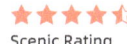

1

16. Gongga Full Route
[贡嘎全线, Gònggā Quánxiàn]

8days
78km

Chengdu
[成都, Chéngdū]
Gathering City

16KM
Longest Single-Day Hike

950M
Maximum Daily Elevation Gain

4,920M
Highest Elevation Along the Route

★★★★½
Scenic Rating

★★★★
Difficulty Level

Credit
Image 1 | ©Majun
Image 2 | ©Huyang
Image 3 | ©Banban
Image 4 | ©Lizi

Mount Gongga is located in the eastern part of the Qinghai-Tibet Plateau, in the central section of the Daxue Mountain Range within the Hengduan Mountains. Its geographical position gives it a distinct advantage, making it the easternmost snow-capped peak over 7,000 meters. The main peak rises to 7,508.9 meters above sea level, with its summit covered in ice and snow year-round. The mountain is renowned for its unique glacial features, and its sharp, imposing edges project the commanding presence of a king, appearing truly spectacular. Surrounding Mount Gongga are more than a hundred ice-covered peaks, each standing between five and six thousand meters high.

Natural Features

The Gongga Mountain region is an area with relatively intact modern glaciers. Several glaciers "rushing" down from the mountain top weave a magnificent crystal crown for the "King of Sichuan Mountains," appearing crystal clear, pure white, and immaculate, like a pure saint.

This place is both a paradise for outdoor enthusiasts and a fairyland for photography lovers. Every photography enthusiast would want to capture a snow mountain, a sunrise, a sunset, and the extraordinary landscapes of western Sichuan at least once in their lifetime. The majestic main peak of Mount Gongga, the floating and surging sea of clouds surrounding the mountains, the colorful pools of the "Little Huanglong" travertine terraces, the golden and splendid sunset at Lengga Lake (冷嘎措, Lénggá Cuò), the radiant sunrise at Zimei Pass (子梅垭口, Zǐméi Yágǒu)... At Mount Gongga, there are countless wonderful landscapes, like a fairy-tale world far from the hustle and bustle, a paradise that is isolated from the world yet within reach.

Would you like to personally visit those millennia-old glaciers? Would you like to free your soul under the sacred mountain? Then let us meet at Gongga, together to chase the dreamlike scenery of the sun illuminating the mountain and the tranquil night sky under Mount Gongga.

May is the time for spring snow on Mount Gongga, and heavy snowfall is possible. However, mid to late May is also the peak of rhododendron bloom, making the combination of snow scenes and rhododendron flowers unmissable. From June to August, it is summer on Mount Gongga, with relatively more rainfall and unstable weather. However, it is also the flowering season, with vast expanses of alpine wildflowers in full bloom. After the rain, natural phenomena like rainbows may also appear.

September marks the transition from summer to autumn in the Gongga Mountain area, with relatively stable weather, making it an ideal time to view the snow-capped peaks. From October to November, the region experiences autumn, offering beautiful scenery, stable weather, and occasional heavy snowfall. The mountains are adorned with vibrant autumn colors, providing a stunning contrast between the snow-covered peaks and the colorful forests.

Notable Attractions

1 Zimei Pass
[子梅垭口, Zǐméi Yágǒu]

One of Mount Gongga's most famous photography spots, this location offers a heartfelt encounter with the "King of Sichuan Mountains." Standing at the pass, the snow-capped peak of Mount Gongga comes into full view, showcasing the "King of Sichuan Mountains" in all its grandeur. The sight is so captivating that it feels as if the snow mountain is within arm's reach.

2 Riwuqie Valley
[日乌且, Rìwūqiě]

While everyone knows about Hailuogou valley (海螺沟, Hǎiluógōu) and Yanzigou valley(燕子沟, Yànzigōu), next to them quietly lies a hidden beauty—Riwuqie.

Walking in the Riwuqie Valley, you're surrounded by four mountains over 6,000 meters: Little Gongga (小贡嘎, Xiǎo Gònggā) at 6,027 meters; Jiazi Peak (嘉子峰, Jiāzǐ Fēng) at 6,540 meters; Riwuqie Peak (日乌且峰, Rìwūqiě Fēng) at 6,376 meters;And Leduomanyin (勒多曼因, Lèduō mànyīn) at 6,112 meters.

Little Gongga is a three - ridged peak with a straight pyramid shape that deeply attracts one's gaze; Jiazi Peak is one of the famous satellite peaks of Mount Gongga; Riwuqie Peak and Leduomanyin Peak also await our visit with their majestic postures.

3 Lengga Lake
[冷嘎措, Lénggá Cuò]

Lengga Lake is located on a mountain at an elevation of about 4,530 meters to the left of Yulong West Village in Gongga Mountain Township. It is a typical cirque-type alpine lake, with its opening directly facing the main peak of Mount Gongga.

Due to its close proximity to the peak, it has become a popular spot for outdoor hiking enthusiasts and photography lovers, offering a perfect vantage point to capture the reflection of Mount Gongga and the sunset. This spot is often referred to as the "Dressing Mirror of Mount Gongga."

4 Travertine Terraces
[泉华滩, Quánhuá Tān]

This is a colorful calcite pool located in a concave valley surrounded by mountains on three sides. It was formed by chemical precipitation from spring water rich in various chemicals, which deposits on the surface.

The terraces stretch over 900 meters in length and more than 100 meters in width, forming 8 travertine platforms descending along the mountain. Each platform has pools of different colors, shapes, and sizes, blending with the reflection of the blue sky, creating breathtaking beauty.

5 Bawang Lake
[巴王海, Bāwáng Hǎi]

Located at the junction of Kangding County and Shimian County in Ganzi Prefecture, Sichuan Province, it belongs to the heartland of Mount Gongga. The name "Bawang Lake" actually originates from the nearby Gongbu Glacier (贡布冰川, Gòngbù Bīngchuān). This glacier is shrouded in thick clouds and fog year-round, making it difficult to fully see its true form.

As a result, local Tibetans named it "Bawang Glacier," which suggests that one might have to look back eight times to catch a glimpse of it. Due to the differences in communication between Tibetan and Han cultures, "Bawang" (八望, Bāwàng, meaning "eight looks") was eventually pronounced as "Bawang" (巴王, Bāwáng), a name with the same pronunciation but different characters.

The lake near the glacier was subsequently named "Bawang Lake." Bawang Lake is narrow and beautiful, quietly nestled in a lush green canyon, surrounded by mountains and forests. The lake is scattered with many dead trees, creating a striking contrast with the vibrant, lively surroundings of the mountains and forests.

Itinerary

Day1 Gather in Chengdu (成都)

Day2 Chengdu - Kangding (康定 2,600m) - Laoyulin Power Station (老榆林电站) - Gexi Grassland Campsite (格西草原营地 3,400m)
Driving: 310km, 5 hours
Trekking: 3km, 1 hours

We drive through Kangding County to reach Laoyulin Village (老榆林村, Lǎoyúlín Cūn), where we will switch to local minibuses to reach the trailhead at Laoyulin Power Station. From here, we will begin our hike to Gexi Grassland for camping, or alternatively, take local private cars directly to the Gexi Grassland Campsite.

Day3 Gexi Grassland Campsite - Two-Fork River (两岔河) - Lower Riwuqie Campsite - Upper Riwuqie Campsite (4,350m)
Trekking: 15km, 950m ascent, 7 hours

We head towards the Upper Riwuqie Valley, taking in the magnificent highland scenery along the way. About two hours after departure, we reach Two-Fork River, with expansive red stone beaches visible across the water.

Continuing forward, we enjoy views of Tianhaizi Snow Mountain (田海子雪山, Tiánhǎizǐ Xuěshān) at 6,070 meters, Little Gongga at 6,027 meters, and Jiazi Peak at 6,549 meters. After passing the Lower Riwuqie Campsite, we continue on to the Upper Riwuqie Campsite, where we will set up camp for the night.

Day4 Upper Riwuqie Campsite - Riwuqie Pass (4,920m) - Moxi Valley End Campsite (莫溪沟尾营地3,900m)
Trekking: 16km, 570m ascent, 1020m descent, 8 hours

We depart to cross the highest pass of the entire journey, Riwuqie Pass. The continuous climb allows you to experience firsthand the changes in alpine vegetation.

After crossing the pass, we descend all the way, walking through low shrubs and meadows. In the evening, we will camp at Moxi Valley End Campsite.

Day5 Moxi Valley End Campsite - Yulong West Pass (玉龙西垭口 4,500m) - Yulong West Village (玉龙西村 3,800m)
Trekking: 15km, 600m ascent, 700m descent, 7 hours

We continue along Moxi Valley, walking through shrubs and alpine meadows, to cross the 4,500m Yulong West Pass. The route primarily involves traversing and ascending.

From here, you'll be treated to a breathtaking view of Mount Gongga, the King of Sichuan Mountains, along with more than a dozen surrounding snow-capped peaks. Afterward, we descend through alpine meadows to reach the roadside of Yulong West Village.

From there, we'll take local minibuses to reach Yulong West Village for overnight accommodation.

Day6 Yulong West Village - Travertine Terraces (4,000m) - Lengga Lake (4,500m) - Yulong West Village
Trekking: 14km, 500m ascent/descent, 6 hours

In the morning, we will hike to the Travertine Terraces, also known as the "Little Five-Colored Pools," for sightseeing. Afterward, we will return down the mountain the same way and take a local minibus to the trailhead at the foot of Lengga Lake Mountain to begin our hike upward. We will trek through shrub forests, with the majestic Gongga Mountain range towering behind us.

As we walk with our backs to Mount Gongga, we will gradually ascend, then traverse a short section to reach the 4,500-meter Lengga Lake. Here, we can capture stunning photos of the magnificent Gongga sunset.

Afterward, we will return the same way to the trailhead and take transportation back to Yulong West Village for overnight accommodation.

Day7 Yulong West Village - Zimei Pass (4,500m) - Zimei Village - Bawang Lake (3,100m) - Caoke (草科 1,500m)
Driving: 70km, 2 hours
Trekking: 15km, 5 hours

We will take transportation to Zimei Pass to watch the sunrise and photograph Mount Gongga from a different angle. Afterward, we will drive down the mountain to Lower Zimei Village (下子梅村, Xià Zǐméi Cūn) and begin our hike to Bawang Lake.

The scenery along the way is stunning as we travel along the riverside through primeval forests, passing dense sea buckthorn trees and hundred-year-old shrub forests.

After reaching the 3,100-meter Bawang Lake, we will continue hiking to the endpoint at the Bawang Lake Parking Lot. From there, we will take transportation to Caoke.

Day8 Caoke - Ya'an (雅安) - Chengdu
Driving: 355km, 7 hours

Important Notes

● Best Season: June to October

● Suitable For: Healthy individuals aged 18-65 years with high-altitude long-distance trekking and camping experience

● Potential Risks: 1. High-altitude hiking: Be mindful of the risks of altitude sickness.

      2. If heavy snow occurs at Riwuqie Pass, it will become very difficult to cross, and extra caution is required.

      3. After descending from Riwuqie Pass, there are many forking paths, making it easy to get lost, so stay close with the team.

      4. During the rainy season, landslides or road submersion may occur near Bawang Lake, please follow the team leader to find the safest paths.

17. Joseph Rock Route

[洛克线, Luòkè Xiàn]

8days
64km

Chengdu
[成都, Chéngdū]
Gathering City

16KM
Longest Single-Day Hike

1,000M
Maximum Daily Elevation Gain

4,750M
Highest Elevation Along the Route

★★★★
Scenic Rating

★★★★
Difficulty Level

Every traveler who yearns to visit the highlands—whether a travel expert, hiking enthusiast, photography aficionado, or travel novice—would likely include one name on their "must-visit destinations" list: Daocheng Yading (稻城亚丁, Dàochéng Yādīng).

The popular "Daocheng Yading" refers to the Yading Scenic Area (亚丁风景区, Yādīng Fēngjǐng Qū), located in Yading Village, Shangri-La Town (香格里拉镇, Xiānggélǐlā Zhèn), formerly known as Riwa Town in Daocheng County, Ganzi Prefecture, Sichuan Province. It is often referred to as the "Soul of Shangri-La." In the Western world, Shangri-La is synonymous with "utopia" or "paradise on earth," and the origin of this title is closely linked to the American explorer Joseph Rock from the early 20th century.

Cultural Significance

In 1923, four young couples from a Naxi ethnic village in Yunnan took their own lives out of love. During the "Great Wind Sacrifice" ceremony held for them by the local Dongba religion, Joseph Rock, who was residing in the area, learned that the "paradise" and the "Third Kingdom of the Jade Dragon" described in the scriptures were not merely fictional, but actually existed in the Gongga Ridge mountain area of western Sichuan. Determined to explore this region,

Rock decided to travel through Muli, but was turned away by the King of Muli.

The following year, Rock arrived in Muli without prior permission. The newly enthroned King of Muli explained that the full name of the area was "Nyainqêntanglha Jambeyang Gonpo" (念青贡嘎日松贡布, Niànqīng Gònggā Rìsōng Gòngbù), a region protected by three sacred mountains, collectively known as the "Three Protector Snow Mountains" (三怙主雪山, Sān Hùzhǔ Xuěshān). This was a holy site that every Tibetan aspired to pilgrimage to. However, the area was plagued by bandit gangs who not only looted and killed but also circumambulated the mountains to atone for their sins, making it far too dangerous for anyone to visit.

In 1928, with the mediation of the new King of Muli and a bandit leader, Rock was able to enter the Yading mountain area twice. His third attempt was forced to end when he was believed to have offended the mountain deity, causing hailstorms. However, Rock's photographs and articles were serialized by National Geographic, creating a sensation.

In April 1933, James Hilton used Joseph Rock's exploration articles and photographs as material to create the famous novel "Lost Horizon." The "Shangri-La" described in the novel captivated the world and sparked a global trend of searching for Shangri-La. Meanwhile, the route that Joseph Rock took from Muli to the Gongga Ridge area during his expedition was later named the "Joseph Rock Route" by later generations.

Due to harsh natural conditions, the Joseph Rock Route has not been commercially developed to this day. Those who wish to witness its breathtaking scenery must tread the ancient Tea Horse Road (茶马古道, Chámǎ Gǔdào) that has existed for thousands of years, hiking deep into the three sacred mountains to glimpse the splendor invisible to ordinary people.

Notable Attractions

1 Nyainqêntanglha Jambeyang Gonpo
[念青贡嘎日松贡布,
Niànqīng Gònggā Rìsōng Gòngbù]

This means "the sacred place of three guardian deity snow mountains with eternal snow that never melts," referring to Chenrezig peak (仙乃日, Xiānnǎirì), Jambeyang peak (央迈勇, Yāngmàiyǒng), and Chanadorje peak(夏诺多吉, Xiànuòduōjí).

The three sacred mountains are arranged in a triangular formation and rank 11th among the 24 Buddhist holy sites in the world. The mountain cultures, symbolizing compassion, wisdom, and power, has built a massive mandala of faith across thousands of square kilometers.

2 Jambeyang peak
[央迈勇, Yāngmàiyǒng]

"Under the clear sky before me stands the unparalleled Jambeyang snow peak; it is the most beautiful snow mountain I have ever seen."

These were Rock's words upon seeing Jambeyang. If someone asks which of the three sacred mountains in Yading is the most beautiful, I would answer without hesitation: Jambeyang.

When walking the Joseph Rock Route, you can admire Jambeyang from at least three different angles. That sense of satisfaction is something only mountain lovers can understand.

3 Chanadorje peak
[夏诺多吉, Xiànuòduōjí]

This is a pyramid-shaped peak with its pointed top cut off. Its two wings extend into broad ridges, resembling the wings of a giant bat... People who see Chanadorje for the first time are immediately struck by its grandeur!

Above the clouds are numerous angular peaks, while below are lush primeval forests and jade-blue alpine lakes. When you see it, you'll understand why so many people travel great distances just to catch a glimpse.

4 Chenrezig peak
[仙乃日, Xiānnǎirì]

The Tibetan name means "Avalokitesvara Bodhisattva." It is the highest of the three sacred mountains, standing at 6,032 meters above sea level.

It is the highest peak in Daocheng County and the fifth highest peak in Sichuan Province. The shape of Chenrezig Peak resembles a throne, as if it were designed for a living Buddha to sit and meditate upon.

5 Five-Color Lake
[五色海, Wǔsè Hǎi]

The surface of the lake is circular, and under the sunlight, it shimmers in multiple colors. It is a renowned sacred lake in Tibetan regions, believed to have the power to "replay history and predict the future."

The plants at the bottom of the lake grow luxuriantly, and when they die, they form various strange patterns, further enhancing the mystery surrounding the Five-Color Lake.

6 Milk Lake
[牛奶海, Niúnǎi Hǎi]

At the foot of Jambeyang, in a mountain valley, there is a lake. Legend has it that when spring comes and flowers bloom, the lake water becomes as pure white as milk, hence its name, Milk Lake. It is formed by meltwater from the Jambeyang Glacier and is shaped like a water droplet.

Surrounded by snow mountains on all sides, the lake's color changes, from black to emerald green to blue. Standing by the lake, looking at this mysterious and beautiful body of water, one feels as if in a dream.

7 Pearl Lake
[珍珠海, Zhēnzhū Hǎi]

Known as "Drolma Latso" (卓玛拉措, Zhuómǎ Lācuò) in Tibetan, it is the ideal spot to capture the reflection of Chenrezig.

Under the sunlight, the surface of the lake shimmers, and the sacred mountain is mirrored in the crystal-clear water, creating the illusion of another world beneath the surface.

Itinerary

Day1 Gather in Chengdu (成都)

Day2 Chengdu - Xichang (西昌) - Muli County (木里县 2,000m)
Driving: 690km, 11 hours

After breakfast, we gather and depart, traveling along the Ya'an-Xichang Expressway through Shimian to Xichang. This expressway, often referred to as "the Most Beautiful Highway in Western Sichuan," winds through tunnels and bridges, offering breathtaking views.

From Xichang, we continue our journey toward Muli County, a Tibetan Autonomous County. Muli holds historical significance as the starting point of Joseph Rock's cultural journey. The local people are known for their warmth and honesty, and the county serves as the last supply point before heading into the mountains.

Day3 Muli County - Shuiluo Township (水洛乡) - Jialuo Village (甲洛村 2,700m)
Driving: 225km, 6 hours

After breakfast, we take a bus to Shuiluo Township. Located in a remote area with rough road conditions, the journey proves to be quite challenging.

We arrive in the afternoon and transfer to local minibuses that take us to Jialuo Village. Situated at a lower elevation, Jialuo Village is surrounded by stunning scenery and marks the final stop before entering the mountains.

Day4 Jialuo Village - Baishui River (白水河) - Baishui River Campsite (白水河营地 3,700m)
Driving: 20km, 0.5 hours
Trekking: 14km, 1000m ascent, 6 hours

In the morning, we drive to Baishui River, where the Joseph Rock trek begins. Following the river, we pass several stunning waterfalls along the way. If time permits, we make a stop at Dulu Monastery (嘟噜寺, Dūlū Sì) to pray for blessings. Afterward, we continue past the Shuiluo Gold Mine and begin our ascent into the primeval forest.

The elevation steadily increases as we enter a valley filled with towering trees and striking rock formations. By evening, we reach the Baishui River Campsite, where we set up camp for the night.

Day5 Baishui River Campsite - Zangbie Cattle Farm (藏别牛场) - Wanhuachi Cattle Farm Campsite (万花池牛场营地 4,250m)
Trekking: 12km, 550m ascent, 6 hours

In the morning, we depart from the campsite and journey through the primeval forest, eventually reaching a vast and beautiful meadow.

Not far from the meadow lies the Zangbie Cattle Farm (also known as Xiari Cattle Farm), where we get our first glimpse of one of the three guardian deity mountains: Chanadorje.

We continue our trek, following the path alongside Chanadorje until we reach the Wanhuachi Cattle Farm Campsite, located just below Zabala Pass.

Day6 Wanhuachi Cattle Farm Campsite - Zabala Pass (杂巴拉垭口 4,750m) - Xinguo Cattle Farm Campsite (新果牛场营地 4,200m)
Trekking: 12km, 550m ascent/descent, 7 hours

After leaving the campsite, we begin our ascent from the southern slope of Chanadorje,

crossing the steep 4,750-meter Zabala Pass. The climb is challenging, but rewarding.

Once over the pass, we descend into a pasture and continue on through three sections of traversing scree slopes, eventually reaching a dense forest. We follow the forest path upward to the summit at 4,400 meters, where we are treated to a breathtaking view of the canyon below.

From here, we descend all the way to the Xinguo Cattle Farm Campsite, nestled on the southern slope of Jambeyang.

Day7 Xinguo Cattle Farm Campsite - Black Lake Pass (黑湖垭口 4,700m) - Black Lake Campsite (黑湖营地 4,500m)
Trekking: 7km, 500m ascent, 200m descent, 5 hours

Today's trek takes us primarily above 4,000 meters, making it a demanding journey. Along the way, we cross several unnamed passes and pass by the Black Lake (黑湖, Hēihú), its waters dark as ink.

Afterward, we continue past Xiadu Cattle Farm (呷独牛场, Xiádú Niúchǎng) on the southwest slope of Jambeyang, where we catch sight of the Rock Stone (also known as Butterfly Stone). Depending on the conditions, tonight's campsite will either be at Black Lake Campsite or Rock Stone Campsite.

Day8 Black Lake Campsite - Songduo Pass (松多垭口 4,650m) - Yading Scenic Area (亚丁风景区) - Daocheng County Town (稻城县城 3,750m)
Trekking: 16km, 8 hours
Driving: 110km, 3 hours

Today's journey will be long, so it's best to start early. First, we descend to Snake Lake (蛇湖, Shéhú) at an elevation of 4,400 meters, then climb up to cross the 4,650-meter Songduo Pass, entering the Yading Scenic Area.

As we reach the pass, the majestic peaks of Chenrezig and Jambeyang come into view. We pass by Milk Lake and Five-Color Lake before following the scenic area's boardwalk down to Luorong Cattle Farm (络绒牛场, Luòróng Niúchǎng), marking the end of the Joseph Rock Route trek.

From here, we take a shuttle bus out of the scenic area, switch to our vehicle at the entrance, and head to Daocheng County Town for the night's accommodation.

Important Notes

● Best Season: June to October

● Suitable For: Healthy individuals aged 18-65 years with high-altitude long-distance trekking and camping experience

● Potential Risks: 1. High-altitude trekking, be aware of altitude sickness;

2. Crossing the four passes above 4,500 meters presents several risks, including physical exhaustion, the potential for slipping and falling, altitude sickness, and hypothermia.

18. Yading Grand Kora

[亚丁大转, Yàdīng Dà Zhuǎn]

`9 days` `73 km`

Daocheng
[稻城, Dàochéng]
Gathering City

16KM
Longest Single-Day Hike

760M
Maximum Daily Elevation Gain

5,036M
Highest Elevation Along the Route

★★★★★
Scenic Rating

★★★★⯪
Difficulty Level

Tibetan Buddhism believes that worshipping and circumambulating the Three Protector Snow Mountains of Yading can fulfill one's wishes in this life and the next. Circumambulating the mountains once is equivalent to the merit of reciting one hundred million mantras, and circumambulating the Chonggu Temple (冲古寺, Chōnggǔ Sì) at the foot of the sacred mountains 15 times is equivalent to the merit of reciting one hundred million mantras.

There are three methods of circumambulation: the Grand Kora (大转, Dà Zhuǎn), the Middle Kora (中转, Zhōng Zhuǎn), and the Small Kora (小转, Xiǎo Zhuǎn). Tibetans usually choose the Small Kora method in their daily lives, which means circumambulating the Chenrezig Sacred Mountain. However, during their zodiac year, more people choose the Grand Kora. The Small Kora generally takes 1 day, the Middle Kora takes 3 days, and the Grand Kora takes about 7 days.

The Three Protector deities are extremely important principal deities in Vajrayana Buddhism, representing the essence of Buddhist teachings. The Three Protector Snow Mountains of Yading are three completely separate but close snow peaks arranged in a triangular formation. The northern peak, Chenrezig (仙乃日, Xiānnǎirì), means Avalokitesvara Bodhisattva in Tibetan; the southern peak, Jambeyang (央迈勇, Yāng màiyǒng), means Manjusri Bodhisattva in Tibetan; and the eastern peak, Chanadorje (夏诺多吉, Xiànuòduōjí), means Vajrapani Bodhisattva in Tibetan.

The Yading Grand Kora combines the essence of classic routes such as the Joseph Rock Route, the Luhuo-Yading Route, and the Niru-Yading Route. Starting from Chonggu Temple within the Yading Scenic Area, the journey involves a 360-degree trek around the outer perimeter of the three sacred mountains, passing through Bayu Campsite (巴玉营地, Bāyù Yíngdì), Boyong Lake (波拥措, Bōyōng Cuò), Galuo Cattle Farm (嘎洛牛场, Gáluò Niúchǎng), Gongga Zhaze (贡嘎扎则, Gònggā Zhāzé), Zabala Pass (杂巴拉垭口, Zábālā Yákǒu), the pagoda on the southern slope of Jambeyang peak, Xinguo Cattle Farm (新果牛场, Xīnguǒ Niúchǎng), Black Lake Pass (黑湖垭口, Hēihú Yákǒu), Snake Lake (蛇湖, Shéhú), Songduo Pass (松多垭口, Sōngduō Yákǒu), Kasi Cattle Shed (卡斯牛棚, Kǎsī Niúpéng), Songluo Pass (松洛垭口, Sōngluò Yákǒu), Pearl Lake (珍珠海, Zhēnzhū Hǎi), and finally back to Chonggu Temple. The cumulative elevation is about 3,900 meters, with the lowest elevation at 3,990 meters and the highest at 5,036 meters.

Notable Attractions

Chanadorje peak
H5958m

Jambeyang peak
H5958m

Chenrezig peak
H6032

1 Three Sacred Mountains of Yading
[亚丁三神山, Yàdīng Sān Shénshān]

The Tibetan name is "Gongga Risong Gonpo" (贡嘎日松贡布, Gònggā Rìsōng Gòngbù), meaning "the sacred place of three guardian deity snow mountains with eternal snow that never melts." Their Buddhist name is the Three Protector Snow Mountains, ranking 11th among the 24 Buddhist holy sites in the world, "as a sacred place where sentient beings make offerings to the deities and accumulate merit." In the 8th century CE, Guru Padmasambhava blessed the three snow peaks.

The three snow mountains are arranged in a triangular formation, each with a different shape, standing tall and majestic. The Yading Grand Kora offers a 360-degree all-around view of the Three Protector Snow Mountains, allowing for a fresh perspective on the beauty of the hidden paradise of Yading.

▶ **Jambeyang peak**
[央迈勇, Yāngmàiyǒng]

"Under the clear sky before me stands the unparalleled Jambeyang snow peak; it is the most beautiful snow mountain I have ever seen." These were Rock's words upon seeing Jambeyang.

If someone asks which of the three sacred mountains in Yading is the most beautiful, I would answer without hesitation: Jambeyang. When walking the Joseph Rock Route, you can admire Jambeyang from at least three different angles. That sense of satisfaction is something only mountain lovers can understand.

▶ **Chanadorje peak**
[夏诺多吉, Xiànuòduōjí]

This is a pyramid-shaped peak with its pointed top cut off. Its two wings extend into broad ridges, resembling the wings of a giant bat... People who see Chanadorje for the first time are immediately struck by its grandeur! Above the clouds are numerous angular peaks, while below are lush primeval forests and jade-blue alpine lakes.

When you see it, you'll understand why so many people travel great distances just to catch a glimpse.

▶ **Chenrezig peak**
[仙乃日, Xiānnǎirì]

The Tibetan name means "Avalokitesvara Bodhisattva." It is the highest of the three sacred mountains, standing at 6,032 meters above sea level. It is the highest peak in Daocheng County and the fifth highest peak in Sichuan Province. The shape of Chenrezig Peak resembles a throne, as if it were designed for a living Buddha to sit and meditate upon.

2 Snake Lake
[蛇湖, Shéhú]

Its Tibetan name is Lexi Lake (勒西措, Lèxī Cuò), also known as the Sea of Wisdom. Shaped like a large snake, Snake Lake's waters are not as vividly blue as those of Milk Lake.

However, with the majestic peaks of Jambeyang and Chenrezig serving as a backdrop, the lake exudes a clear, distant, and ethereal beauty.

3 Niang Lake
[娘措, Niáng Cuò]

Located in the valley to the north of the Cuogaida Lake group, shrouded in clouds and mist, it is more mysterious than the other lakes and seldom visited by people.

4 Resong Lake
[热松措, Rèsōng Cuò]

Also known as Lapis Lake, the water of the lake is calm and emerald green. Situated on the backside of Chenrezig Mountain, above the Kasi Hell Valley(卡斯地狱谷, Kǎsī Dìyù Gǔ), this area is often frequented by groups of bharal (Himalayan blue sheep). Depending on the season and weather, the surface of the lake reflects a variety of different colors.

5 Cuogaida Lake Group
[措该达湖群, Cuògāidá Hú Qún]

This lake is visible when looking down from Cuogaida Pass. During the wet season, this lake group consists of 2 lakes; during the dry season, it divides into multiple small lakes.

6 Black Lake
[黑湖, Hēihú]

The Tibetan name is Yajiao Chuna (牙脚出纳, Yájiǎo Chūnà), located at the southwestern turning point of the Jambeyang mountain range. The lake water is green-black, like a black pearl, hence the name Black Lake.

7 Milk Lake
[牛奶海, Niúnǎi Hǎi]

At the foot of Jambeyang Sacred Mountain, in a mountain hollow, there is a lake. Legend has it that when spring comes and flowers bloom, the lake water becomes as pure white as milk, hence its name, Milk Lake. It is formed by melt-water from the Jambeyang Glacier and is shaped like a water droplet.

Surrounded by snow mountains on all sides, the water color changes from black to emerald green to blue. From a distance, it looks like a jewel embedded among the mountains. Standing by the lake, looking at this mysterious and beautiful body of water, one feels as if in a dream.

8 Five-Color Lake
[五色海, Wǔsè Hǎi]

Its surface is circular, and under the sunlight, it shimmers in five distinct colors. A famous sacred lake in Tibetan regions, it is believed to have the power to "replay history and predict the future."

The plants at the bottom of the lake grow luxuriantly, and when they die, they form various strange patterns, adding an aura of mystery to the Five-Color Lake.

Itinerary

Day1 Gather in Shangri-La Town, Daocheng (稻城香格里拉镇 2,900m)

Day2 Shangri-La Town - Chonggu Temple (冲古寺 3,990m) - Boyong Cattle Farm (波拥牛场 4,550m) - Boyong Lake (波拥措 4,750m)
Trekking: 7km, 760m ascent, 4 hours

We begin by driving to the visitor center, where we then switch to a shuttle bus. The shuttle ride takes approximately 50 minutes to reach the starting point of the trek, Chonggu Temple. From there, we follow the scenic area boardwalk to the Sacred Water Gate. Upon reaching the gate, we turn left and begin our journey into the primeval forest.

After climbing for some time, we emerge from the forest, and the view gradually opens up, offering breathtaking vistas of the Three Sacred Mountains of Yading.

We continue upward, eventually reaching Boyong Cattle Farm. From there, we follow the gentle slope on the left, making our way to the Boyong Lake campsite, where we will set up camp for the night.

Day3 Free Day at Boyong Lake

The most exquisite part of the Yading Grand Kora is at Boyong Lake. From the campsite, we climb up the ridge behind it, where we are rewarded with an awe-inspiring view. In one direction, all three of the sacred mountains of Yading are visible, and in the distance, you can even spot the King of Sichuan Mountains, Gongga, as well as Meili Snow Mountain in Yunnan.

Boyong Lake's lakeside is one of the best spots for photographing the starry sky, the reflections of the snow-capped mountains, and the golden glow of the sun illuminating the mountainside.

Day4 Boyong Lake - Cuogaida Pass (措该达垭口 5,036m) - Cuogaida Lake (措该达湖) - Niang Lake (娘措) - Galuo Cattle Farm (嘎洛牛场) - Gongga Zhaze (贡嘎扎则 4,100m)
Trekking: 16km, 300m ascent, 940m descent, 8 hours

After departing from the campsite, we embark on a climb that lasts about 2 hours, leading us to Cuogaida Pass. From the pass, we begin our descent past Cuogaida Lake, heading toward the Niang Lake viewing point. From there, we follow a gentle mountain path for over an hour to reach Galuo Cattle Farm.

Continuing onward, we pass through Chagong Cattle Farm before descending into the river valley. We then traverse through a primeval forest, following the Baishui River upstream until we reach the Gongga Zhaze campsite, which is also the closest point to Chanadorje.

Day5 Gongga Zhaze (4,400m) - Chanadorje Transverse Pass (夏诺多吉横向垭口 4,500m) - Campsite Below Zabala Pass (杂巴拉垭口下方营地 4,400m)
Trekking: 7km, 400m ascent, 100m descent, 5 hours

After departing, we continue climbing over several small passes until we reach the Chanadorje Transverse Pass. Once we cross this pass, we traverse along the mountainside, parallel to and above the Joseph Rock Route.

Along the way, we are treated to views of several major cattle farms in the valley below, as well as Dulu Lake on the opposite mountain. Finally, we reach the campsite below Zabala Pass, situated at an elevation of 4,400 meters. This location also marks the point where our route joins the Joseph Rock Route, just above the Wanhuachi Cattle Farm.

Day6 Campsite Below Zabala Pass - Zabala Pass (杂巴拉垭口 4,750m) - Niangxi Cattle Farm (娘西牛场) - Xinguo Cattle Farm (新果牛场 4,300m)
Trekking: 9km, 350m ascent, 450m descent, 5 hours

From the campsite, we begin the climb up Zabala Pass, ascending more than 300 meters over a relatively steep slope, which takes about 2 hours. After reaching the summit, we descend along a gentle slope, passing through Niangxi Cattle Farm and continuing along the mountain path on the right side.

As we pass through several landslide areas and cross the relatively simple Jambeyang Transverse Pass, we finally reach the Xinguo Cattle Farm campsite, located at the foot of the southwestern slope of Jambeyang.

Day7 Xinguo Cattle Farm - Black Lake Pass (黑湖垭口 4,720m) - Butterfly Stone (蝴蝶石) - Snake Lake Pass (蛇湖垭口 4,730m) - Snake Lake (蛇湖 4,500m)
Trekking: 11km, 430m ascent, 230m descent, 6 hours

We climb several small passes and navigate through landslide areas, with distant views of Jambeyang and Chanadorje from the mountainside. Around noon, we reach Black Lake Pass, the turning point for Jambeyang, where we can enjoy distant views of Black Lake.

Following this, we walk along a flat stone path leading to Jiadu Cattle Farm (甲独牛场, Jiǎdú Niúchǎng), where we can observe the iconic "Butterfly Stone." Moving ahead, we reach Jiadu Lake (甲独措, Jiǎdú Cuò). Continuing onward, we arrive at Snake Lake Pass, then descend vertically over 200 meters to set up camp by the tranquil Snake Lake.

Day8 Snake Lake - Songduo Pass (松多垭口 4,670m) - Five-Color Lake (五色海) - Milk Lake (牛奶海) - Resong Lake (热松措) - Kasi Cattle Shed (卡斯牛棚 4,400m)
Trekking: 12km, 270m ascent, 370m descent, 7 hours

Departing from the lakeside, we cross the 4,670-meter Songduo Pass on our way to visit Milk Lake and Five-Color Lake in the Yading Scenic Area. You can climb up to the Double Lake Checkpoint (双湖打卡点, Shuānghú Dǎkǎ Diǎn) at an elevation of 4,770 meters to capture stunning photos before returning to Songduo Pass.

From there, we follow the Small Kora route of Chenrezig, descending past Resong Lake, and finally reach Kasi Cattle Shed, where we will camp for the night.

Day9 Kasi Cattle Shed - Songluo Pass (松洛垭口) - Pearl Lake (珍珠海) - Chonggu Temple (冲古寺 3,990m) - Shangri - La Town - Daocheng
Trekking: 11km, 250m ascent, 600m descent, 6 hours

After departing, we traverse along the slope of Chenrezig Mountain, with the famous Kasi Hell Valley on our left. After approximately 3 hours of hiking, we reach the final pass of the journey—Songluo Pass. This pass is crucial for entering the paradise of Yading from Kasi Hell Valley and is also the pass adorned with the most prayer flags along the route.

Once we cross Songluo Pass, we begin a long descent through a forest, eventually reaching the scenic area boardwalk that leads to Pearl Lake. From there, we hike down to Chonggu Temple, marking the end of the Yading Grand Kora. Finally, we take transportation back to Daocheng.

Important Notes
- Best Season: June to October
- Suitable For: Healthy individuals aged 18-65 years with high-altitude long-distance trekking and camping experience
- Potential Risks: High-altitude hiking, be aware of altitude sickness

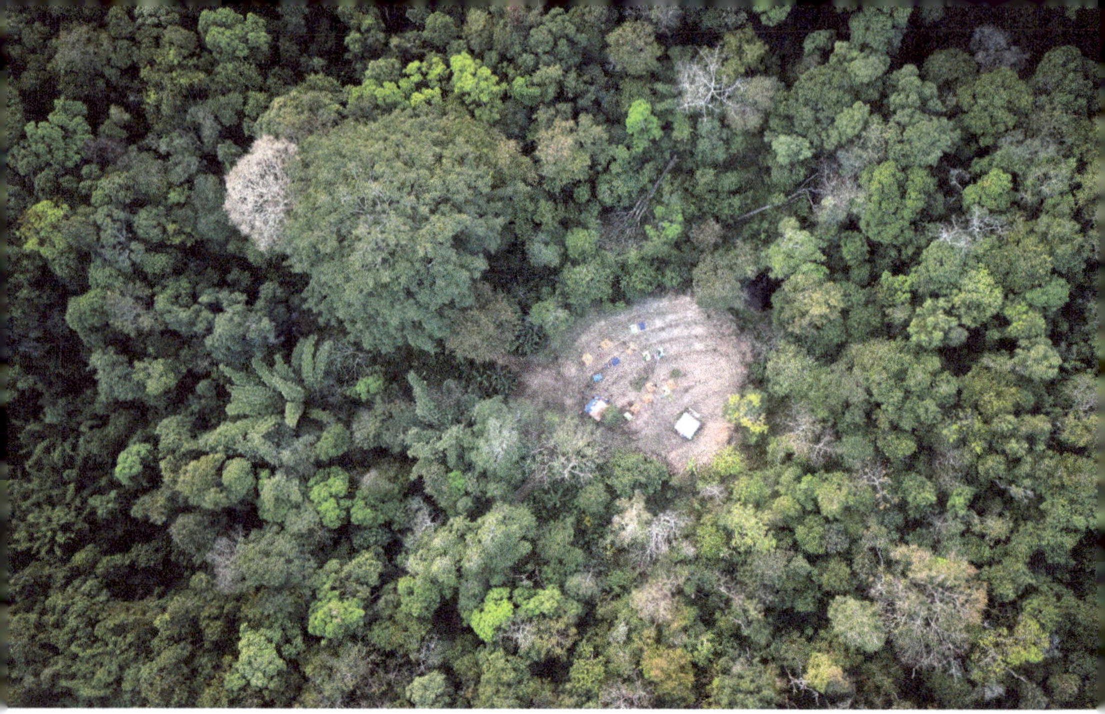

19. Xishuangbanna Rainforest Trek

[西双版纳雨林徒步, Xīshuāngbǎnnà Yǔlín Túbù] 4days 25km

Xishuangbanna
[西双版纳, Xīshuāngbǎnnà]
Gathering City

9KM
Longest Single-Day Hike

500M
Maximum Daily Elevation Gain

1,250M
Highest Elevation Along the Route

★★★
Scenic Rating

★★
Difficulty Level

Credit
© All images in this piece by Harrison

This is a winter haven for those who "fear the cold," with an average annual temperature of around 22°C. The area preserves China's most intact tropical ecosystem and is home to the country's only tropical rainforest nature reserve. It is often referred to as the "Kingdom of Plants and Animals" and a "Biological Gene Bank." Located at the southwestern tip of China, it borders Laos to the southeast and Myanmar to the southwest. It blends with the customs of Southeast Asia, offering an opportunity to experience Southeast Asian culture without leaving the country.

It has the largest botanical garden in China with the richest collection of species–the Xishuangbanna Tropical Botanical Garden of the Chinese Academy of Sciences–also being the largest in the world for displaying the most outdoor-preserved plant species and plant groups to the public.

It also has the largest night market in Southeast Asia. In 2023, it became the only Chinese destination to make Lonely Planet magazine's "Top 10 Best Travel Regions" list. This place combines Southeast Asian characteristics with ethnic minority customs, embodying a myriad of cultural flavors–this is Xishuangbanna (西双版纳, Xīshuāngbǎnnà).

Xishuangbanna is located in the southern extension of the Hengduan Mountains, at the end of the Nu River (怒江, Nù Jiāng), Lancang River (澜沧江, Láncāng Jiāng), and Jinsha River (金沙江, Jīnshā Jiāng). Mountainous hills cover about 95% of the area, while intermountain basins and river valleys make up the remaining 5%.

This diverse landscape offers an abundance of mountain resources highly sought after by outdoor enthusiasts.

Natural Features

Protected by the Ailao Mountains (哀牢山, Āiláo Shān) and Wuliang Mountains (无量山, Wúliàng Shān), which block cold currents from the north, and influenced by the southwest monsoon from the Indian Ocean and the southeast airflow from the Pacific Ocean, Xishuangbanna enjoys a warm and humid climate year-round.

The region does not have four distinct seasons, but only a distinction between dry and wet seasons. The dry season lasts from November of the current year to April of the following year, while the wet season lasts from May to October.

Xishuangbanna also has the only tropical rainforest protection area in China. The protected area covers 242,500 hectares, spanning three regions: Menghai (勐海, Měnghǎi), Jinghong (景洪, Jǐnghóng), and Mengla (勐腊, Měnglà). It is the northernmost limit of the tropical rainforest, a true natural wonder. It wasn't until the 1980s, when Prince Philip, Duke of Edinburgh and then-president of the World Wildlife Fund, personally visited Xishuangbanna and discovered the Parashorea chinensis (望天树, Wàngtiān Shù) trees, that the world finally recognized the unique identity of its tropical rainforest.

How could anyone visit Xishuangbanna and not go on a tropical rainforest trek?

Cultural Significance

This is the most unique and captivating outdoor experience in Xishuangbanna. The deeper you venture, the more it feels like entering a giant tropical forest maze. As far as the eye can see, there are exotic flowers and plants, ancient trees, and secluded forests that you have never seen before in your life. Being in such an environment, the vigorous life force of wild growth is enough to heal anyone worn down by the concrete jungle of city life.

Due to local conservation efforts to protect wild elephants, completing a full traverse of the tropical rainforest in Xishuangbanna is not possible. Travelers are typically allowed to circling the outskirts of the rainforest or embarking on short day trips, as long-distance routes are nearly nonexistent. However, with careful planning, it is possible to break the norm. Without compromising ecological protection, one can trek 25 kilometers, camp for two nights in the rainforest, and unlock the unique experience of tree climbing.

We have chosen Mengla for our tropical rainforest trek. The Mengla area of Xishuangbanna, having been spared from the Quaternary glacial impact, preserves over 30 species of ferns and gymnosperms that flourished in the Paleozoic and Mesozoic eras, which are called plant fossils from a hundred million years ago.

Here, we'll encounter a fascinating array of unusual plants, such as those bearing fruits that produce "salt frost," alongside the iconic buttress-root plants that thrive only in tropical rainforests. Our trek through the tropical rainforest of Xishuangbanna will take us deep into its heart, where we'll experience the rainforest firsthand. We'll sample its natural food, spend the night immersed in its surroundings, and learn survival skills essential for navigating this vibrant ecosystem. By reconnecting with nature, we'll return to simpler times, embracing the role of primitive gatherers as we source ingredients directly from the land.

The Dai people (傣族, Dǎizú) of Xishuangbanna have long held a tradition of gathering raw materials from the forest since acient time.

Today, under the guidance of local experts, we have the opportunity to prepare a meal using tools and ingredients provided by nature—banana leaves as bowls, fruits as sustenance—allowing us to experience what it's like to live as a primitive rainforest inhabitant, fully immersed in nature's abundance. It's a truly immersive experience, one that connects us deeply to the land and its gifts. However, it's essential to remember that without reliable guides, you should never attempt to forage in the rainforest alone.

On this special route, more communication with the guides will yield abundant practical knowledge.

Itinerary

Day1 Gather in Jinghong Xishuangbanna (西双版纳景洪)

Day2 Xishuangbanna - Baka Village (坝卡村) - Laoxiong Gully (老熊沟) - Banyan Tree Campsite (榕树营地)
Trekking: 7km, 500m ascent, 180m descent, 4 hours

After breakfast, we depart by vehicle and, in about two hours, arrive at the starting point of our trek: Baka Village in Mengla County. From there, we begin our first tropical rainforest adventure. Our journey starts as we trek from Baka Village, passing through rubber tree forests and rare plantations before entering the dense rainforest.

We'll follow a creek upstream, encountering an array of unique tropical plants and wildlife, immersing ourselves in the region's rich biodiversity. After trekking along the stream for approximately 3 kilometers, we'll ascend a ridge and continue our climb, ultimately reaching the Banyan Tree campsite where we'll set up camp for the night.

Day3 Banyan Tree Campsite - Tropical Rainforest Small Circuit Trek - Banyan Tree Campsite - Campsite Experience Activities
Trekking: 8km, 350m ascent/desent, 4 hours

After breakfast at the campsite in the morning, we don't need to break camp as we will contin-ue to stay at the Banyan Tree campsite tonight. The trek will start from the campsite, and during the trek, our leader and local guide will introduce the various flora and fauna of the tropical rainforest and teach some survival skills.

After returning to the campsite, we will make a rainforest feast and have tree climbing activities.

Day4 Banyan Tree Campsite - Muntjac Gully (麂子箐) - Hani Village (哈尼族寨子) - Mengla County High-Speed Rail Station
Trekking: 9km, 400m ascent, 600m descent, 5 hours

After breakfast, we pack our personal belongings and assist the leader in breaking camp. Once camp is packed up, we begin today's trek, departing from the Banyan Tree campsite. Our journey takes us uphill to the Married Banyan Trees, then we'll continue ascending to a small pass before descending into Muntjac Gully.

We'll trek along the gully until we reach an abandoned quarry, located near a few scattered households.

After passing through these homes, we re-enter the rainforest, eventually reaching a Hani village. From there, we'll take a vehicle back to Mengla County town, where the tour will come to a close.

Important Notes

- Best Season: October to April of the following year, with slight route adjustments for different season
- Suitable For: Healthy individuals aged 7-65 years
- Potential Risks: 1. Valley stream trekking: Slippery surfaces, prone to slipping and falling.
    2. Rainforest trekking: There are many mosquitoes and insects, so be cautious and take preventive measures.

20. Gaoligong Trek

[高黎贡徒步, Gāolígòng Túbù]

Baoshan

[保山, Bǎoshān]
Gathering City

18KM
Longest Single-Day Hike

600M
Maximum Daily Elevation Gain

3,175M
Highest Elevation Along the Route

★★★
Scenic Rating

★★★
Difficulty Level

Credit
Image 1 | ©HuangHuang
Image 2/3 | ©Huyang

Gaoligong Mountain (高黎贡山, Gāolígòng Shān) does not refer to a specific single mountain, but rather to a massive mountain range situated on the west bank of the Nujiang River (怒江, Nù Jiāng). It spans a north-to-south direction with a low-to-high elevation gradient, and it is characterized by a narrow, elongated shape. The mountain range stretches across Longling (龙陵, Lónglíng), Tengchong (腾冲, Téngchōng), Baoshan, Lushui (泸水, Lúshuǐ), Fugong (福贡, Fúgòng), Gongshan (贡山, Gòngshān), Chayu (察隅, Cháyú), and parts of Kachin State in Myanmar, crossing five latitudes from north to south.

From the highest peak, Gawa Gapu Snow Mountain (嘎哇嘎普雪山, Gáwā Gápǔ Xuěshān) at 5,128 meters, to the lowest point, the Dayingjiang River (大盈江, Dàyíng Jiāng) at 210 meters, Gaoligong Mountain has a nearly 5,000-meter elevation difference. This dramatic variation in altitude, coupled with the region's complex topography, is further influenced by year-round warm, humid airflows from the Indian Ocean, resulting in heavy rainfall and consistently high humidity levels. This has created a vertical climate in Gaoligong Mountain where "one mountain spans four seasons, and ten miles can have different weather." This also forms the foundation for nurturing rich biodiversity.

Natural Features

Entering Gaoligong Mountain is like stepping into a giant tangible natural science textbook. It always brings surprises, vividly demonstrating biodiversity. The rugged, fragmented terrain often forms small environments isolated from their surroundings. Combined with multiple factors, this allows plants and animals that originally lived in different environments to find suitable habitats in Gaoligong Mountain. For a long time, the Gaoligong Mountain area was little-known and difficult to access, thus preserving its relatively pristine appearance, full of mystery and wildness. Here, besides having opportunities to encounter various amazing plants and animals, you can also see natural landscapes such as tropical rainforests, bamboo seas, waterfalls, streams, and hot springs. The historical traces left by the "Southern Silk Road" and the Expeditionary Army have also given Gaoligong Mountain profound historical significance, making the hidden ancient paths in the mountains a paradise for photography and hiking enthusiasts.

Even if you have visited many primeval forests, you will still be captivated by its charm. The morning sunlight weaves through the dense mountain forest, casting its glow on the tree roots and moss. This scene, reminiscent of Alice's adventures in Wonderland, unfolds every day in Gaoligong Mountain.

Beyond the natural scenery, the historical traces left by the Expeditionary Army also evoke reflections and sighs.

Gaoligong was one of the key battlefields of the China-Burma Campaign during the War of Resistance against Japanese Aggression. As the main southwestern front, it was described by American forces at the time as "the highest-altitude battlefield of World War II."

The ancient mountain paths are strategically crucial, with treacherous terrain, making them important strategic locations. More than seventy years ago, the 198th Division of the 54th Army of the Chinese Expeditionary Army's 20th Group fought bloody battles with Japanese forces on these ancient paths. They achieved victory at the cost of even more than ten times the Japanese casualties—a tragic victory that should be remembered. If you want to learn more comprehensively about this campaign, you can visit the China-Burma War Memorial Museum in Tengchong after hiking. There, this history is recorded in particular detail.

The best time to enter Gaoligong Mountain is from autumn and winter through to April of the following year. The rainy season recedes, and all living things, nourished by prolonged rainfall, become more vibrant. There is a special feeling in traversing this primeval dense forest with ancient towering trees and walking along ancient stone paths covered with moss.

2

Notable Attractions

1 Baihualing
[百花岭, Bǎihuā Lǐng]

This is a "five-star bird-watching sanctuary in China." To date, 431 bird species have been recorded here, nearly a third of the total number of wild bird species in China, making it a paradise for all bird enthusiasts.

2 Yubi Ancient Path
[玉璧古道, Yùbì Gǔdào]

According to historical records, Tengchong's Yubi Ancient Path may have been established as early as the Three Kingdoms period when Zhuge Liang conducted southern expeditions to expand territory.

It is one of the sections of the ancient official postal road from Baoshan to Tengchong, known for its highest standard of construction, best-preserved road surface, and most beautiful natural scenery.

3 Heshun Ancient Town
[和顺古镇, Héshùn Gǔzhèn]

Heshun is an important town for commercial avtivities on the Silk Road, where the culture of Central Plains, Western regions, and neighboring countries converge, forming a unique caravan culture and overseas Chinese culture.

The daily life customs from more than 600 years ago continue to thrive today, and it remains a vibrant ancient town.

4 Tengchong Ginkgo Village
[腾冲银杏村, Téngchōng Yínxìng Cūn]

Tengchong Ginkgo Village is renowned as "China's Premier Ginkgo Village," featuring a 600-year-old settlement, over 30,000 ginkgo trees, and more than 10,000 acres of ginkgo forest.

The village is home to more than 1,200 ginkgo trees that are over 100 years old, with the oldest believed to be over 1,300 years old.

Itinerary

Day1 Gather in Baoshan (保山)

Day2 Baoshan - Gaoligong Mahogany Ancient Path Selected Section Traverse (高黎贡红木古道精选段穿越) - Lujiang (潞江)
Driving: 150km, 4 hours
Trekking: 15km, 500m ascent/descent, 4 hours

After breakfast, we drive to the southern section of Gaoligong Mountain, passing through the "Lifeline for Anti-Japanese battle"–the Stilwell Road, built during the War of Resistance against Japanese Aggression. After reaching the hiking starting point, we begin to traverse the southern section of Gaoligong. Along the way, the sounds of insects and birds, coupled with the dense forest, all highlight the vibrant vitality of the primeval forest. We hike along this Tea Horse Ancient Road, following in the footsteps of revolutionary predecessors, witnessing the rise and fall of history.

Day3 Lujiang - Double Rainbow Bridge (双虹桥) - Primeval Forest Trek - Wild Hot Springs - Baihualing (百花岭)
Driving: 50km, 1 hour
Trekking: 7km, 100m ascent/descent, 3 hours

After breakfast, we travel through the picturesque and fertile Lujiang Basin, following the Nujiang Grand Canyon until we reach the Double Rainbow Bridge. Standing on the ancient bridge, we are immersed in the turbulence of over 200 years of history.

Next, we head toward the undeveloped hot springs of Gaoligong Mountain—Yinyang Valley Hot Springs (阴阳谷温泉, Yīnyáng Gǔ Wēnquán). Nestled deep within the mountains and shrouded in mist, two hot springs rise between volcanic rock layers. During festivals and holidays, locals come here to bathe, using the hot spring water for healing and wellness.

After a good bath, we can take out our pre-prepared binoculars to enjoy birdwatching in this national 5A-level bird-watching sanctuary. As evening falls, we stay at Baihualing farmhouse, enjoying the tranquility and charm of the countryside.

Day4 Baihualing - Gaoligong South Zhai Gonglange Traverse (高黎贡南斋公房穿越) - Tengchong (腾冲)
Driving: 60km, 1 hour
Trekking: 20km, 1200m ascent, 1000m descent, 8 hours

Today, we will experience the highlight of this trip: traversing the primeval forest of Gaoligong Mountain and retracing the path of the Expeditionary Army.

As an important component of the Three Parallel Rivers World Natural Heritage site, Gaoligong Mountain is the only place on Earth that still preserves large areas transitioning from humid tropical forests to temperate forests.

Following the counterattack route of the Expeditionary Army, we climb up the mountain. Standing at the top of Gaoligong Mountain, looking out at the mist-shrouded Nujiang Canyon, one feels a sense of commanding the landscape and viewing all mountains as small.

Afterward, following the footsteps of the caravan of the past, we emerge from the primeval forest, drive to Tengchong, and check into a hot spring hotel.

Day5 Tengchong - Jietou Canola Flowers (界头油菜花) - Daying Mountain Flower Sea (打鹰山花海) - Tengchong
Driving: 50km, 1 hour
Trekking: 8km, 200m ascent/descent, 3 hours

After breakfast, we head to the Jietou Canola Flower Sea, which has been rated by "China National Geographic" as "the most beautiful place in Yunnan" and by the National Ministry of Agriculture as having "most beautiful rural landscape in China." At the foot of Gaoligong Mountain, 150,000 acres of canola flowers spread out in a crisscross pattern, creating a harmonious scene.

The title "Eden at the Foot of Gaoligong Mountain" is well-deserved. Afterward, we head to Daying Mountain, the highest active volcano in Tengchong, surrounded by dozens of volcanoes. The top of the mountain is a depression formed by the contraction after magma eruption.

The seasonal lake on the mountain, reflecting the azure sky, has been given the beautiful name "Mirror of the Sky." After completing the hike, we return to Tengchong where the group disperses.

Important Notes

● Best Season: November to March of the following year
● Suitable For: Healthy individuals aged 7-65 years
● Potential Risks: 1. Pay attention to waterproofing and warmth, and make sure to bring a raincoat.
   2. Hot spring bathing can be physically exhausting, it's advisable to prepare some snacks in advance.
   3. Birdwatching is a seasonal activity, so avoid wearing bright colors like red.

21. Shangri-La Niru Traverse

[香格里拉尼汝穿越, Xiānggélǐlā Nírǔ Chuānyuè]

6days

54km

Lijiang
[丽江, Lìjiāng]
Gathering City

16KM
Longest Single-Day Hike

1,400M
Maximum Daily Elevation Gain

4,200M
Highest Elevation Along the Route

★★★★⯪
Scenic Rating

★★★
Difficulty Level

When discussing hiking within China, one must mention the magical land of Yunnan Province. The north-south streched Great Hengduan Mountains have created its unique landforms, endowing it with more possibilities. The pursuit of the extreme, the hidden, and the unknown is our driving force to explore and discover this world. Persistent and determined people cross mountains, traverse forests, and search for one secret paradise after another that few people know about.

Shangri-La has been yearned for by people around the world since it appeared in the famous novel "Lost Horizon" in the 1930s. Niru (尼汝, Nírǔ), located within Shangri-La, is known as the "hidden gem within the hidden gem," a secluded Tibetan village surrounded by primeval forests. Entering Niru is like stepping into paradise on earth.

Natural Features

Niru, meaning "a place bathed in sunshine" in Tibetan, is a small Eden that was once virtually unknown. It is located in the unparalleled World Natural Heritage site—the Three Parallel Rivers region, where the Jinsha River (金沙江, Jīnshā Jiāng), Nujiang River (怒江, Nù Jiāng), and Lancang River (澜沧江, Láncāng Jiāng) flow from north to south, parallel but never converging. The village nestled among the mountains, together with high mountains and valleys, grasslands and pastures, primeval forests, rushing waterfalls, blue skies, and colorful clouds, forms a dreamy Eden.

Here, mountains are lush, giant trees create canopies that block the sun, and all living things grow vebrantly. This area preserves intact biological communities from warm temperate, temperate, cold temperate, and frigid climate zones, making it one of the world's richest regions in terms of biodiversity. It is also a paradise where red pandas, civets, musk deer, Tibetan eared pheasants, and other rare and exotic animals roam freely. This place is also a famous pasture in Shangri-La, with vast grasslands and lush vegetation. Every spring and summer, herds of cattle and sheep wander around the highland pastures and lakesides.

Officials from the UNESCO World Heritage Centre have visited this place. Regarding Niru's unique ecological environment, beautiful natural scenery, and rich ethnic culture, they wrote: "Niru—my dream of China, the true Shangri-La, the world's premier village."

Entering this Tibetan village, you will find that the residents work from sunrise to sunset, decorating their homes with grain seedlings, cattle, sheep, chickens, ducks, and unceasing kitchen smoke, living a life where "paths crisscross, chickens and dogs can be heard from neighboring homes, and the elderly and young live in contentment." The beauty here is quite gentle, like a cloud rising tenderly from the foot of the mountain.

It is not a well-known travel destination, but a Tibetan village lost to time. Only those travelers with an adventurous spirit in their nature, who are not content with ordinary journeys, can have the fortune to discover its mysterious face. Niru gives travelers searching for the dreamlike Shangri -La a reason to stay.

During the trek, we will cross five major pastures, each with different scenery and unique characteristics. The landscapes also vary with the seasons: June is a romantic time, with alpine rhododendrons and a variety of wildflowers in full bloom, creating a sea of color, while herds of cattle and sheep roam freely. July is a paradise for mushrooms, and autumn paints the landscape with vibrant forests and endless hues of fall.

Notable Attractions

1 Shudu Lake and Bita Hai
[蜀都湖和碧塔海, Shǔdū Hú hé Bìtǎ Hǎi]

Two beautiful freshwater lakes, the main attractions of Pudacuo National Park (普达措国家公园, Pǔdácuò Guójiā Gōngyuán), are known as "highland pearls."

Standing by the lakes, watching herds of cattle and sheep, feeling the wind brushing the lake water, one can't help but sense the joy of the wind as it sweeps through the forest.

2 Seven-Colored Waterfall
[七彩瀑布, Qīcǎi Pùbù]

A huge group of waterfalls cascading down from a fan-shaped calcium carbonate terrace about 20 meters high, washing over pristine tundra.

Even with a camera, one cannot capture a tenth of its beauty.

Itinerary

3

Day1 Gather in Lijiang (丽江 2,400m)

Day2 Lijiang - Shangri-La (香格里拉 3,300m) - Shudu Lake in Pudacuo National Park (普达措国家公园属都湖 3,580m) - Dijitang Pasture (迪吉塘牧场 3,800m)
Driving: 200km, 4 hours
Trekking: 8km, 300m ascent, 4 hours

Departing from Lijiang in the morning, we drive to Pudacuo. After purchasing tickets to enter the scenic area, we take the shuttle bus to Shudu Lake, a journey of about 40 minutes. Upon arriving at Shudu Lake, we begin hiking, passing through Conggu Pasture (葱古牧场, Cōnggǔ Mùchǎng), and trek to Dijitang Pasture to set up camp.

Today's hike has relatively gentle slopes, mainly on mountain paths, with a very high level of safety.

Day3 Dijitang Pasture - Seven-Colored Waterfall (七彩瀑布 2,900m) - Niru Village (尼汝村 2,800m)
Trekking: 15km, 7 hours

Departing from Dijitang Pasture, we walk along a gentle mountain path, followed immediately by trekking through primeval forest, all downhill until we reach the Seven-Colored Waterfall.

The section from the Seven-Colored Waterfall to Niru Village consists entirely of scenic area boardwalks, which are more comfortable to walk on than dirt paths. Following the river

valley downward will lead us to Niru Village. Today's hiking trails are in good condition, and it's easy to stay on track.

Day4 Niru Village - Xirenlong Pasture (习仁龙牧场 3,350m) - Selie Lake (色烈湖 4,000m) - Nanbao Pasture (南宝牧场 4,200m)
Trekking: 15km, 1400m ascent, 7 hours

Today is the day with the most elevation gain. After breakfast, we depart from Niru Village and walk along a rural road for a while before entering the primeval forest. The road conditions are relatively good as we ascend toward the marshy meadows.

A little further ahead lies Selie Lake. Beyond Selie Lake, the trail condition gets better, and the slopes become gentler. We'll spend the night at the Nanbao Pasture campsite.

Day5 Nanbao Pasture - Shuoe Pasture (硕俄牧场 3,900m) - Dingru Lake (丁汝湖 4,000m) - Niru Village (2,800m)
Trekking: 16km, 1400m ascent, 6 hours

From Nanbao Pasture, we pass through Shuoe Pasture to reach Dingru Lake, with gentle slopes both up and down and good road conditions.

From Dingru Lake onward, the terrain descends gradually, with some sections covered in loose gravel, which can make it easy to slip.

Day6 Niru Village - Shangri-La - Lijiang
Driving: 290km, 6 hours

Important Notes

- Best Season: May to November
- Suitable For: Healthy individuals aged 10-65 years
- Potential Risks: Numerous uphill and downhill sections, with muddy roads during rainy weather, make it easy to slip and fall.

1

22. Tiger Leaping Gorge + Stone City
[虎跳峡+石头城, Hǔtiào Xiá + Shítou Chéng] 6days 56km

Lijiang
[丽江, Lìjiāng]
Gathering City

15KM
Longest Single-Day Hike

760M
Maximum Daily Elevation Gain

2,660M
Highest Elevation Along the Route

★★★
Scenic Rating

★★★
Difficulty Level

The Jinsha River (金沙江, Jīnshā Jiāng), after rushing thousands of miles from the Qinghai-Tibet Plateau, suddenly encounters two massive mountains—Haba Snow Mountain (哈巴雪山, Hābā Xuěshān) and Jade Dragon Snow Mountain (玉龙雪山, Yùlóng Xuěshān). The river channel instantly narrows, and the 216-meter huge drop makes the previously calm waters suddenly become "furious," with surging waves, thunderous roars, and unstoppable force. This place is Tiger Leaping Gorge (虎跳峡, Hǔtiào Xiá).

The canyon walls on both sides of Tiger Leaping Gorge are at a 90-degree vertical angle to the river surface, with an average drop of more than 3,000 meters. The narrowest part of the canyon is less than 30 meters wide. On both sides of the canyon, the towering Jade Dragon Snow Mountain and Haba Snow Mountain stand like two silver barriers between heaven and earth.

Natural Features
As one of "Top Ten Most Beautiful Canyons in China," Tiger Leaping Gorge is "dangerous, extraordinary, and beautiful." To truly appreciate its beauty, one must hike through it. Trekking the high path of Tiger Leaping Gorge is like walking along a natural barrier, either looking up at snow mountains or looking

down into deep valleys. In terms of difficulty, this route might not be the most challenging one, but in terms of magnificence, it is unparalleled by any other hiking routes. Snow-capped mountains stand on both sides of the route, with Haba Snow Mountain as a companion on the left, and the Thirteen Peaks of Jade Dragon (玉龙十三峰, Yùlóng Shísān Fēng) visible on the right.

Walking on the stone step path that resembles pages of a book, one can't help but marvel at how such an ingenious natural creation could exist. "Read ten thousand books, travel ten thousand miles"—Could this famous proverb be a reflection of the ancients as they walked these paths? And there are ibexes everywhere, living in mountains and valleys on cliffs and precipices. Sometimes they watch the backpackers coming and going, sometimes they lower their heads to graze, just as they have for centuries.

The trekking route passes through a part of the "Tea Horse Ancient Road" (茶马古道, Chámǎ Gǔdào). This historical concept, with specific meaning, represents a vast transportation network—a corridor for economic and cultural exchanges among ethnic groups in southwestern China. It is also a world-class natural scenic belt, brimming with endless cultural heritage. Hiking along this ancient road, amid the steep canyon scenery, one seems to hear echoes of history.

Following the ancient path, trekking through Tiger Leaping Gorge, crossing Prince's Pass (太子关, Tàizǐ Guān), and passing through ancient tunnels, with the winding, majestic Jinsha River by your side and the narrow path clinging to the cliff beneath your feet, one can't help but marvel at the wonders of nature. This route has little of modern convenience, no luxury restaurants or hotels, only pristine natural ecology. Multiple ethnicities have lived and multiplied here, continuously enacting magnificent and stirring history. Venture into the mountains and enter Naxi villages—this is both a return-to-nature journey and an adventure and discovery journey.

Notable Attractions

Stone City
[石头城, Shítou Chéng]

A Naxi (纳西族, Nàxī Zú) castle on a cliff, hidden deep in the Jinsha River canyon in Yunnan, is home to more than a hundred Naxi households. Stone City is built on a mushroom-shaped giant rock, with one side facing the river and three sides facing cliffs, naturally formed and ingeniously crafted by nature.

In ancient times, a Naxi leader, weary of prolonged warfare, recognized the strategic importance of this location—ideal for both offense and defense. He ordered gates to be constructed and walls to be built upon this massive rock, thus creating a 'naturally fortified city. Local people adapt to the rock formations; houses, beds, and stools are all carved out of the rock, which is amazing.

Walking here, one occasionally encounters local elder people, either sitting by the roadside basking in the sun or carrying bamboo baskets up the steps. They are very friendly; even though they don't speak Mandarin, they warmly greet visitors when they encounter outsiders. There are no cars here, and the transportation of goods in and out relies entirely on horses and mules, thus there is less hustle and bustle, only tranquility.

2 Thirteen Peaks of Jade Dragon
[玉龙十三峰, Yùlóng Shísān Fēng]

A famous snow mountain in Yunnan, majestic and breathtaking. The main peak is 5,596 meters above sea level.

The thirteen snow peaks stretch continuously, covered in clouds and snow year-round, resembling a "giant dragon" leaping and dancing, hence the name "Jade Dragon."

Itinerary

Day1 Gather in Lijiang (丽江 2,400m)

Day2 Lijiang - Tiger Leaping Gorge Town (虎跳峡镇) - Naxi Yage (纳西雅阁) - 28 Bends (28 道拐 2,660m) - Middle Trail Inn (中途客栈 2,350m)
Trekking: 16km, 760m ascent, 7 hours

After breakfast, we depart from Lijiang and drive for about 2 hours to reach the starting point of the Tiger Leaping Gorge high trail.

We rest at Naxi Yage, and in the afternoon, we climb the famous Twenty-Eight Bends. With determination, we can reach the pass in about 1.5 hours, where we can fully appreciate the Thirteen Peaks of Jade Dragon Snow Mountain.

After that, we hike downhill for about 2 hours to reach the Tea Horse Ancient Road Inn, and then continue hiking for about 2.5 hours to reach the Middle Trail Inn.

Day3 Middle Trail Inn - Guanyin Waterfall (观音瀑布) - Teacher Zhang's Inn (张老师客栈) - Middle Tiger Leaping (中虎跳) - Heaven's Ladder (一线天天梯) - Teacher Zhang's Inn (1,800m)
Trekking: 13km, 760m ascent, 5 hours

In the morning, we depart from the Middle Trail Inn, pass by Guanyin Waterfall, and arrive at Teacher Zhang's Inn.

Then, we descend to Middle Tiger Leaping, and return to Teacher Zhang's Inn via the thrilling Heaven's Ladder.

Day4 Teacher Zhang's Inn - Daju Ferry (大具渡口) - Ahai Power Station (阿海电站) -

Stone City (石头城 1,720m)
Driving: 2 hours | Boating: 1 hour

Leaving Middle Tiger Leaping Gorge, we drive to Daju Ferry. Upon reaching Daju Ferry, we cross the Jinsha River by ferry with our vehicle, then drive to Ahai Power Station, and finally take a boat to Stone City for self-guided exploration.

Day5 Stone City - Yanshuangluo (岩双洛 1,860m) - Liuqing (柳青 2,800m)
Driving: 50km, 3 hours
Trekking: 15km, 1080m ascent, 3 hours

This is the most challenging day of the journey, as we hike through Prince's Pass. The main difficulty lies in the significant elevation gain and the sandy, slippery path, with some sections being particularly steep.Crossing Prince's Pass involves passing through two mountain tunnels.

Along the hike, we'll be treated to the most stunning views of the Jinsha River canyon, with distant glimpses of Baoshan Stone City and terraced fields.

Day6 Liuqing - Jinsha River Pier (金沙江码头) - Ahai Power Station - Lijiang
Trekking: 8km, 3 hours

After breakfast, we depart from Upper Liuqing, pass through Middle Liuqing, and continue downhill to the Jinsha River Pier.

We take a boat to Ahai Power Station and then switch to vehicles and return to Lijiang.

Important Notes

- Best Season: Year-round; in summer, the river water is turbid and surging; in winter, the river water is emerald and tranquil
- Suitable For: Healthy individuals aged 7-65 years
- Potential Risks: The journey involves climbing cliff, people with a fear of heights should think twice.

23. Abujicuo Trek
[阿布吉措, Ābùjí Cuò]

6days
39km

Lijiang
[丽江, Lìjiāng]
Gathering City

12KM
Longest Single-Day Hike

765M
Maximum Daily Elevation Gain

4,405M
Highest Elevation Along the Route

★★★★☆
Scenic Rating

★★★
Difficulty Level

Shangri-La (香格里拉, Xiānggélǐlā) has long been a popular tourist destination, with attractions like Pudacuo (普达措, Pǔdácuò), Dukezong Ancient Town (独克宗古城, Dúkèzōng Gǔchéng), Songzanlin Monastery (松赞林寺, Sōngzànlín Sì), and Tiger Leaping Gorge (虎跳峡, Hǔtiào Xiá) already familiar to many. After outdoor activities gained popularity, ordinary scenic spots could no longer satisfy the demands, and finding lesser-known hidden gems became a necessity for travelers. Subsequently, some landscapes that can only be seen by hiking have emerged, and with the tailwind of the self-media era, they have gained the title of "internet celebrities." Abujicuo (阿布吉措, Ābùjí Cuò) is one such example.

Abujicuo became popular because it truly deserves recognition; its beauty has moved the vast majority of visitors. The beauty of Abujicuo differs from the curated beauty of trending establishments. It requires no careful adornment, no selective angles, no layers of filters. Every corner here is stunning; even the most casual snapshot captures breathtaking scenery.

Natural Features
Abujicuo is a transliteration from the Naxi language, where "Abuji" means "magical place" and "Cuo" means lake. This highland lake in Xiaozhongdian (小中甸, Xiǎozhōngdiàn), Shangri-La, surrounded by snow mountains on three sides, is known as "the last pure land of Shangri-La." According to local guides, a Naxi herdsman, while searching for his lost cattle, followed their hoof prints all the way to the mountain top and discovered the dazzling pearl-like Lake Abujicuo. Thus, the beautiful name of Abujicuo spread.

This magical body of water is nestled within the lotus petal-shaped mountain of Tianbao Snow Mountain (天宝雪山, Tiānbǎo Xuěshān). Deep and clear, with sharp peaks reflected in its mirror-like surface, it creates the illusion of being in a heavenly paradise. Here, the mountains exude their own grandeur, the water its own tranquility, and the clouds their own sense of freedom. In spring and summer, alpine rhododendrons and high mountain vegetation bloom around the lake, forming a vibrant tapestry. Looking from afar, the undulating sea of flowers across the mountains creates breathtaking panoramic views. It's worth mentioning that in good weather, standing at the open pass, one can see Meili Snow

Credit
© All images in this piece by Harrison

Mountain (梅里雪山, Méilǐ Xuěshān), the Three Sacred Mountains of Daocheng (稻城三神山, Dàochéng Sān Shénshān), and Haba Snow Mountain (哈巴雪山, Hābā Xuěshān) from different directions. In autumn, Abujicuo becomes beautiful and bright, with an incredibly blue sky that makes one lose track of time. In winter, Abujicuo turns fierce, blanketed in white, with gale-force winds at the pass hurling ice pellets against one's face. To see the gentleness of the sacred lake, one must first endure the hardship of wind and snow.

Many versions of the Abujicuo trek can be found online, with most tourists choosing to go via Xiaozhongdian toward Abujicuo for a single-day trip. For 'greedy' outdoor enthusiasts, having journeyed all the way to Shangri-La and with the rare opportunity to see Abujicuo, a one-day trip simply doesn't satisfy their appetite.

Therefore, we designed this multi-day trekking loop centered around Abujicuo, with a total length of about 39 kilometers. Along the way, there are many other highlights except for Abujicuo.

For example, this route offers close-up views of Tianbao Snow Mountain. As one of the seven snow mountains of Shan-gri-La, it has steep and rugged terrain with a fantastical beauty. Another major attraction along the way is the Meteorite Crater Group (陨石天坑群, Yǔnshí Tiānkēng Qún). It is said that these craters were formed by meteorite impacts, creating nearly 40 small lakes of various sizes. They differ in shape and color, and when viewed from above, they resemble gems scattered by fairies.

On the way to Abujicuo, you will also pass through dense primeval forests and alpine pastures, which are havens for plants and animals. The Spanish moss hanging leisurely from trees, mushrooms quietly peeking out, birds singing in the forest, and cattle and sheep grazing contentedly on the meadows, all convey a sense of ease and comfort.

However, the extreme beauty of Abujicuo is also accompanied by dangers. The elevation of 4,405 meters, the changeable weather on the plateau, the risks of getting lost, hypothermia, and encounters with wild animals all pose potential hazards. An important aspect of respecting nature is ensuring your own safety. Outdoor conditions are complex and unpredictable, so remember to make adequate preparations before setting out.

Notable Attractions

1 Meteorite Crater Group
[陨石天坑群, Yǔnshí Tiānkēng Qún]

It is said that these craters were formed by meteorite impacts, creating nearly 40 small lakes of various sizes. Each lake has its unique shape and color.

Hidden within this forested meadow, the reflections on the lake surfaces, combined with the occasional mist, make this place seem like a fairyland. Viewed from the sky, the dense cluster of lakes is quite spectacular.

Itinerary

Day1 Gather in Lijiang (丽江 2,400m)

Day2 Lijiang - Shangri-La (香格里拉) - Washbasin Pass (洗脸盆垭口) - Three Cattle Camp (三牛场) - Gebeng Campsite (格崩营地 3,960m)
Driving: 200km, 4 hours
Trekking: 8km, 765m ascent, 6 hours

We drive from Lijiang, pass through Shangri-La, and proceed via Three Cattle Camp, enjoying views of Tianbao Snow Mountain and the nearly 40 lakes surrounding the Meteorite Crater Group, ultimately arriving at Gebeng Campsite.

Day3 Gebeng Campsite - Meteorite Crater Group (陨石天坑群) - Abujicuo Pass (阿布吉措垭口) - Abujicuo - Golden Pillar Pass (金柱垭口) - Golden Pillar Campsite (金柱营地 4,105m)
Trekking: 10km, 340m ascent, 7 hours

In the morning, after hiking a short distance, we reach the Meteorite Crater Group. Later, we cross over Abujicuo Pass, where we can admire the panoramic view of Abujicuo.

After descending from the pass to the lakeshore for appreciation, we set off to cross Golden Pillar Pass, then head downhill all the way to Golden Pillar Campsite. During hiking, in good weather, we can clearly see the Three Sacred Mountains of Daocheng and Meili Snow Mountain.

Day4 Golden Pillar Campsite - Tianbao Mountain Pass (天宝山垭口) - Xinshangong-ga (新山贡嘎) - Benghuo Campsite (崩火营地 3,670m)
Trekking: 9km, 700m ascent, 7 hours

Departing from Golden Pillar Campsite, we pass through Tianbao Mountain Pass, Xinshangong-ga, and Despair Slope (绝望坡, Juéwàng Pō), setting up camp at Benghuo Campsite.

The route today is mostly uphill, with a steep downhill section after reaching Xinshan Pass.

Day5 Benghuo Campsite - Nine Dragon Cattle Camp (九龙牛场) - Sheep Camp (羊场) - Shangri-La
Trekking: 12km, 6 hours

Today, we first descend a gentle slope to reach Nine Dragon Cattle Camp, then ascend a gentle slope to a farm road.

Along the way, we will pass through primeval forests and large rhododendron forests, eventually reaching the end of our trek, from where we drive back to Shangri-La.

Day6 Shangri-La - Lijiang
Driving: 170km, 2.5 hours

Important Notes

- Best Season: April to December
- Suitable For: Healthy individuals aged 12-65 years
- Potential Risks: Steep mountain paths; Muddy and slippery when raining.

24. Haba Western Slope

[哈巴西坡, Hābā Xī Pō]

5days
45km

Lijiang
[丽江, Lìjiāng]
Gathering City

10KM
Longest Single-Day Hike

530M
Maximum Daily Elevation Gain

4,370M
Highest Elevation Along the Route

★★★
Scenic Rating

★★★
Difficulty Level

Credit
© All images in this piece by Harrison

"Haba" in the Naxi language means "flower like gold." The main peak of Haba Snow Mountain (哈巴雪山, Hābā Xuěshān) stands at 5,396 meters above sea level and is located on the north bank of the Jinsha River (金沙江, Jīnshā Jiāng) in the southeast of Shangri-La (香格里拉, Xiānggélǐlā). It faces Jade Dragon Snow Mountain (玉龙雪山, Yùlóng Xuěshān) across the river on the south bank, and in ancient Naxi legends, it is the twin brother of Jade Dragon Snow Mountain.

When outdoor enthusiasts mention Haba Snow Mountain, the first thought that often comes to mind is "the first snow-capped peak of one's life." For many, Haba Mountain marks the beginning of their climbing journey. However, Haba Snow Mountain is not just a desolate, cold paradise; instead, the massive vertical drop from the foot of the mountain at Tiger Leaping Gorge Town (虎跳峡镇, Hǔtiào Xiá Zhèn) to the peak of Haba Snow Mountain encapsulates the entire natural landscape of northwestern Yunnan: primeval forests, alpine meadows, rhododendrons, coniferous forests, alpine lakes, pastures, snow slopes... Various landscapes are well-arranged, creating breathtaking scenery.

Natural Features

Avoiding the bustling crowds on Haba's eastern slope, the western slope of Haba is more like a secret paradise rarely visited by people. The splendid rhododendrons of early summer and the colorful coniferous forests of autumn are its most unmissable beauties.

The western slope of Haba boasts various species of rhododendrons. In summer, rhododendrons of different colors bloom all over the mountains. Immersed in this wanderland, one can feel the magnificent vitality of nature.

The western slope of Haba in autumn is a visual feast. Sunlight spills onto the layered forests, dyeing the entire hillside gold and red. Whether you're walking on the slopes, in the pastures, in the forest, or beside an alpine lake, every step feels like stepping on a canvas. Everything around appears so vibrant and full of life. The wind rustling through the leaves has a gentle and healing power. Autumn is also the best season for hiking on the western slope of Haba. Walking here, the majestic Haba Snow Mountain is right before your eyes, like a sleeping giant, magnificent and grand. The sprawling alpine meadows and the golden autumn leaves shimmer in the sunlight, like a golden carpet spread across the earth. Not far away, a few small wooden cabins of the herdsmen dot the landscape, with the faint sound of flowing water, as if nature is whispering.

According to local guides, the western slope of Haba was only developed in 2021 and was previously a place where locals grazed livestock and gathered mushrooms. Not having been developed for many years, this route has preserved its pristine ecological environment. It's an entry-level hiking route with well-maintained trails, featuring a daily elevation gain of 300-500 meters.

On this route, you can enjoy not only the grandeur and awe of close proximity to alpine snow mountains, but also primeval forests, river valleys, alpine meadows, serene lakes, and other natural landscapes.

Throughout the changing seasons of the year, you can appreciate the pristine natural scenery. Being there, your heart will likely expand with the endless extension of these wild mountains, becoming increasingly stronger and broader.

Notable Attractions

Black Lake
[黑海, Hēihǎi]

It is a beautiful alpine lake along the way. As the eye of Haba Snow Mountain, it sits on a plateau over 4,000 meters above sea level, serene and beautiful.

Speaking of Black Lake, one cannot miss that fiery red "wishing tree." Many people travel thousands of miles, crossing mountains and ridges, just to see it, just to stand quietly in its shade for a while, to daydream. Some might think this is too much trouble, but how many times in one's life can one experience such peaceful moments?

Lijiang
[丽江, Lìjiāng]

Mountains and plateaus account for about 94% of Yunnan Province's total territory. Nestled within the mountains and plateaus of Yunnan are numerous relatively flat basins, small alluvial plains formed by rivers, and other gentle landscapes—locally referred to as "bazi" (坝子, bàzi).

Lijiang City is one such "bazi." From the streets of Lijiang, a glance upwards reveals the majestic figure of Jade Dragon Snow Mountain. At night, amidst the colorful lights, one can wander in the romantic and bustling Old Town of Lijiang (丽江古城, Lìjiāng Gǔchéng).

Setting out the next day, one encounters a different kind of quiet yet captivating mountain and wilderness scenery.

Itinerary

Day1 Gather in Lijiang (丽江 2,400m)

Day2 Lijiang - Tiger Leaping Gorge Town (虎跳峡镇) - Old Medicine Mountain Village (老药山村) - Baicaopo Campsite (百草坡营地 3,680m)
Driving: 18km, 1 hours
Trekking: 8km, 530m ascent, 4 hours

After breakfast, we depart from Lijiang and drive to Tiger Leaping Gorge Town in Shangri-La. We then switch to smaller vehicles to reach the starting point of our hike, Old Medicine Mountain Village.

From there, we hike 8 kilometers to Baicaopo Campsite. The entire route primarily consists of small paths through mountain forests, with relatively gentle slopes.

Day3 Baicaopo Campsite - Yuanbao Mountain (元宝山) - Lower Jizhi (下吉支) - Upper Jizhi Campsite (上吉支营地 3,960m)
Trekking: 10km, 450m ascent, 6 hours

In the morning, we depart from Baicaopo Campsite. The first half of the journey is mostly walking through primeval forests. After passing Yuanbao Mountain, we reach an open area strewn with rocks.

Throughout the day, we can closely observe Haba Snow Mountain.

The hiking route is relatively gentle, with good trail conditions, following relatively established caravan routes.

Day4 Upper Jizhi Campsite - Twin Lakes (双湖) - Twin Lakes Pass (双湖垭口 4,370m) - Green Sea (绿海) - Black Lake Campsite (黑海营地 4,100m)
Trekking: 9km, 400m ascent, 6 hours

After breakfast, we hike to Twin Lakes at an elevation of 4,080 meters, which is an excellent photography spot for capturing the reflection of Haba Snow Mountain. We then cross Twin Lakes Pass at an elevation of 4,370 meters.

From the pass, we can see the other side of Haba Snow Mountain and the lakes of various sizes in the direction of Black Lake spread out before us.

After a brief rest, we traverse southeast toward Green Sea at an elevation of 4,260 meters, then descend to Small Lake Pass (小海垭口, Xiǎohǎi Yágǒu) at 4,200 meters. This is an excellent location for viewing Black Lake. From Small Lake, we descend all the way to Black Lake Campsite.

Day5 Black Lake - Couple Lakes (夫妻海) - Pot Bottom Depression (锅底洼) - Horse Hiding Place Campsite (马躲处营地 3,780m)
Trekking: 8km, 350m ascent, 6 hours

We rise up early to explore Black Lake at leisure. After breakfast, we climb to Couple Lakes and then descend all the way to Horse Hiding Place Campsite, which is the best location for viewing Haba Snow Mountain throughout the entire journey. Along the way, Haba Snow Mountain and Black Lake together create a beautiful landscape painting.

Day6 Horse Hiding Place Campsite - Orchid Flat (兰花坪) - Sheep House Pasture (羊房牧场) - Haba Village (哈巴村) - Lijiang
Trekking: 10km, 4 hours

After watching the golden mountain illuminated by the sun at Horse Hiding Place Campsite, we begin today's hike, descending all the way, passing through Orchid Flat Pasture and Sheep House Pasture, to reach the end of our trek. We then drive back to Lijiang.

Important Notes

- Best Season: April to December
- Suitable For: Healthy individuals aged 12-65 years
- Potential Risks: 1. The plateau climate is highly variable, so be sure to take precautions for waterproofing and warmth.

  2. There is a risk of altitude sickness, so pay attention to your physical condition.

25. Yubeng Kora

[雨崩转山, Yǔbēng Zhuǎnshān]

6days

56km

Lijiang
[丽江, Lijiāng]
Gathering City

17KM
Longest Single-Day Hike

1,000M
Maximum Daily Elevation Gain

3,800M
Highest Elevation Along the Route

★★★★
Scenic Rating

★★★
Difficulty Level

Meili Snow Mountain (梅里雪山, Méilǐ Xuěshān) is located at the junction of Yunnan, Sichuan, and Tibet provinces, in the middle section of the Hengduan Mountains between the Nujiang River (怒江, Nù Jiāng) and Lancang River (澜沧江, Láncāng Jiāng). It connects with Adong Geni Mountain in Tibet to the north and Biluo Snow Mountain (碧罗雪山, Bìluó Xuěshān) to the south. Meili is not the name of a single peak, but rather a series of peaks with an average elevation of over 6,000 meters, commonly known as the "Prince's Thirteen Peaks" (太子十三峰, Tàizǐ Shísān Fēng). By coincidence, "Kawagebo" (卡瓦格博, Kǎwǎgébó) has become the name card of the main peak of Meili Snow Mountain. Yet for Tibetan believers, regardless of its name, it is the irreplaceable "God of Snow Mountains," a sacred site for circumambulation that has continued to this day, standing as the foremost among the eight sacred mountains of the Tibetan region.

Yubeng (雨崩, Yǔbēng), nestled among the mountains of Meili Snow Mountain, is a place frequently mentioned by outdoor enthusiasts. This remote and sacred small village was only discovered by the outside world in the mid-20th century. According to legend, at the foot of Meili Snow Mountain, an old man often went to Xidang Village (西当村, Xīdāng Cūn) to borrow grain, but no one knew where he actually lived. Therefore, the villagers of Xidang followed him, but they always lost track of him.

Later, someone came up with an idea: the next time the old man came to borrow grain, the villagers said, "This time we won't lend you highland barley, nor wheat, only millet." They made a small hole in the bag of millet, which left a trail as the old man walked, until it disappeared under a huge rock. When they moved the rock, they discovered a small village hidden underneath—this is today's Yubeng.

Natural Features

Although it became an internet sensation a decade ago, Yubeng's popularity has not waned on the internet with the passage of time. Twelve years ago, Yubeng Village had no electricity and was truly a paradise away from the world; twelve years later, Yubeng Village is filled with guesthouses and coffee shops, yet many people still come to walk the classic Yubeng trekking route and see the legendary Meili Snow Mountain.

From Deqin (德钦, Déqīn) to Feilai Temple (飞来寺, Fēilái Sì), snow mountains stretch on the left, prayer flags at the temple tear through the sound of the wind, and the tinkling of wind chimes under the eaves adds a touch of dreaminess to the scene before your eyes. Most first-time visitors to Meili will wait at Feilai Temple for a sunrise over the Meili peaks. Most who wait for the sunrise will also hear others say: some people have come more than a dozen times and still haven't had the luck to witness the sun illuminating the golden mountains. If by chance at this moment, the sunlight gradually extends to cover the tops of the thirteen snow mountains, how unexpectedly honored one would feel. At sunrise and sunset, as clouds gather and disperse, the longing for and reverence toward nature always overflows at such moments.

The yearning for sacred mountains is not always about conquering them. The main peak of Meili Snow Mountain, Kawagebo, remains an unclimbed virgin peak to this day. In 2001, legislation was enacted prohibiting climbing this mountain, making it the first peak banned from climbing for cultural protection reasons.

The topographical features of the Three Parallel Rivers region bring abundant moisture, fostering a rich and diverse natural environment with distinct climates. Towering snow-capped mountains and glaciers, along with significant elevation changes, combine to create a wealth of plant and animal life, making the Meili Snow Mountain area a stunning showcase of biodiversity. In the summer, the landscape is lush and green, and trekking through the mountains feels like stepping into a natural oxygen bar. During August and September, the mountains are blanketed with vibrant blooms, captivating all who venture there. From mid-October to late November, the golden hues of autumn leaves blend with the pristine white of snow and ice, creating a breathtaking and unique beauty. If you come for scenery, Meili will not disappoint you.

Among the many routes for viewing Meili Snow Mountain, the circumambulation trail centered on Yubeng Village stands out as the most iconic and a favorite starting point for outdoor enthusiasts. There's no need to camp in the wilderness—simply rest up in Yubeng Village before setting out on your journey to Sacred Lake (神湖, Shén Hú), Sacred Waterfall (神瀑, Shén Pù), Ice Lake (冰湖, Bīng Hú), and more. As you trek, you'll pass through lush forests and meadows, encountering stacks of mani stones (玛尼堆, Mǎní Duī) by streams, and, at times, catch a breathtaking, unexpected glimpse of the towering Meili Snow Mountain. After completing your hike, you can return to your hotel for a refreshing hot shower, indulge in a delicious meal with your companions, and relax on the terrace while gazing at the stars–just imagining it is enough to stir the soul.

Notable Attractions

1 Feilai Temple
[飞来寺, Fēilái Sì]

Feilai Temple is located 8 kilometers outside Deqin County town, beside the Dian-Tibet Highway (滇藏公路, Diān-Zàng Gōnglù). Feilai Temple was initially built in the 42nd year of the Wanli period of the Ming Dynasty (1614), with a history of over 410 years.

It is the best location for viewing the golden sunrise on Meili Snow Mountain and Mingyong Glacier (明永冰川, Míngyǒng Bīngchuān).

2 Mianzimu
[缅茨姆, Miǎncímǔ]

At 6,054 meters, Mianzimu is often referred to as Kawagebo's "wife," tenderly guarding its southern flank. With her gentle, graceful shape, she is said to resemble a mother cradling her child.

Her serene and elegant form has earned her the title of "Goddess Peak" (神女峰, Shénnǚ Fēng) among locals.

3 Kawagebo
[卡瓦格博, Kǎwǎgébó]

At 6,740 meters, Kawagebo is the highest peak of the Prince's Thirteen Peaks and holds deep spiritual significance for various religious groups, especially among the local Tibetan communities. It is considered a sacred mountain, and to this day, it remains unclimbed.

In 2001, local legislation officially banned climbing on Kawagebo, making it the first mountain to be prohibited from ascent for cultural protection.

4 Sacred Waterfall
[神瀑, Shén Pù]

This waterfall holds a deep sacred significance as a true pilgrimage site in the hearts of local Tibetans. Its waters flow from Kawagebo, and it is believed that taking a holy bath beneath the falls grants the protection of the spirits. Along the path to the Sacred Waterfall, you'll encounter numerous prayer flags, fluttering in the wind, worn by countless gusts over time.

Many Tibetans come here to pay their respects, and if you cross their path, it's customary to offer a Tibetan blessing: "Tashi Delek" (扎西德勒, Zhāxī Délè).

Itinerary

Day1 Gather in Lijiang (丽江 2,400m)

Day2 Lijiang - Xiaozhongdian (小中甸) - Moon Bay (月亮湾) - Feilai Temple (飞来寺)
Driving: 360km, 8 hours

After breakfast, we depart from Lijiang by vehicle, passing through Xiaozhongdian, where the wind sweeps low over the grass, revealing herds of cattle and sheep, immersing ourselves in the serene grassland scenery of Shangri-La (香格里拉, Xiānggélǐlā).

Our journey continues as we reach Benzilan (奔子栏, Bēnzilán) for lunch, before heading through Moon Bay and finally arriving at Feilai Temple. From the temple's observation deck, we are treated to a breathtaking view of Meili Snow Mountain.

Day3 Feilai Temple - Xidang (西当) - Nanzhong Pass (南争垭口 3,729m) - Yubeng Village (雨崩村 3,000m)
Trekking: 11km, 6 hours

We rise early to head to the Meili Snow Mountain viewing platform, where we can witness the golden sunrise illuminating the Meili peaks.

After breakfast, we drive to Xidang Village to begin our hike. We ascend 1,200 meters to reach Nanzong Pass, then make our descent, arriving in Yubeng Village by evening. (Please note that due to ongoing local road construction, the classic Xidang entrance will be temporarily closed starting June 2024, and entry will be via Ninong (尼农, Nínóng).)

Day4 Yubeng Village - Xiaonong Base Camp (笑农大本营) - Ice Lake (冰湖 3,800m) - Yubeng Village
Trekking: 14km, 7 hours

We depart from Yubeng Village and begin our hike towards Ice Lake. Along the way, we pass through vibrant sea buckthorn forests and venture into pristine, untouched woodlands.

We continue on to Xiaonong Base Camp, which once served as the campsite for the Sino-Japanese joint mountaineering expedition to climb Kawagebo Peak.

After resting and replenishing our energy, we continue our ascent to Ice Lake. We then retrace our steps back to Yubeng Village via the same route.

Day5 Yubeng Village - Sacred Waterfall (神瀑 3,800m) - Yubeng Village
Trekking: 14km, 7 hours

After breakfast, we set off, crossing the Yubeng River and passing through Lower Yubeng Village (雨崩下村, Yǔbēng Xià Cūn), where lush green mountains and crystal-clear waters stretch beside us, while the sky above is a canvas of blue and white clouds.

We then hike through untouched forests and alpine pastures, where the absence of human presence enhances the natural beauty. Our journey leads us to the Sacred Waterfall, cascading down from Meili Snow Mountain. From here, we enjoy a stunning panoramic view of Goddess Peak and Five Crown Peak (五冠峰, Wǔguān Fēng).

After taking in the breathtaking scenery, we retrace our steps back to Yubeng Village.

Day6 Yubeng Village - Ninong Grand Canyon (尼农大峡谷) - Deqin (德钦) - Lijiang
Trekking: 17km, 6 hours

After breakfast, we begin our journey, following the Yubeng River as it gently winds downhill toward the Ninong Grand Canyon. As we enter the canyon, we are immersed in its serene depths, surrounded by lush greenery and soft, drifting clouds.

The trail here narrows in places, so it's important to stay cautious while hiking. After exploring the canyon, we reach the Ninong Village parking lot and make our way back to Lijiang.

Important Notes

- Best Season: Year-round, with unique characteristics in each season
- Suitable For: Healthy individuals aged 10-65 years
- Potential Risks: The weather on the plateau is changeable, so pay attention to waterproofing and keeping warm.

26. Meili North Slope
[梅里北坡, Méilǐ Běi Pō]

Lijiang
[丽江, Lìjiāng]
Gathering City

17KM
Longest Single-Day Hike

1,000M
Maximum Daily Elevation Gain

5,200M
Highest Elevation Along the Route

★★★★½
Scenic Rating

★★★½
Difficulty Level

Is there a hiking route that features towering mountains and snow-capped peaks alongside streams, pastures, and picturesque bridges... and importantly, has few visitors, is easily accessible, and not overly challenging? Indeed, there is! This place is the Meili North Slope.

Out of our love for snow-capped mountains and fascination with Meili, we have made numerous journeys into the Meili region over the years, traversing untouched areas and developing several breathtaking hiking routes. In 2019, we finally selected a trekking route through the northern group of peaks in the Meili Snow Mountain range. Starting from Yagong Village (亚贡村, Yà Gòng Cūn), the trail runs along the base of the north slope, offering comprehensive views of the various peaks and glaciers of Meili's north face. This unique vantage point presents an even more magnificent perspective of the Meili Snow Mountain, giving this route its name: "Meili North Slope."

Since its emergence, the Meili North Slope has ranked among Yunnan's most popular trekking routes consecutively. The "Meili North Slope" refers not to a single mountain, but to the group of peaks on the northern side of the Meili Snow Mountain range. From east to west, these peaks include Lairi Gongka (来日贡卡, Lái Rì Gòng Kǎ, 6300 meters), Nairi Dingka (奶日顶卡, Nǎi Rì Dǐng Kǎ, 6379 meters), Mangkang Laka Ka (芒框腊卡, Máng Kuàng Là Kǎ, 6040 meters), and Kawagebo Peak II (卡瓦格博 II 峰, Kǎ Wǎ Gé Bó Èr Fēng, 6509 meters).

The extreme elevation range has endowned this region diverse ecosystems on the Meili North Slope. This natural oxygen bar boasts rich flora and fauna, attracting countless researchers for scientific exploration. It is precisely because of the rich vegetation resources that it is rarely heard of anyone experiencing altitude sickness here, so hikers can easily put this concern aside.

Leaving the trailhead at Yagong Village, you follow a winding forest path that gradually penetrates deeper into the forest, where the magic and wonder of Meili's hidden realm begins to unfold. Walking on soft soil and fallen pine needles, surrounded by the sounds of wind, water, insects, and birds, you can occasionally glimpse snow-capped peaks through the sparse trees, solemn and sacred. As you ascend, passing through the coniferous forest belt, the view suddenly opens up, revealing a breathtaking panorama. Snow-covered mountains, glaciers, rivers,

Credit
Image 1 | ©Banban
Image 2/4 | ©Harrison
Image 3 | ©Majun
Image 5 | ©Zijun

121.

and the vast wilderness rush into view, creating an overwhelming, soul-stirring experience that words can hardly capture.

Trekking in high altitude region, mountain passes are nightmares for each hikers, but also a form of self-challenge. To complete the Meili North Slope trek, trekkers are required to cross Ciding Pass and the Dian-Tibet Pass. Ciding Pass (次丁垭口, Cì Dīng Yàkǒu) stands at 4770 meters. Along the way to or standing at the pass, you can capture excellent photos of the snow mountains and glaciers of Meili North Slope. On the fourth day of hiking, you'll reach the highest point of the journey, the Dian-Tibet Pass (滇藏垭口, Diān Zàng Yàkǒu) at 5200 meters. This pass marks the boundary between Yunnan and Tibet provinces, hence its name.

Another highlight of the Meili North Slope is its excellent camping experience. Each site has its own characteristics, and every one could be considered a five-star campsite, but the most beautiful are Pojun Campsite and Pojiang Campsite, which offer stunning viewpoints of the Meili North Slope. You'll reach Pojun Campsite on the second day of trekking; on the third and fourth days, you'll stay at Pojiang Campsite, with the two sites separated by a mountain ridge.

Cultural Significance

In recent years, geologists and botanists have been conducting scientific expeditions to the Meili North Slope. Due to the extreme elevation difference (nearly 5000 meters), maritime modern glaciers wind down from the main peaks along the valleys, with glacial tongues extending to forest areas as low as 2700 meters. Such low-elevation glacier terminals are rare in the world, making this a unique case study for glacier research in China and globally. The diverse, complex, and well-preserved environmental characteristics have also created a rich variety of flora, fauna, and landscapes in the Meili Snow Mountains.

Because of global warming, the snow mountains and glaciers of the Meili North Slope are melting at an unprecedented rate. Local villagers say that twenty or thirty years ago, the glacier was below the Pojun Campsite. But now, the glacier has retreated upward from the campsite by at least several kilometers, with a surprising rate of melting. Perhaps Meili will soon no longer display such magnificent glaciers. While the glaciers are still there, don't hesitate to take a look at this enchanting hidden realm of Meili!

2

Notable Attractions

1 Pojun
[坡均, Pō Jūn]

In Tibetan, it means "valley bottom where immortals live," located at an elevation of 4120 meters. It serves as a gathering campsite for locals and is an excellent base for photographing the Meili North Slope landscape.

From the campsite, you can closely observe Lairi Gongka, Nairi Dingka, Mangkuangla Ka, and their glaciers.

2 Mangkuangla Ka Snow Mountain
[芒框腊卡雪山,Máng Kuàng Là Kǎ Xuěshān]

Located to the west of Nairi Dingka, it consists of two snow peaks, with the main peak on the western side.

Below the eastern subsidiary peak, there is also a large glacier belt. From Pojun Campsite, you can admire its golden sunrise glow on the mountain.

3 Nairi Dingka Glacier
[奶日顶卡冰川, Nǎi Rì Dǐng Kǎ Bīngchuān]

Formed by the convergence of north slope glaciers from two snow mountains—Nairi Dingka (6379 meters) and Lairi Gongka (6300 meters). From a distance, the massive glacier belt displays a captivating pale blue color.

4 Cuogei Glacier
[错给冰川, Cuò Gěi Bīngchuān]

Located on the northern slope of Kawagebo Peak II, the Cuogei Glacier extends downward for over a thousand meters into the glacial valley. Compared to the Nairi Dingka Glacier, it is more undulating, with its base filled with numerous small glacial lakes—an apparent testament to the effects of climate change.

5 Lion Throne Sacred Mountain
[狮子座神山, Shīzi Zuò Shénshān]

Kawagebo Peak II, at 6509 meters, is the second highest peak in the Meili Snow Mountain range and also the northernmost peak of the Meili Snow Mountains.

The mountain is massive and stands proudly, like the guardian of the northern Meili Snow Mountains.

Itinerary

Day1 Gather in Lijiang (丽江 2,400m)

Day2 Lijiang - Shangri-La (香格里拉 3300m) - Feilai Temple (飞来寺 3450m)
Driving: 380km, 8 hours

Day3 Feilai Temple - Yagong Village (亚贡村 3000m) - Zhangjia Campsite (涨价营地 3500m)
Trekking: 9km, 550m ascent, 5 hours

We wake up early at Feilai Temple to witness the golden glow of the sunrise over Meili Snow Mountain. After breakfast, we depart by vehicle, embarking on a 2-hour drive to Yagong Village, the starting point of our trek. Situated above the Lancang River (Mekong) and near the north slope of Meili, this village offers stunning surroundings.

As we stroll through the primary forest and bamboo groves, the distant snow-capped peaks occasionally come into view. The hike lasts about 4 hours, during which we cross a wooden bridge, navigate a scree slope, and continue onward to reach Zhangjia Campsite.

Day4 Zhangjia Campsite - Bamboo Forest - Pojun Campsite (坡均营地 4100m)
Trekking: 8km, 600m ascent, 5 hours

After breakfast, we depart from the campsite and head toward the snow-capped mountains, following a small river. Our path first leads us through a vast bamboo forest, and as the elevation gradually rises, the full outline of the distant snow peaks begins to emerge.

We continue through forests, navigating rocky terrain, until Mangkuangla Ka Peak comes fully into view. Passing an abandoned cattle yard, we cross a wooden bridge, then ascend a slope. As we reach higher ground, the Nairi Dingka and its glacier come into focus. Pushing onward, we eventually arrive at Pojun Campsite.

Day5 Pojun Campsite - Ciding Pass (次丁垭口 4770m) - Pojiang Pasture Campsite (坡将牧场营地 4200m)
Trekking: 7km, 670m ascent, 570m descent, 5 hours

We wake up early at the campsite to capture the breathtaking golden sunrise on the Meili North Slope. After breakfast, we begin our ascent, passing through a small pasture before tackling the climb. The trail first crosses a steep scree slope, then continues upwards along the mountainside. As we reach 4500 meters, we enter the glacial valley remnants, a prime photography spot to capture the stunning Meili North Slope glaciers.

From here, we push higher to Ciding Pass,

which stands at 4770 meters—one of the most challenging part of the journey. Throughout the climb, we are treated to spectacular views of the snow-capped peaks and glaciers of Meili North Slope. Beyond the pass, we face a steep, long descent of more than 500 meters to reach the valley floor. After hiking a bit further, we finally reach Pojiang Pasture Campsite, located at 4200 meters.

Day6 Pojiang Pasture Campsite - Dian-Tibet Border Pass (滇藏界垭口 5200m) - Twin Lakes - Pojiang Pasture Campsite
Trekking: 9km, 1000m ascent/descent, 7 hours

After breakfast, we proceed toward Tibet. The Dian-Tibet Border Pass, at 5,200 meters, is the most challenging part of the entire journey, not only due to its high elevation but also because of the treacherous path conditions. With no clear trails on either side of the pass, walking requires extra caution. As you ascend, Kawagebo Peak II gradually comes into view, and the Nairi Dingka Glacier is once again fully visible. From the pass, a panoramic view of the Meili North Slope unfolds, while on the other side lies Tibet, with Mukong Snow Mountain and other peaks visible in the distance.

Continue along the ridge, then descend to the right along the scree path to reach the beautiful Twin Lakes. Afterward, we return to the Pojiang Pasture Campsite via the same route.

Day7 Pojiang Pasture Campsite - Dala Transverse Pass (达拉横向垭口 4350m) - Yagong - Feilai Temple
Trekking: 17km, 500m ascent, 1700m descent, 6 hours

After breakfast, we depart from the campsite and enter the forest. The trail begins with a downhill section, followed by a steady ascent to the Dala Yigu Pasture. After a rest here, we continue climbing, gaining more than 100 meters in elevation to reach the Dala Transverse Pass, where a breathtaking view of the entire Meili North Slope snow mountain range awaits.

Following a section of traversing, we reach an abandoned cattle shed before re-entering the forest and descending toward Yagong. As the elevation drops, the vegetation grows denser, and streams flow through the woods. Along the way, we cross several wooden bridges, eventually exiting the mountains and returning to the trek's starting point at Yagong Village. From there, we drive back to Feilai Temple.

Day8 Feilai Temple - Shangri-La - Lijiang
Driving: 380km, 9hours

Important Notes

● Best Season: May to November

● Suitable For: Healthy individuals aged 18-65 years

● Potential Risks: High elevation with risk of altitude sickness

27. Infinite Guizhou Trek

[无限黔徒, Wúxiàn Qián Tú]

6 days

64km

Guiyang
[贵阳, Guìyáng]
Gathering City

16KM
Longest Single-Day Hike

900M
Maximum Daily Elevation Gain

1,800M
Highest Elevation Along the Route

★ ★ ★
Scenic Rating

★ ★ ★
Difficulty Level

According to official data released in February 2024, more than 1.28 billion visits were made to Guizhou in 2023, with total tourism revenue of approximately 1.46 trillion yuan, ranking first among China's "Top Ten Tourism Revenue Provinces in 2023." While most people explore Guizhou in a conventional way, few realize that the lesser-known wilderness areas represent Guizhou's true essence. Guizhou boasts unique tourism agvantages, including caves, mountains, canyons, and numerous undeveloped outdoor resources. Hiking is the best way to explore authentic Guizhou.

"Land without three square feet of flat ground, sky without three days of continuous sunshine." This is the truest reflection of Guizhou's terrain and climate. This region boasts 1.258 million peaks and 984 rivers streching 10 kilometers long. It's home to the world's largest radio telescope—China's "Heavenly Eye" (中国天眼, Zhōngguó Tiānyǎn), 47 of the world's top 100 highest bridges, and national data centers… Many miracles occur in this mountainous land.

Without visiting this place, you could never imagine that alongside the highways, hidden in mountain valleys, lie "wonders" that are worth half a day to explore. Walking downhill from a gap in the guardrail of National Highway 356, you'll find a place called "Monkey King's Eye" (大圣之眼, Dà Shèng Zhī Yǎn). The initial scree slopes and steep inclines are nothing compared to the path leading to the "Monkey King's Eye," which offers a real challenge. Using both hands and feet is the only way to navigate this section—it's the true way to unlock the magical door of Guizhou.

Hollywood blockbuster scripts often include an "almost rock-bottom" plot twist before the perfect grand finale, and the "Monkey King's Eye" knows exactly how to capture visitors'hearts. Just when people are on the verge of despair, the "Monkey King's Eye" reveals its trump card—suddenly appearing at the bottom of the valley. This extraordinary natural landscape is tucked away so deeply. As the short journey comes to an end and you climb back to the road, watching vehicles continue on their way, you can't help but feel a twinge of sympathy for the people in those cars—unaware of the beautiful world just a kilometer away, waiting to be discovered.

In addition, Guizhou is home to a magical landscape that can achieve spatial folding, connecting the land above and below, forming a unique ecosystem. This is the power of karst topography. The Sheepskin Cave Waterfall (羊皮洞瀑布, Yángpí Dòng Pùbù) near the Wu River is a wonder created by karst landforms.

The "Yelang Sky Road" (夜郎天路, Yèláng Tiān Lù) on Dragon Ridge Mountain along the Zangke River (牂牁江, Zāngkē Jiāng) in Guizhou Province is another highlight of our journey, also known as "Dragon Ridge Sky Road" (龙脊天路, Lóngjǐ Tiān Lù). Speaking of famous southwestern regions in ancient times, the Yelang Kingdom must be mentioned. Legend has it that this area was once the core region of the ancient Yelang Kingdom, and the Moon Cave on the opposite Old King Mountain is said to be the burial place of the king and queen of the Yelang Kingdom.

The Zangke River (also known as the North Pan River) winds past the foot of Dragon Ridge Mountain like a blue gem inlaid between mountains. On this pristine mountain path, rarely visited by travelers, mountains and waters harmonize beautifully, offering panoramic views where you can fully immerse yourself in the awe and tranquility of nature.

When speaking of Guizhou, people often think of the Xijiang Thousand Household Miao Village or the Dong villages in eastern Guizhou. Guizhou is home to 49 ethnic minorities, making it one of the provinces with the highest concentration of ethnic minorities in China. In addition to its indigenous ethnic groups, this land in China's southwestern transverse mountain region also bears the cultural influence of the north. A prime example is the Tunpu culture in Anshun, which traces its origins to Emperor Zhu Yuanzhang's "Northern Expedition to the South" during the early Ming Dynasty. After the Ming army arrived in Anshun, they stationed troops and began farming the land. Hundreds of thousands of soldiers and civilians built homes and settled there, eventually forming the unique Tunpu culture, which continues to thrive to this day.

Notable Attractions

1 Sheepskin Cave Waterfall
[羊皮洞瀑布, Yángpí Dòng Pùbù]

Unlike most waterfalls, the Sheepskin Cave Waterfall is formed by an "underground stream" gushing from a cave opening. Aesthetically, it embodies "Chinese aesthetics," surrounded by lush greenery and accompanied by the cheerful songs of birds and the soothing sound of flowing water. With these gentle, natural white noises, the cascading waterfall feels anything but loud—its elegance creates a serene harmony with the surroundings.

2 Yunfeng Tunpu
[云峰屯堡, Yúnfēng Túnbǎo]

As a complex of buildings designed for both military and civilian use, every detail showcases the wisdom of people from 600 years ago and the architectural sophistication of the cold weapon era. Here, alleys intertwine, households are closely connected, and everything is made of stone—stone houses, stone walls, stone roads, and even stone benches and water vats. During the Ming Dynasty, these newly arrived soldiers and civilians utilized the karst topography to its fullest potential. Today, they still maintain their appearance from hundreds of years ago, which is truly impressive!

Itinerary

Day1 Gather in Guiyang (贵阳)

Day2 Guiyang - Sheepskin Cave Waterfall (羊皮洞瀑布) - Guiyang
Driving: 150km, 3 hours
Trekking: 10km, 500m ascent, 4 hours

We take a vehicle to the Sheepskin Cave Waterfall for hiking, and the route features mainly waterfall, cave, and canyon scenery.

The hike to Sheepskin Cave Waterfall begins with steep mountain roads, and during the rainy season, the paths can become muddy, so it's recommended to wear non-slip shoes.

After descending to the bottom of the canyon, you'll have the chance to admire the "famous" Sheepskin Cave Waterfall, where you can take photos in front of the stunning cascade. Lunch will be served as a roadside meal at the basin. In the afternoon, you'll explore a mysterious cave before completing the looped hike back to the parking area. Finally, you'll take a vehicle back to Guiyang city.

Day3 Guiyang - Monkey King's Eye (大圣之眼) - Anshun (安顺)
Driving: 150km, 3 hours
Trekking: 9km, 500m ascent, 4 hours

After breakfast, we take a vehicle to the starting point of the Monkey King's Eye hike, trekking through sinkholes, cliff caves, karst caves, and underground river valleys. In the afternoon, we exit the karst cave and continue crossing sinkhole valleys, rocky slopes, and shrub forests to reach the second underground river.

We are treated to the stunning view of the Monkey King's Eye, and pass through caves, and then exit the mountains, following a country road back to the starting point. Afterward, we drive to Anshun and check into a hotel.

Day4 Anshun - Yelang Sky Road (夜郎天路) - Anshun
Driving: 150km, 3 hours
Trekking: 16km, 600m ascent, 7 hours

After breakfast, we drive to the Yelang Sky Road. We will begin hiking from the country road at the foot of the mountain, pass through villages, and climb along a narrow path to the top of Dragon Ridge Mountain at over 2,000 meters above sea level, overlooking the Zangke River and Old King Mountain along the way.

After reaching the summit, we continue along mountain peaks that resemble an "alien planet" before descending to return to the gathering point and driving back to Anshun.

Day5 Anshun - Guanling Glacial Potholes (关岭冰臼) - Anshun
Trekking: 9km, 200m ascent, 3 hours

After breakfast, we drive to the Guanling Glacial Potholes and hike through the pothole valley to explore Triassic glacial relics. At noon, we share packed lunches with each other.

Then we continue hiking to enjoy the glacial pothole scenery before driving back to the hotel in Anshun.

Day6 Anshun - Yunjiu Mountain (云鹫山) - Yunfeng Tunpu (云峰屯堡) - Guiyang
Trekking: 8km, 2 hours

After breakfast, we drive to Yunfeng Tunpu and explore the 600-year-old ancient village, home to one of Guizhou's eight wonders— buildings with stones used as roof tiles. We then climb Yunjiu Mountain to visit the temple, offering prayers for blessings while enjoying panoramic views of the surrounding landscape.

Next, we visit a nearby ancient village, tour traditional mansions, and learn about the unique Tunpu culture, concluding the last day with a cultural feast, and then we drive back to Guiyang to end the tour.

Important Notes

● Best Season: Year-round
● Suitable For: Healthy individuals aged 8-65 years
● Potential Risks: The steep sections of the road can be slippery during the rainy season, so it's recommended to wear non-slip shoes and bring a change of clothes.

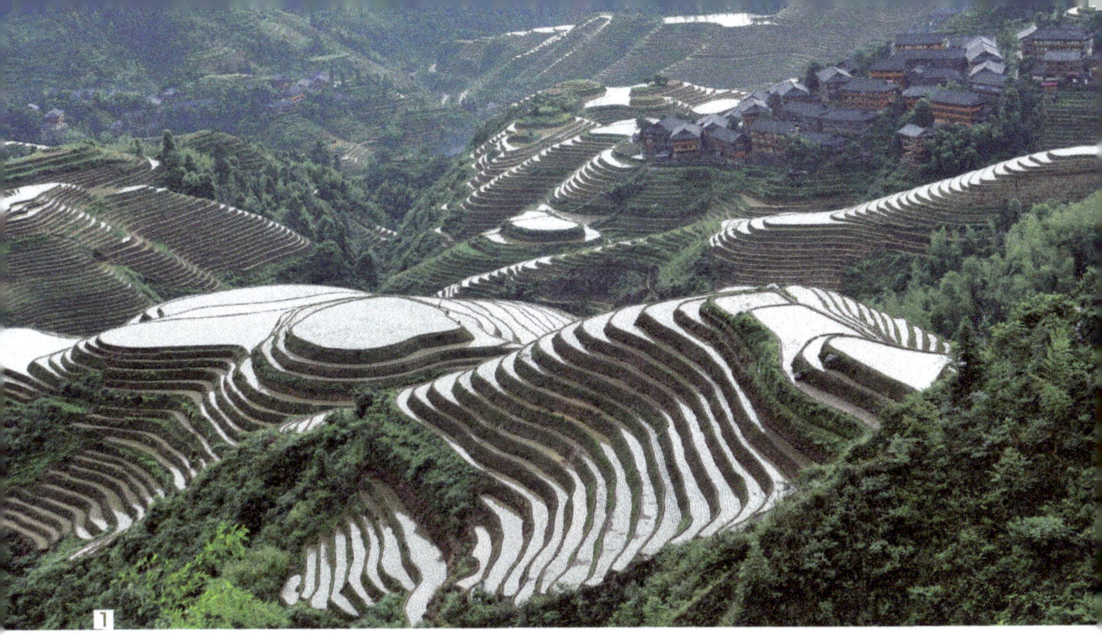

1

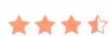

28. Longji Rice Terraces Trek

[龙脊梯田徒步, Lóngjǐ Tītián Túbù]

6days

47km

Guilin
[桂林, Guìlín]
Gathering City

18KM
Longest Single-Day Hike

400M
Maximum Daily Elevation Gain

2,142M
Highest Elevation Along the Route

★★★½
Scenic Rating

★★½
Difficulty Level

Millions of years ago, the region where the Five Ridges (五岭, Wǔlǐng) are located was covered by the ocean, forming thick limestone layers. Later, during tectonic movements, magma continuously rose and solidified underground, forming massive layers of granite. As the land was uplifted, both layers of rock simultaneously emerged above the surface, and both developed numerous cracks. These cracks led to constant collapses, creating huge gaps in what was originally a continuous mountain range. Through ongoing weathering and erosion, the once unified mountain range eventually transformed into five separate mountain ridges.

The Five Ridges are situated at the junction of Guangdong, Guangxi, Hunan, and Jiangxi provinces, forming China's largest east-west transverse mountain range south of the Yangtze River. They serve as a natural watershed, dividing the Yangtze and Pearl River basins. Acting as a formidable east-west barrier, the Five Ridges have long isolated the enigmatic Lingnan Baiyue region from the Central Plains. Throughout history, these mountains also became a favored place of exile for disgraced officials.

It wasn't until the Song and Ming dynasties that transportation across the region became increasingly convenient and efficient. However, the natural barrier of the Five Ridges continued to reinforce the significant differences between the areas

Credit
Image 1/2 | ©Majun
Image 3 | ©Ningle

north and south of the range—one of the key reasons why Lingnan culture has remained remarkably distinctive for over a thousand years.

Natural Features

Due to this special geographical environment, a variety of natural and man-made landscapes has been developed throughout Lingnan, with rice terraces being one of them. Chinese rice terraces are widely known to most people, not unique to the Lingnan region. These natural artworks, crystallized from the wisdom and strength of working people, never fail to bring tremendous awe to the world. Guangxi Longji Rice Terraces (龙脊梯田, Lóngjǐ Tītián), Yunnan Hani Rice Terraces (哈尼梯田, Hāní Tītián), Guizhou Qiandongnan Rice Terraces (黔东南梯田, Qián Dōngnán Tītián), and Jiangxi Wuyuan Rice Terraces (婺源梯田, Wùyuán Tītián) are all paradises for photographers and sacred travel destinations for leisure and sightseeing. Yet unlike other rice terraces, the representative of the Lingnan region—Longji Rice Terraces—is also a paradise for outdoor enthusiasts to enjoy hiking.

The Longji Rice Terraces began construction during the Yuan Dynasty and were completed in the early Qing Dynasty, boasting a history of over 650 years. Revered as the "Crown of the World's Rice Terraces," this breathtaking landscape is defined by its majestic grandeur, cloud- kissed mountain peaks, and vibrant ethnic traditions, creating a stunning panoramic view. Often referred to as the "Dragon's Backbone" (龙脊, Lóngjǐ), this place calls upon the imagination to envision the full scale of its awe-inspiring beauty. As the Chinese often call themselves the "descendants of the dragon," the name feels especially fitting, inviting one to appreciate the grandeur and mystery of this unique region.

Cultural Significance

The Longji Rice Terraces primarily comprise two scenic areas: the Ping'an Rice Terraces (平安梯田, Píng'ān Tītián) and the Jinkeng Rice Terraces (金坑梯田, Jīnkēng Tītián), representing the cultures of the Zhuang (壮族, Zhuàngzú) and Yao (瑶族, Yáozú) ethnic groups, respectively. Both areas showcase a striking blend of grandeur and artistic delicacy. With their distinct mountain formations, each offers a unique, poetic, and picturesque landscape, reflecting different yet equally captivating cultural flavors.

When hiking in this area, two days are enough to explore both the Ping'an and Jinkeng Rice Terraces. Of the two, the Jinkeng Rice Terraces are larger in scale and more awe-inspiring. Their layout is neat and layered, with predominantly curved lines that cascade gracefully across the mountainsides. These flowing curves resemble colorful ribbons drifting down from the sky, creating a dynamic beauty and rhythmic harmony that evoke a synesthetic experience—much like listening to a piece of music. If Jinkeng Rice Terraces excel in scale, then Ping'an Rice Terraces are superior in shape, making them more exquisite and giving people a startling sense of amazement.

"Seven Stars Accompanying the Moon" (七星伴月, Qīxīng Bàn Yuè) is one of the essence scenic spots of Ping'an Rice Terraces. The "Seven Stars" refer to seven small mounds left when the fields were first developed. They look like seven twinkling stars accompanying the silver shining paddy field at the mountaintop. From a distance, it looks like seven stars accompanying a bright moon, making people marvel at the greatness of the working people who created such an extraordinarily beautiful landscape.

Notable Attractions

2

The Longji Rice Terraces offer breathtaking beauty in all four seasons, with each type of weather adding its own unique charm. On sunny days, the terraces appear grand and radiant, while on rainy days, they take on a softer, more serene character. Shrouded in mist and rain, the landscape becomes veiled in mystery—dreamlike and reminiscent of a fairy tale. While in most places one might hope for sunshine, here, it's the rain you'll find yourself longing for.

After completing the Longji Rice Terraces trek, there are still little-known secret places in northern Guangxi to explore. For example, places like "Sky-Touching Ridge" (摩天岭, Mótiān Lǐng), which is named for its towering height reaching into the clouds, Cat Mountain (猫儿山, Māo'ér Shān), and Longtan River Gorge (龙潭江峡谷, Lóngtán Jiāng Xiágǔ) are not to be missed.

1 Cat Mountain
[猫儿山, Māo'ér Shān]

The largest of the Five Ridges and the highest peak of the 400-mile Yuecheng Ridge mountain system. The summit is a giant granite boulder shaped like a reclining cat, hence the name Cat Mountain. Its elevation reaches 2,141.5 meters, making it not only the highest peak in Guangxi but also the highest peak in South China, earning the reputation as the "Crown of Five Ridges, Peak of South China."

2 Yellow Mud Pond Waterfall
[黄泥塘瀑布, Huángnítáng Pùbù]

The waterfall at Sky-Touching Ridge is spectacular with clear water, making it very suitable for summer heat relief, water play, and stream trekking. So after breaking camp, we put on stream trekking shoes and begin to enjoy a 5-kilometer thrilling waterfall stream climbing route.

3 Sky-Touching Ridge
[摩天岭, Mótiān Lǐng]

A less-traveled, comfortable, beautiful, and stunning five-star alpine meadow stargazing campsite. Sky-Touching Ridge has an elevation of over 1,000 meters and features alpine meadows comparable to those of Wugong Mountain. It is also home to South China's largest wind farm, with large wind turbines scattered across the ridge's grassy slopes, making it the best viewpoint for observing wind farms in the entire South China.

3

Itinerary

Day1 Gather in Guilin (桂林)

Day2 Guilin - Longsheng Dazhai Xiaozhai (龙胜大寨小寨)
Driving: 2 hours
Trekking: 9km, 400m ascent, 5 hours

After breakfast, we drive to the Longsheng Longji Rice Terraces scenic area and transfer to the shuttle bus to Dazhai Village. Here, we can try local oil tea of Yan ethnic group, "medicinal chicken" and other folk delicacies.

After lunch, we begin our hike through Longsheng's Dazhai and Xiaozhai. We enjoy the sunset over the terraces from "Golden Buddha Peak" (金佛顶, Jīn Fó Dǐng), followed by dinner featuring Yao cuisine.

Day3 Dazhai (大寨) - Ping'an Village (平安寨) - Sky-Touching Ridge (摩天岭)
Driving: 2 hours | Trekking: 18km, 7 hours

After breakfast, we begin hiking the Longji Rice Terraces at Ping'an Village, eventually reaching Jinjiang Yao Village (金江瑶寨, Jīnjiāng Yáo Zhài). After the hike, the entire group drives to Sky-Touching Ridge to enjoy the sunset over the alpine meadows and stay at the tent campsite.

Day4 Sky-Touching Ridge - Yellow Mud Pond Waterfall (黄泥塘瀑布) - Foot of Cat Mountain (猫儿山脚)
Trekking: 5km, 3 hours

We wake up early to watch the sunrise. After breakfast, we begin hiking, exploring the mountain streams, valleys, and waterfalls, enjoying the pleasure of stream trekking and climbing along the way. After lunch at a rural restaurant, we drive to Cat Mountain and stay at a guesthouse at the foot of the mountain.

Day5 Foot of Cat Mountain - Ten-Mile Grand Canyon (十里大峡谷) - Summit of "South China's Peak" Cat Mountain (猫儿山顶)
Trekking: 9km, 300m ascent, 4 hours

After breakfast, we visit the "Ten-Mile Grand Canyon" at the foot of Cat Mountain, walking along stone steps through bamboo forests to reach the "Dragon Pool" (龙潭, Lóngtán) waterfall. We experience "stream trekking, and climbing" along the granite rocks by the stream, reaching the confluence of two streams where we can choose either to wade through the stream or return via the scenic area steps.

We then drive to the top of Cat Mountain to visit the "Three Rivers Source" (三江源, Sānjiāng Yuán) and "Old Border Mountain" (老界山, Lǎo Jiè Shān). We hike the summit loop trail to see the "South China Tiger" (华南虎, Huánán Hǔ), Buddha Light Rock (佛光岩, Fó Guāng Yán), Single Line Sky (一线天, Yīxiàn Tiān), and other features, sitting at the "Peak of South China" to enjoy the sunset.

Day6 Cat Mountain Summit - Longtan River (龙潭江) - Guilin
Trekking: 6km, 2 hours

After breakfast, we drive down from Cat Mountain to the Longtan River scenic area for hiking, experiencing the "jelly water" of the Longtan River mountain stream. After lunch, we drive back to Guilin and the group disperses.

Important Notes
- Best Season: year-round, with autumn being the most beautiful
- Suitable For: Healthy individuals aged 8-65 years
- Potential Risks: Take care to protect your knees when going downhill.

1

29. Kula Kangri Trek
[库拉岗日, Kùlā Gǎngrì]

7days

32km

Lhasa
[拉萨, Lāsà]
Gathering City

10KM
Longest Single-Day Hike

800M
Maximum Daily Elevation Gain

5,363M
Highest Elevation Along the Route

★★★★
Scenic Rating

★★★
Difficulty Level

Deep in the Shannan(山南, Shānnán) Prefecture in Tibet lies a hidden natural paradise–Kula Kangri (库拉岗日, Kùlā Gǎngrì). This is a heaven for outdoor enthusiasts, with snow-capped mountains, lakes, meadows, and temples... every scene is like a poem or painting, intoxicating visitors.

If not for Kula Kangri, few people would take notice of Shannan (山南, Shānnán)—let alone the little-known Lhozhag County (洛扎县, Luòzhā Xiàn) or Se Township (色乡, Sè Xiāng). Yet this region is where Tibet's first king, Nyatri Tsenpo (聂赤赞普, Niè Chì Zànpǔ), was born, and where the first palace, Yumbulagang (雍布拉康, Yōngbù Lākāng), was built. It is widely regarded as the "cradle of Tibetan national culture," and even celebrated as the very "birthplace of Tibetan civilization."Tibet's glory has long been associated with Lhasa, dominated by the Potala Palace and Jokhang Temple. As a result, many are surprised to learn that "Lhasa Gonggar International Airport" is actually in Shannan, or that the holy lake Yamdrok Tso (羊卓雍措, Yángzhuō Yōngcuò) also belongs to this region.

Shannan is located on China's southwestern border, nestled between the Gangdise Mountain Range and the Himalayas, and shares a boundary with Bhutan. Along its 600-kilometer border stretch countless snow-capped peaks, while the Yarlung River Valley nourishes the land on both sides—where grain fields and sacred spiritual sites have long coexisted in harmony. This is where you'll find the holy lake Yamdrok Tso, the sacred mountain Kula Kangri, the earliest Tibetan Buddhist monasteries, the oldest Tibetan palace, and the birthplace of the ancient Tubo Kingdom. Shannan defies the stereotypical image of Tibet—it is both mysterious and welcoming, grand yet serene.

Natural Features

Among the many classic trekking routes in Tibet, Kula Kangri undoubtedly stands out for its uniqueness and beauty. As one of the four sacred mountains in central Tibet, Kula Kangri reaches an elevation of 7,538 meters, making it the highest peak in the Shannan region. Standing on the main ridge line of the middle section of the Himalayas, it forms a magnificent ice and snow barrier alongside six neighboring 7,000-meter-level snow mountains. On its northern side, canyon glaciers lie horizontally, creating spectacular scenery, while beyond the glaciers, plateau lakes quietly rest in groups.

In the snow-covered plateau where mountain deity worship predates Buddhist beliefs, Kula Kangri is the southern sacred mountain in folk religion. It guards the region, protects homes, and safeguards dharma; the fortunes and misfortunes of humans, and the favorability of natural conditions, are all under its control. Today, myths and legends have not disappeared with time. Wherever footsteps can reach, temples for worshipping mountain deities, prayer flags flying in the wind, and juniper incense smoke permeating the air are evidence that Kula Kangri still lives in faith.

Below the Kula Kangri snow mountain are several sacred lakes, which are like treasures fallen to the mortal world, each with different colors that captivate the soul. Among them, Baima Lincuo (白玛林措,

Báimǎ Líncuò) has blue, green, and white intermingling lake colors. Legend has it that people can see their past and present lives through this lake water. In mythology, there is also a palace built with jewels to its south, where the hero King Gesar resides. Zhegong Sancuo (折公三措, Zhégōng Sāncuò) is located below the Gula Karji (过拉卡日, Guòlā Kǎrì) peak. Climbing up the ridge, three plateau lakes come into view, with the blue-green mixed with milky white Jiejiu Lake (介久措, Jièjiǔ Cuò) being the most eye-catching one. On clear days, Kare Jiangfeng (卡热疆峰, Kǎrè Jiāng Fēng) and Kula Kangri are reflected in it, creating breathtaking scenery of lakes and mountains. On the way to the Kula Kangri mountain group, we will also encounter lakes such as the well-known Yamdrok Tso and Pumo Yongcuo (普莫雍措, Pǔmò Yōngcuò) in the Tibet.

Cultural Significance

The Yarlung culture in the Shannan region is considered the birthplace of Tibetan culture, with its palaces and temples scattered throughout the area serving as the most significant and enduring symbols of its sacred heritage. During the journey, you will also encounter famous monasteries such as Tuiwa Monastery (推瓦寺, Tuīwǎ Sì), Rituo Monastery (日托寺, Rìtuō Sì), Samye Monastery (桑耶寺, Sāngyē Sì), Kajiu Monastery (卡久寺, Kǎjiǔ Sì), and Saika Gutuo Monastery (塞卡古托寺, Sāikǎ Gǔtuō Sì).

Located in Shannan, this mountain holds deep cultural significance as a cornerstone of Tibetan culture and Tibetan Buddhism. It is the highest peak in Shannan and one of the four traditional sacred mountains. In terms of scenery, six majestic peaks—each over 7,000 meters—stand alongside it, forming a towering barrier of ice and snow that stretches into the sky. From afar, the view is awe-inspiring; up close, vast valley glaciers, dramatic ice cliffs, and sheer walls dominate the landscape. In summer, vibrant alpine flowers bloom; in winter, the mountains are cloaked in striking blue ice. Each season offers its own breathtaking beauty.

In terms of accessibility, the journey from Lhasa to the trek's starting point takes only about 10 hours by car, assuming no stops at scenic sites along the way. A nearby village offers convenient accommodation close to the trailhead. Along the route, supplies are readily available, emergency evacuation is manageable, and the overall trip is both time-efficient and relatively effortless.

In terms of broad appeal, the combination of stunning scenery, rich cultural experiences, and gentle trekking makes this route ideal for most travelers. The three-day trek covers less than 10 kilometers per day on average, with a moderate intensity and well-maintained trails. Most importantly, this remains a relatively undiscovered route–offering beautiful landscapes, fewer crowds, and no need for camping. It's perfectly suited for those with average fitness, limited time, and a love for nature.

Notable Attractions

1 Pumo Yongcuo
[普莫雍措, Pǔmò Yōngcuò]

At an elevation of 5,010 meters, it is the highest lake in the world, formed by thousands of years of meltwater from Kula Kangri. In winter, it freezes over, and under the sunlight, huge blue ice blocks, ice cracks, and ice bubbles are clearly visible, with blue ice beauty comparable to Lake Baikal.

When the ice layer is at its thickest, the lake surface year after year stages the scene of sheep herds migrating, which is both dreamy and adorable.

2 Samye Monastery
[桑耶寺, Sāngyě Sì]

This monastery has a central Buddha hall that combines Han, Tibetan, and Indian styles, along with black, white, red, and green pagodas. They are laid out according to the structure of the "Great Thousand World" in Buddhist scriptures, forming a huge building complex in the form of a "mandala."

The bottom floor houses a statue of Shakyamuni carved from a natural huge rock, the middle floor corridor has nearly hundred-meter-long "Tibetan History" murals, and the hall contains bronze statues of Guru Padmasambhava, Shakyamuni, and Amitabha Buddha.

The upper floor has double rows of swastika-shaped pillars, with the Buddha in the center, surrounded by the Eight Great Bodhisattvas and many Blissful Buddhas.

3 Kajiu Monastery
[卡久寺, Kǎjiǔ Sì]

Located on the mountain peak behind Lakang Town in Lhozhag County, surrounded by lush vegetation, under the shroud of clouds and mist, the monastery appears like a celestial palace, sometimes visible, sometimes hidden.

Walking along the circumambulation path of Kajiu Monastery, every step offers a different view, and with luck, you might see Bhutan's national bird, the blood pheasant, foraging.

Itinerary

Day1 Gather in Lhasa (拉萨 3,650m)

Day2 Lhasa - Samye Monastery(桑耶寺 3,680m) - Yumbulagang (雍布拉康 3,600m) - Tsetang (泽当 3,560m)
Driving: 300km, 6 hours

Day3 Tsetang - Zhegu Lake (哲古措) - Kajiu Monastery(卡久寺 4,019m) - Se Township (色乡 3,800m)
Driving: 200km, 6 hours
After breakfast, we drive to Zhegu Lake. Along the way is the endless Zhegu Grassland, with distant views of the Yala Xiangbo (雅拉香波, Yǎlā Xiāngbō) Snow Mountain Range.

Afterward, we drive to Kajiu Monastery, enjoying beautiful scenery along the way. Lhozhag Kajiu Monastery, fully named "Auspicious Hermitage," was built in 1570 CE and is located on a cloud-shrouded mountain peak called "Jiapujin" behind Lakang Town in Lhozhag County, 75 kilometers from the county town, at an elevation of 4,019 meters. After visiting, we drive to Se Township for overnight stay.

Day4 Se Township - Cuoyu Village (措玉村 4,160m) - Baima Lincuo (白马林措 4,500m) - Cuoyu Village
Trekking: 10km, 200m ascent/desent, 3 hours
After breakfast, we drive to the Baima Lincuo parking lot to officially begin our trekking journey today.

We walk along the right side of Baima Lincuo to the end of the lake to Baima Lin Monastery, visit Guru Padmasambhava's practice site, overlook the Kare Jiang (卡热疆, Kǎrè Jiāng) Snow Mountain, and admire Baima Lincuo—its color appears in blue, green, and white due to different depths merged with the surrounding scenery.

Afterward, we return to the parking lot and drive to Cuoyu Village to stay at a Tibetan guesthouse.

Day5 Cuoyu Village - Zhegong Three Lakes (折公措三湖 4,600m) - Cuoyu Village
Trekking: 12km, 400m ascent/desent, 7 hours
Today we climb up along the ridge to the right of Baima Lincuo towards Zhegong Three Sacred Lakes under Kula Kaji (库拉卡日, Kùlā Kǎrì).

We climb from an elevation of 4,500 meters to 4,900 meters. Standing at the high point, the three sacred lakes and the majestic Kula Kangri are right in front of us, which is one of the highlights of our journey. We begin our return journey before 2 PM, arriving back at Cuoyu Village before dark for overnight stay.

Day6 Cuoyu Village - Jiejiu Lake (介久措 4,600m) - Saika Gutuo Monastery (赛卡古托寺) - Lhozhag (洛扎 3,800m)
Trekking: 10km, 300m ascent/desent, 6 hours
Starting from the Baima Lincuo parking lot, we trek along the left hillside to climb up to a ridge, reaching a viewing platform where the beautiful sacred Jiejiu Lake is in front of us. In good weather, we can see the huge Kula Kangri and Kari Jiang (卡日疆, Kǎrì Jiāng) snow mountains. We return to the parking lot, then drive to Saika Gutuo Monastery. After visiting, we drive to Lhozhag County town for overnight stay.

Day7 Lhozhag - Monda La Pass (蒙达拉垭口 5,363m) - Pumo Yongcuo (普莫雍措 5,100m) - Yamdrok Tso (羊卓雍措 4,400m) - Lhasa
Driving: 300km, 7 hours
After breakfast, we drive back to Lhasa. Along the way, we follow the Lhozhag River Valley, ascending all the way to cross the Monda La Pass at an elevation of 5,363 meters, looking back at the Kula Kangri snow mountain group.

Afterward, we reach the shore of Pumo Yongcuo, which offers different scenery in different seasons. We make a brief stop at Tui Village (推村, Tuī Cūn), then drive to Yamdrok Tso, one of Tibet's three holy lakes, where lakes, snow mountains, islands, pastures, wild animals and plants, and temples integrate into one landscape. We arrive in Lhasa in the evening, where the tour ends.

Important Notes

- Best Season: year-round
- Suitable For: Healthy individuals aged 18-65 years
- Potential Risks: 1. The high altitude makes the visitors prone to altitude sickness.
  2. There is no signal in the mountains, so never travel alone!

1

30. Winter Southeast Tibet Trek
[冬季藏东南, Dōngjì Zàng Dōngnán] `11days` `33km`

Nyingchi
[林芝, Línzhī]
Gathering City

12KM
Longest Single-Day Hike

600M
Maximum Daily Elevation Gain

4,600
Highest Elevation Along the Route

★★★★★
Scenic Rating

★★★★½
Difficulty Level

To truly understand Southeast Tibet, one must first understand the Nyenchen Tanglha Mountain Range (念青唐古拉山脉, Niànqīng Tánggǔlā Shānmài). Stretching across central and eastern Tibet, this range continues eastward from the Gangdise Range and extends southeast to merge with the southwestern reaches of the Hengduan Mountains. Its central section forms the watershed between the Yarlung Tsangpo and Salween Rivers, effectively dividing Tibet into three distinct regions: Northern, Southern, and Eastern Tibet. Cold air masses channeled between the ranges bring abundant snowfall and precipitation, nurturing vast glacier systems and shaping a spectacular landscape of towering ice-covered peaks.

Influenced by the southwest monsoon from the Indian Ocean, this region receives abundant rainfall, resulting in a relatively low snowline and large, impressive mountain glaciers. Most of the peaks are shaped with razor-sharp edges, creating a striking and aesthetically pleasing landscape. Each winter, trekkers who venture into Southeast Tibet are captivated by its myriad wonders. Here, you'll find China's most concentrated cluster of pyramid-shaped snow-capped mountains, the richest marine-type glacier systems, countless alpine lakes, lush forests, and the enchanting essence of Tibetan culture.

Natural Features

From 2021 to 2024, we explored the vast Southeast Tibet region, including Bomi County in Nyingchi Prefecture, Jiali County in Nagqu Prefecture, and Bingba, Basu, Dengqen, Baqing, and Suo counties in Chamdo Prefecture. Due to its towering mountains, deep valleys, and remote location, this area remains rarely visited. Many of its snow-capped peaks, lakes, and glaciers were introduced to the world for the first time through our explorations.

Among them, the most renowned is Namcha Barwa (南迦巴瓦, Nánjiā Bāwǎ), standing at 7,782 meters as the highest peak in Nyingchi Prefecture. In the hearts of Himalayan-region Buddhists, Namcha Barwa is a sacred site of Tibet's ancient Bon religion and is venerated as the "Father of Tibetan Mountains." China National Geographic once honored it as "China's Most Beautiful Mountain Peak."

Besides Namcha Barwa, along this route, we will explore the eastern section of the Nyenchen Tanglha Range, discovering dozens of unknown pyramid-shaped mountain peaks through trekking and off-road exploration. These include Nailang Peak (乃朗峰, Nǎilǎng Fēng 6,870 meters), Malapo (玛拉波, Mǎlābō 6,018 meters), Chuqiepo (初切波, Chūqiēbō 6,550 meters), Kongla Snow Mountain (孔拉雪山, Kǒnglā Xuěshān 6,313 meters), Resong Gompo (热松贡布, Rèsōng Gòngbù 6,378

meters), Kongga Gabu (孔嘎嘎布, Kǒnggā Gābù 6,488 meters), Bengbula Peak (崩布拉峰, Bēngbùlā Fēng 5,739 meters), Gongyada Peak (贡亚达峰, Gòngyàdá Fēng 6,423 meters), Baima Snow Mountain (白马雪山, Báimǎ Xuěshān), and Dapo Snow Mountain (达波雪山, Dábō Xuěshān). Only by venturing deep into Southeast Tibet can you truly experience the awe and endless charm it brings.

Snow mountains are always accompanied by glaciers. However, to appreciate magnificent glaciers, one doesn't need to go to the Arctic, Antarctic, or Northern Europe. Tibet actually has the world's richest glacier resources, many of which are highly accessible and extraordinarily beautiful, such as the Laigu Glacier Group (来古冰川群, Láigǔ Bīngchuān Qún).

The Laigu Glacier Group consists of six glaciers: Meixi (美西, Měixī), Yalong (雅隆, Yǎlóng), Ruojiao (若骄, Ruòjiāo), Dongga (东嘎, Dōnggā), Xiongjia (雄加, Xióngjiā), and Niuma (牛马, Niúmǎ). During winter, visitors can walk directly on the frozen glacial lake, offering a rare opportunity to get up close to the ice and even reach the massive, blue glacier tongue. Please note that the lake is typically frozen only from mid-December to early March.

Yalong Glacier is the most spectacular in the Laigu Glacier Group. It extends from the main peak of Gangrigabu Mountain (岗日嘎布山, Gǎngrì Gābù Shān) at 6,606 meters to Gangrigabu Lake at around 4,000 meters. Its massive "3"-shaped ice tongue makes the Yalong Glacier one of the few highly accessible glacier travel destinations in China with second-to-none scenery. The Yalong Glacier has a zebra-like appearance, with its surface showing three colors—blue, white, and gray—resembling the frozen planet in the movie "Interstellar", creating a stunning, atmospheric backdrop for photos.

2

Cultural Significance

Beyond snow mountains and glaciers, lakes are another highlight not to be overlooked in Southeast Tibet. Gongcuo lake(贡措, Gòngcuò) at the foot of the Yalong Glacier begins to freeze around December each year, with ice thickness reaching over 20 cm, making it safe to walk on the ice surface. On the frozen lake stand scattered ice pillars, ridges, and mounds, and in the distance, one can see spectacular blue ice walls, reminiscent of the North in the TV series "Game of Thrones," giving it an epic quality.

When winter arrives, Ranwu Lake (然乌湖, Ránwū Hú), another major lake in Southeast Tibet, reveals its most beautiful appearance. Its waters freeze to a crystal-clear blue, with crack patterns covering the lake surface, as if it were an exquisite work of art carved by God's own hands.

Additionally, Bingba's Three-Color Lake (三色湖, Sānsè Hú), Resong Gompo's Xianggela Glacier Lake (祥格拉冰川湖, Xiánggēlā Bīngchuān Hú), Baima Snow Mountain's Bojiu Co (泊泅措, Bóqiú Cuò), Dapo Snow Mountain's Zhenmu Co (阵木措, Zhènmù Cuò), Jinling Township's Jionglacuo (炯拉措, Jiǒnglā Cuò), and Lepu Co (勒普措, Lèpǔ Cuò) all transform into enchanting ice lakes during the winter months. Crystal-clear and resembling uncut gems, these lakes showcase a mesmerizing array of blue ice, ice caves, ice cracks, and bubble ice. If you happen to visit when the sunlight hits just right, you'll be immersed in a truly dreamlike world of stunning blue ice.

Entering Southeast Tibet, you'll be immersed in the region's deep cultural heritage and the warmth of its people. This is a land steeped in mystery, rich with myths and legends. The stories of love and rivalry between the Sapu family and the Guobu Zhaxi Tajie family evoke a unique romantic atmosphere, offering a glimpse into the timeless spirit of this enchanting place. People have lived here for generations following water and grass, and due to inconvenient transportation and the blockade of surrounding mountains, they have avoided many wars in Tibet while preserving the unique human history of Eastern Tibet. Local people claim this is a pure land where Guru Padmasambhava hid, an ideal Orgyen Padma Ling world, similar to utopia or a peach blossom paradise—an earthly fairyland. Perhaps this is just the local people's yearning for a happy life, but when you truly get close to them, you will definitely be deeply moved by the people here.

Notable Attractions

1 Namcha Barwa

[南迦巴瓦, Nánjiā Bāwǎ]

In Tibetan, its name means "a spear piercing the sky," a fitting description of its striking, towering form. Influenced by the unique climate of the Yarlung Tsangpo Grand Canyon, the summit of Namcha Barwa is often veiled in clouds and mist, making it elusive and rarely seen. Like a shy maiden reluctant to reveal her face, it has earned the nickname "Shy Maiden Peak."

On average, the summit is visible only about 60 days a year. However, during the winter months, the drier climate and reduced precipitation often provide clearer views of the majestic main peak.

Itinerary

Day1 Gather in Nyingchi (林芝 3,100m)

Day2 Nyingchi - Sejila Mountain (色季拉山 4,702m) - Lulang (鲁朗) - Bomi (波密 2,750m)
Driving: 230km, 5 hours

After breakfast, we set out by car, crossing the Sejila Mountain Pass at 4,702 meters. In good weather, we can see Namcha Barwa Peak piercing directly into the sky. Then we travel through winding canyons to reach Lulang, known as "Little Switzerland of Tibet." Here there are vast stretches of primeval forests, surrounded by snow-capped mountains and winding streams, like a fairyland.

After lunch in Lulang, we continue along National Highway 318, accompanied by snow mountains all the way, and stay overnight in Bomi County Town, known as the "Snow Mountain Fairyland."

Day3 Bomi - Laigu Yalong Glacier (来古雅隆 冰川 4,200m) - Rituo Camp (日托营地 4,300m)
Driving: 150km, 3 hours
Trekking: 3km, 3 hours

We rise early to enjoy the golden sunrise on the mountains in Bomi. After breakfast, we drive along the beautiful Parlung Zangbo (帕隆藏布, Pàlóng Zàngbù) towards Laigu Glacier. "Laigu" in Tibetan means "a hidden utopian village." The Laigu Glacier Group consists of six glaciers: Meixi, Yalong, Ruojiao, Dongga, Xiongjia, and Niuma, originating from the Gangrigabu Mountain Range. Among them, Yalong Glacier is the most magnificent and spectacular.

From late December to around March of the following year is the freezing period. We will trek up the Yalong Glacier, where the ten-thousand-year-old blue ice within reach will excite everyone. With luck, we will see incomparable ice cracks and bubble ice. Afterward, we return to the beautiful Rituo Pasture (日托牧场, Rituō Mùchǎng) to camp.

Day4 Rituo Camp - Laigu Dongga Glacier Cave (来古东嘎冰洞 4,500m) - Bomi
Trekking: 5km, 5 hours

We rise early to enjoy the golden sunrise on the mountains from our camp. After breakfast, we head to the Laigu Dongga Ice Cave. The Dongga Ice Cave is a recently discovered, incredibly beautiful blue ice cave, with a round-trip trek of 5 kilometers. The huge blue ice cave and its astonishing deep blue color make you feel as if you are on another planet—super stunning. After the trek, we drive back to Bomi.

Day5 Bomi - Tongmai (通麦) - Yigong Township (易贡乡) - Niwu Township (尼屋乡 3,100m)
Driving: 200km, 6 hours

After breakfast, we drive from Bomi County Town, leaving National Highway 318 at Tongmai Bridge and entering the Yigong Zangbo River Valley.

We travel along the Yigong Zangbo River Valley towards Bagai and Niwu. The Yigong Zangbo River Valley can be called a world-class scenic canyon. Both sides of the river valley are covered with forest and shrubs. Due to the presence of glaciers and glacial lakes, ice waterfalls often develop on both sides of the valley, forming forest waterfalls, while the Tiffany-blue river water is absolutely the most magical color you have ever seen. We stay overnight in Niwu Township.

Day6 Niwu Township - Jinling Township (金岭乡) - Lepu Valley Glacier Lake (勒普沟冰川 湖 4,200m) - Jionglacuo (炯拉措 3,900m)
Driving: 120km, 3 hours
Trekking: 12km, 6 hours

After breakfast, we drive to Jinling Township, following a stunning snow mountain scenic highway. Along the way, we pass dozens of striking, pyramid-shaped peaks—many of them still unnamed. We travel through a stretch of ancient seabuckthorn forest, over a thousand years old and extending more than 20 kilometers.

Eventually, we arrive at the breathtaking Jionglacuo, a vast glacial lake where massive, unmelted ice blocks float in its emerald-green waters. On the right side of the lake, a narrow path used by local villagers to collect caterpillar fungus leads us deeper into the snow-covered mountains. This trail allows for a 12-kilometer round-trip trek. We set up camp by the lake and spend the night in this serene alpine wonderland.

Day7 Jionglacuo - Xiagongla Mountain (夏 贡拉山) - Three-Color Lake (三色湖) - Xiangela Glacier (祥格拉冰川 4,150m)
Driving: 200km, 5 hours

We rise early to see the golden sunrise on the mountains. After breakfast, we drive across Xiagongla Mountain, the most famous high snow mountain on the central Tibet-Sichuan route, once known as the "First Dangerous Pass into Tibet." In 2023, the Xiagongla Tunnel was completed, turning a formidable barrier into an easy passage. Afterward, we head to the Three-Color Lake, consisting of the Black Lake, White Lake, and Yellow Lake.

To the south of the "Three-Color Lake" are three very beautiful snow mountains that locals call "Resong Gompo" (热松贡布, Rèsōng Gòngbù), representing three bodhisattvas: Manjushri, Vajrapani, and Avalokiteshvara. Below the sacred Resong Gompo Mountain is a glacier lake called Xianggelacuo. Tonight we camp by the lake, enjoying the beautiful sunset on the sacred mountain and the starry night sky.

Day8 Xianggela Glacier - Kongga Gabu Glacier Ice Cave (孔嘎嘎布冰川冰洞 4,300m) - Bianba County (边坝县 4,000m)
Driving: 60km, 1 hours
Trekking: 8km, 5 hours

We rise early to enjoy the golden sunrise on the three sacred mountains of Resong Gompo. After breakfast, we trek to explore the mysterious ice caves of the Kongga Gabu Snow Mountain Glacier.

This area has been barely explored before, and you can't find any relevant information or introduction online, but when you trek in, you will be deeply amazed by the snow mountains, glaciers, and ice caves. After the trek, we drive to Bianba County Town to stay in a hotel.

Day9 Bingba - Zizhu Monastery(孜珠寺 4,500m) - Dingqen (丁青 3,800m)
Driving: 240km, 6 hours

After breakfast, we depart from Bianba County Town and drive to Zizhu Monastery, a sacred site of the Yungdrung Bon religion with a history spanning over three thousand years. Perched high in the mountains, the monastery resembles a celestial city, leaving visitors in awe with its majestic presence. Nearby, Jianxing Peak (见性峰, Jiànxìng Fēng) of Zizhu Mountain features a striking natural hollow that resembles a suspended

mirror—an unforgettable sight.

As the sun sets, we descend from Zizhu Monastery and continue our journey to Dingqen County Town.

Day10 Dingqen - Bujia Snow Mountain Glacier (布加雪山冰川 4,600m) - Suo County (索县 3,900m)
Driving: 280km, 5 hours
Trekking: 5km, 5 hours

After breakfast, we depart from Dingqen and drive west along National Highway 317 to reach the Bujia Snow Mountain Glacier. Bujia Snow Mountain, one of Tibet's seven sacred mountains, remains a lesser-known and mysterious gem, shrouded in secrecy.

Currently, there are five mature giant hanging glaciers on its northern and southern slopes. The longest, Poge Glacier (坡戈冰川, Pōgē Bīngchuān), cascades down from the 6,238-meter-high Bujia Snow Mountain peak, forming a hanging glacier body with a drop of 2,100 meters. If you are lucky enough, you will see the incomparable Bujia blue ice. After the trek, we drive to Suo County to stay in a hotel.

Day11 Suo County - Nagqu(那曲 4,500m) - Lhasa
Driving: 600km, 9 hours

Today's journey is long and challenging. Our off-road vehicle convoy departs from Suo County early in the morning. The winter sky of Northern Tibet is an astonishing shade of blue, almost surreal in its brilliance.

As we make our way back to Lhasa along the Nyenchen Tanglha Mountain Range, we pass by Qizi Peak, Luzi Peak, and the majestic Nyenchen Central Peak. We finally arrive in Lhasa in the evening, marking the end of our tour.

Important Notes
- Best Season: December to March of the following year
- Suitable For: Healthy individuals aged 18-65 years
- Potential Risks: Cold weather, stay warm.

31. Namcha Barwa Base Camp Trek

40km/7days

[南迦巴瓦大本营徒步, Nánjiā Bāwǎ Dàběnyíng Túbù]

Lhasa
[拉萨, Lāsà]
Gathering City

18KM
Longest Single-Day Hike

900M
Maximum Daily Elevation Gain

4,400M
Highest Elevation Along the Route

★★★★
Scenic Rating

★★★★
Difficulty Level

Credit
Image 1 | ©Majun
Image 2 | ©Liangshuang

A massive triangular peak pierces the sky like a spear tip protruding above surrounding mountains. The mountain shape is steep and towering, and on clear days, you can see the magnificent texture of the rock layers—this is Namcha Barwa Peak (南迦巴瓦峰, Nánjiā Bāwǎ Fēng).

Namcha Barwa Peak is located at the intersection of the Himalayan Range, Nyenchen Tanglha Range, and Hengduan Mountains. It is the highest peak in the Nyingchi region of Tibet, with an elevation of 7,782 meters. Its massive triangular peak is covered in snow year-round and shrouded in clouds and mist, rarely revealing its true face. Legend has it that nine out of ten people never get to see it, earning it the nickname "Shy Maiden Peak." It is also a sacred site of Tibet's ancient Yungdrung Bon religion. In the 2005 "Beautiful China" contest by China National Geographic magazine, Namcha Barwa Peak ranked first.

Although Namcha Barwa is breathtakingly beautiful, for most people, it remains out of reach. This mountain is extremely difficult to climb, with only a handful of successful summit records in history. However, that's not a problem—we can get close to it in another way by traveling deep into the Nyingchi region of Tibet and trekking to the Namcha Barwa Base Camp.

Natural Features

Speaking of the Nyingchi region, it is perhaps the least Tibet-like part of Tibet. Due to its unique terrain and climate, when most regions of China are still in the transition between cold and warm weather, Nyingchi has already entered a lush period of spring warmth with wild peach blossoms and bright sunshine, earning it the nickname "Tibet's Jiangnan" (Jiangnan refers to the fertile region south of the Yangtze River in eastern China). It combines the majestic snow mountains of Tibet with the beautiful flower seas of Jiangnan, showcasing Tibet's most romantic and beautiful spring.

Nyingchi is located in southeastern Tibet, adjacent to Lhasa, Shannan, Nagqu, and Chamdo. It features the ancient and simple Kongpo culture, distinct Menba customs, and Lhoba ethnic flavor. It boasts a large number of renowned natural landscapes such as the Yarlung Tsangpo Grand Canyon, Namcha Barwa Peak, and Basum Tso (巴松措, Bāsōng Cuò). It is home to historical sites like the ancient city of Taizhao and thousand-year-old castle groups, as well as red heritage sites like Yigong General Building and Bomi Red Building. The three world-class mountain ranges—the Himalayas, Nyenchen Tanglha, and Hengduan Mountains—stretch across the Nyingchi area, yet they also face the Indian Ocean through several gaps. The warm currents from the Indian Ocean can thus enter, and the Yarlung Tsangpo River makes a horseshoe bend here. The abundant moisture and the topographical features with an elevation drop of 7,627 meters make Nyingchi a collection point for beautiful landscapes including meadows, flower seas, forests, canyons, glaciers, and snow mountains.

If there were a true Peach Blossom Spring (a utopia) in the world, it would undoubtedly be Nyingchi. Every March and April, China's most beautiful snow-capped mountain, Namcha Barwa, reaches toward the sky, its massive triangular peak resembling a sharp spearhead. The clear, tranquil waters mirror the endless blue sky, while wisps of smoke rise from Tibetan homes nestled among the vibrant peach blossoms. In this breathtaking landscape, grandeur and beauty, mysticism and daily life, intertwine seamlessly, creating a living painting.

Cultural Significance

If you search online for "best places to view peach blossoms in Nyingchi," Gala Peach Blossom Village (嘎拉桃花村, Gāla Táohuā Cūn) is sure to be on the list. It takes only about half an hour to reach Galala Peach Blossom Village from downtown Nyingchi. The scenic area entrance is right by the roadside, accessible as soon as you get off the vehicle. Under the peach blossom forest, there are costume rentals for photo shoots, food vendors, coffee sellers... a comprehensive one-stop scenic spot service. The tourists coming and going make the originally spacious peach forest seem somewhat crowded and congested.

For those accustomed to the natural outdoor environment, being too "developed" is the original sin. In March, Nyingchi has so many wonderful places that it's not necessary to spend too much time here.

We will then head to another classic scenic spot—Suosong Village (索松村, Suǒsōng Cūn). Along the way, mountains stand in clusters. The villages and peach blossoms at the foot of distant mountains are spring's gentle offerings, while the Yarlung Tsangpo River and Nyang River are the exquisite ribbons tied around this gift.

As the wheels roll, this gift box opens layer by layer. In Suosong Village, besides viewing peach blossoms, you can also trek to the Namcha Barwa Climbing Base Camp to face the magnificent snow mountain up close.

In Bomi County (波密县, Bōmì Xiàn), east of Suosong Village, there is also the largest peach blossom valley in China. The peach blossoms there bloom vigorously and beautifully, and it has been selected for the "100 Most Beautiful Viewing and Photography Spots in Tibet" list by China National Geographic magazine.

It's worth noting that although Bomi Peach Blossom Valley is only about 200 kilometers from downtown Nyingchi, there is the Sejila Mountain (色季拉山, Sèjìlā Shān) in between, and even in the spring of March and April, the weather can still be unpredictably snowy and windy. Crossing the 4,728-meter Sejila Mountain Pass is like "Schrödinger's cat"—it might take four to five hours to pass smoothly, or you might get stuck in traffic for half a day or a whole day, which is quite normal.

In addition, we will visit the stunning Basum Tso and trek through the enchanting Gangyun Cedar Forest (岗云杉林, Gǎngyún Shānlín), allowing for a deeper appreciation of Nyingchi's natural beauty. Nyingchi, with its majestic Namcha Barwa, holds countless stories and breathtaking sights—waiting for you to explore and uncover them.

Notable Attractions

1 Gala Peach Blossom Village
[嘎拉桃花村, Gālā Táohuā Cūn]

This village is known as the "Premiere Peach Blossom Village in Nyingchi." The annual Nyingchi Peach Blossom Festival has gradually brought it into public attention from a quiet little village.

Surrounded by mountains on three sides, wild peach trees grow along the ravines, extending for miles, with flowers blooming like a red sea of clouds.

2 Suosong Village
[索松村, Suǒsōng Cūn]

Directly facing Namcha Barwa, it offers an excellent viewpoint to observe China's most beautiful mountain. Here, peach blossoms and snow mountains perfectly complement each other. The coexistence of magnificence and elegance has fascinated countless landscape photographers.

2

3 Bomi Peach Blossom Valley
[波密桃花沟, Bōmì Táohuā Gōu]

It is China's largest peach blossom valley, selected for the "100 Most Beautiful Viewing and Photography Spots in Tibet" list by China National Geographic. The peach blossoms here are the most beautiful and extensive.

In the distance, mountains intersect, while at their feet, peach blossoms compete to bloom. Nearby villages and wheat fields are also decorated with pink peach trees.

4 Basum Tso
[巴松措, Bāsōng Cuò]

Located in Gongbo'gyamda County, Nyingchi. Basum Tso lake is not only an officially certified 5A-level scenic area but also a sacred place in the hearts of Tibetans. Trekking around the lake through dense forests, you'll discover that the water color changes with the section, angle, and weather, presenting different shades of blue.

5 Gangyun Cedar Forest
[岗云杉林, Gǎngyún Shānlín]

It contains China's largest, best, and last primeval forest, selected as one of the "Ten Most Beautiful Forests in China" by China National Geographic many years ago. Walking through it allows you to deeply experience another side of Nyingchi.

Itinerary

Day1 Gather in Lhasa (拉萨 3,650m)

Day2 Lhasa - Basum Tso Circuit - Basum Tso (巴松措 3,700m)
Driving: 350km, 5 hours
Trekking: 8km, 3 hours

Today we travel along China's most beautiful expressway, the Nyingchi-Lhasa Highway (林拉公路, Línlā Gōnglù), arriving at Basum Tso to begin a lake circuit trek. Unlike other sacred lakes in Tibet, Basum Tso is completely surrounded by lush primeval forests.

The lake water presents an intoxicating emerald green, with different shades of green appearing from different angles. Walking around the lake, you'll see dark green mountains with year-round snow at their peaks and reflections of snow mountains and forests in the lake, providing an ultimate visual feast.

Day3 Basum Tso - Xincuo (新措) - Nyingchi (林芝 3,500m)
Trekking: 6km, 3 hours

After photographing the golden morning light on the mountains, we will trek deep into Xincuo, covering about 6 kilometers round trip. This area is rarely visited and undeveloped.

It's also a paradise for unclimbed peaks; in the eastern section of the Nyenchen Tanglha Range centered around Basum Tso, there are dozens of unclimbed peaks between 6,000-7,000 meters. Along the way, we can get close views of King's Throne Peak, Champa Peak, Burning Flame Peak, Puganglo Peak, Jibu Naigori Peak, and others. After trekking, we drive to Nyingchi to stay in a hotel.

Day4 Nyingchi - Yarlung Tsangpo Grand Canyon - Suosong Village Camp (索松村露营 3,000m)
Driving: 100km, 3 hours
Trekking: 4km, 2 hours

Today we reach Suosong Village, known as "Tibet's Jiangnan." Due to its relatively low elevation, it's suitable for us to make adaptation and take a rest. Suosong Village is located on the north bank of the Yarlung Tsangpo Grand Canyon, directly facing Namcha Barwa.

The Yarlung Tsangpo River flows at the foot of the village, and this spot offers an excellent view of Namcha Barwa, China's most beautiful mountain. Walking around Suosong Village, scenery is everywhere.

Day5 Suosong Village Camp - Namcha Barwa Viewing Platform - Namcha Barwa Base Camp (南迦巴瓦大本营 3,500m)
Trekking: 4km, 570m ascent, 4 hours

A massive triangular peak pierces the sky like a spear tip protruding above surrounding mountains. The mountain shape is steep and towering—this is Namcha Barwa Peak, the first among China's top ten most beautiful mountains.

After breakfast, we drive to the starting point of the trek (elevation 2,930 meters) and trek to the Namcha Barwa Climbing Base Camp for a romantic encounter with China's most beautiful mountain. Walking along a small path on the halfway point of the canyon, the distant villages and forests are very beautiful, making you stop and look back to appreciate them from time to time.

Finally, we pass through a dense primeval forest to reach the Namcha Barwa Climbing Base Camp and set up camp. When you open your tent, you can see Namcha Barwa Peak, China's most beautiful mountain.

Day6 Namcha Barwa Base Camp - Nalacuo (那拉措 4,400m) - Namcha Barwa Base Camp
Trekking: 18km, 900m ascent/desent, 10 hours

After breakfast, we pack our equipment and set out for Nalacuo. This is the most strenuous day! Nalacuo is located deep in the Himalayan Range at an elevation of 4,400 meters, like a bright pearl set among snow mountains, mysterious and beautiful. Because its jade-like lake water comes from Namcha Barwa, it is also known as "Namcha Barwa's Tears."

Afterward, we return to the Namcha Barwa Base Camp by the same route.

Day7 Namcha Barwa Base Camp - Nyingchi

Important Notes

● Best Season: March-April, October-November
● Suitable For: Healthy individuals aged 16-65 years
● Potential Risks: In the autumn and winter seasons, the temperature can vary greatly, so be sure to take precautions against the cold and stay warm.

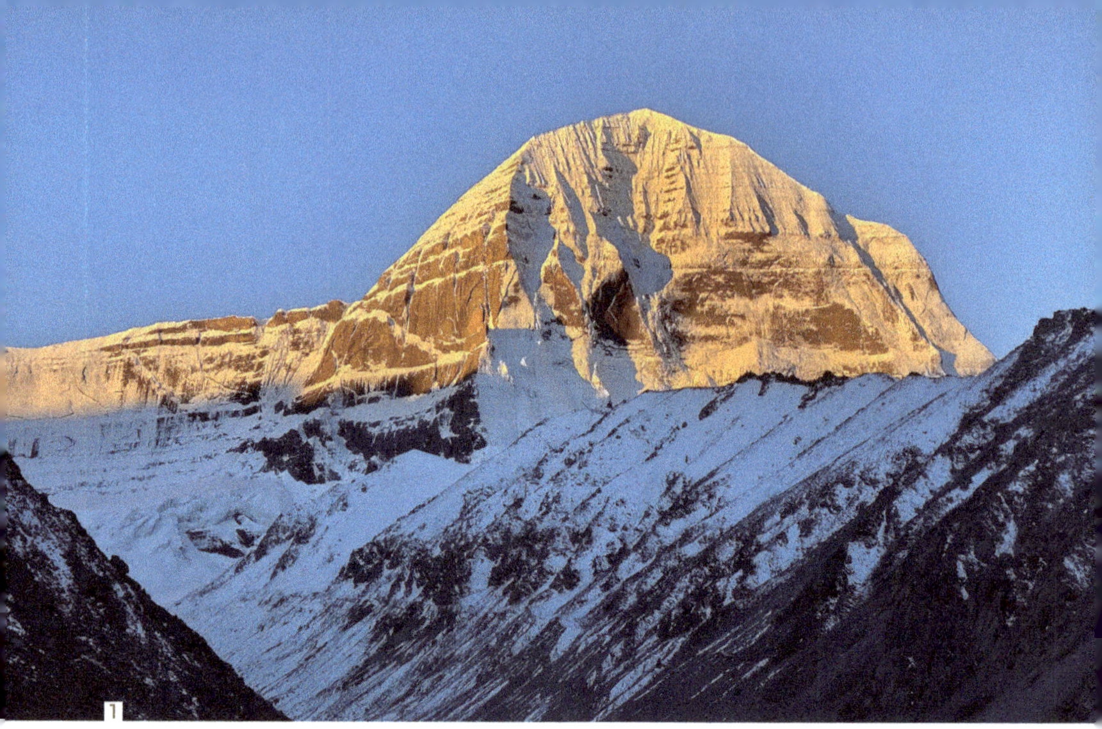

1

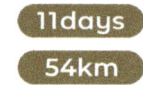

32. Ali Pilgrimage Trek

[阿里转山, Ālǐ Zhuànshān]

11days

54km

Lhasa
[拉萨, Lāsà]
Gathering City

32KM
Longest Single-Day Hike

530M
Maximum Daily Elevation Gain

5,630M
Highest Elevation Along the Route

★★★★★
Scenic Rating

★★★★½
Difficulty Level

Credit
Image 1 | ©Majun
Image 2 | ©Baoyu

Some say that if you haven't been to Ali (阿里, Ālǐ), you haven't truly been to Tibet.

The word "Ali" is a transliteration from Tibetan, meaning "territory." It is the "most Tibetan" part of Tibet. The Ali region covers an area of approximately 345,000 square kilometers, accounting for one-quarter of the entire Tibet area, larger than the combined area of Zhejiang, Jiangsu, and Fujian provinces. Within Ali are numerous famous mountain ranges. This is a sanctuary of mountains, where six 8,000-meter snow peaks including Mount Everest stand, and Mount Kailash (冈仁波齐, Gāngrén Bōqí), one of the four sacred mountains of Tibetan Buddhism, is also located in this region.

Mount Kailash (elevation 6,656 meters), located in Pulan County of Ali region, is the main peak of the Gangdise Mountain Range (冈底斯山脉, Gāngdǐsī Shānmài). The Gangdise Mountain Range is situated in the southwestern part of the Tibet Autonomous Region, close to where China borders India and Nepal. It stretches between the Kunlun Mountains and the Himalayas, covering nearly 1,100 kilometers in a northwest-southeast direction, with an average elevation ranging from 5,500 to 6,000 meters. The term "Gangdise

Sacred Mountain" usually refers specifically to the main peak, Mount Kailash. Its pyramid-shaped body has exactly four sides, like the four pointers of a compass pointing in different directions, and has long been called the "Center of the World."

Cultural Significance

But why is Mount Kailash, the "most Tibetan" part of Tibet, considered the center of Tibet and the center of the world?

According to records in the Indian epic "Ramayana" and Tibetan historical texts such as "Chronicles of the Gangdise Mountains and Lakes," it is speculated that worship of Mount Kailash dates back to around 1000 BCE. The unique geography of the Tibetan Plateau—the "Roof of the World"—with its unpredictable climate of wind, snow, and hail, has shaped Tibetan culture, which is defined by a deep respect for nature, animism, and the belief in harmonious coexistence between humans and the environment. Tibetans observed that towering mountains held powerful forces that influenced daily life. This awareness led them to pilgrimage and worship. Over time, these sacred mountains were personified and seen as divine, and the reverence for them became an essential part of Tibetan culture and spirituality.

As an early major religion of the Tibetan people, the Bon religion (苯教, Běnjiào), centered around the Gangdise Mountain area, absorbed this thinking and gave these spirits greater power and influence.

After the 7th century CE, Buddhism was introduced to Tibet and engaged in a long competition with the Bon religion, gradually marginalizing Bon culture. In Buddhism, the Gangdise Mountain is made of four treasures—gold, silver, lapis lazuli, and glass—symbolizing the center of the entire Buddhist universe. Mountain worship was still preserved in the form of Tibetan Buddhism, and the Gangdise Sacred Mountain remained an important object of worship and an unchanging emotional connection for the Tibetan people.

The Gangdise Mountains are often called the "source of thousands of waters," as they hold vital water resources for both the Tibetan region and the South Asian continent. They give rise to some of Asia's most important rivers—the Yarlung Tsangpo, the Ganges, and the Indus. This means that although the Gangdise range lies deep in the remote Ali region, its unique geographic location and natural features have a direct and lasting impact on the civilizations of both Tibet and South Asia.

Over the course of thousands of years, pilgrimage traditions centered around the Gangdise Mountains have gradually taken shape, with rituals such as circumambulation and ascetic practice becoming deeply ingrained in spiritual life. Devotees widely believe that circumambulating the mountain once can cleanse a lifetime of sins; completing the circuit ten times can spare one from five hundred years of suffering in hell during the cycle of reincarnation; and making the journey a hundred times can lead to enlightenment and Buddhahood. The Year of the Horse holds particular significance, as it is believed that a single circumambulation during this Tibetan zodiac year is equivalent to thirteen circumambulations in an ordinary year.

Beginning with Mount Kailash, but not ending with Mount Kailash! Perhaps your reason for going to Ali begins with Mount Kailash, but please believe that beyond the sacred mountain, there are many more beauties and temptations in this land, such as Mount Naimona'nyi (那木那尼峰, Nàmù Nàní Fēng), Everest Base Camp, Lake Manasarovar (玛旁雍措, Mǎpáng Yōngcuò), Lake Rakshastal (拉昂措, Lā'áng Cuò), and more.

1 Everest Base Camp
[珠峰大本营, Zhūfēng Dàběnyíng]

When the wandering wind of the wilderness blows away the last wisp of cloud, Mount Everest is like a newborn child, wrapped layer by layer by the mountains, with a clear space between heaven and earth...

At the Everest Base Camp, at an elevation of over 5,000 meters, you can appreciate the grandeur and magnificence of Mount Everest up close!

2 Lake Rakshastal
[拉昂措, Lā'áng Cuò]

In Tibetan, it means "poisonous black lake." Due to the mysterious nature of the lake water, it is regarded by locals as the "ghost lake." The lake water tastes bitter, and neither humans nor animals can drink it.

There are no plants or sheep and cattle around the lake, making it appear "desolate" and lifeless. Despite this, the scenery of Lake Rakshastal is no less beautiful than Lake Manasarovar.

3 Lake Manasarovar
[玛旁雍措, Mǎpáng Yōngcuò]

Meaning "the eternal jade lake," it is one of the "Three Holy Lakes" along with Lake Namtso and Lake Yamdrok.

It is the natural freshwater lake with the highest water transparency and is a sacred place in the hearts of followers of Yungdrung Bon, Hinduism, and Tibetan Buddhism, considered the most sacred and beautiful place in the world.

4 Mount Naimona'nyi
[纳木那尼峰, Nàmù Nàní Fēng]

Mount Naimona'nyi, located in the western Himalayas, and Mount Kailash, the towering peak of the Gangdise Range, are not only iconic mountains but also revered as the "source of hundreds of rivers." Surrounding the main peak of Mount Naimona'nyi, 358 glaciers have formed, while the region around Mount Kailash is home to 208 glaciers.

Along with the glaciers of Mount Longger and the Qiangtang Plateau, these icefields serve as the perennial source of vitality for the region of Ali.

Itinerary

Day1 Gather in Lhasa (拉萨 3,650m)

Day2 Lhasa - Zhaxi Temple (扎基寺) - Tashilhunpo Monastery (扎什伦布寺) - Shigatse (日喀则 3,800m)
Driving: 270km, 6 hours

Zhaxi Temple, located on Zhaxi Road in the northern suburbs of Lhasa, is the only temple in Tibet dedicated to the Wealth Deity. Though modest in size, it enjoys a thriving incense offering and attracts many devoted worshippers.

After paying our respects at Zhaxi Temple, we drive to Shigatse to visit Tashilhunpo Monastery. As the largest monastery in the Shigatse region, Tashilhunpo Monastery holds great significance and belongs to the Gelug sect of Tibetan Buddhism.

Day3 Shigatse - Lhatse (拉孜) - Gawula Pass (加乌拉山口 5,210m) - Everest Base Camp (珠峰大本营 5,200m)
Driving: 350km, 7 hours

We depart from Shigatse and head west towards Everest Base Camp. Along the way, we can overlook five snow mountains with elevations above 8,000 meters from the Gawula Pass—from east to west: Mount Makalu, Mount Lhotse, Mount Everest, Mount Cho Oyu, and Mount Shishapangma.

Our destination for the day, Everest Base Camp, is at an elevation of 5,200 meters, with a straight-line distance of only 19 kilometers from the summit of Mount Everest. This is also the closest place to Mount Everest that ordinary people can reach.

Day4 Everest Base Camp - Mount Shishapangma (希夏邦马峰) - Peykutso Lake (佩枯措) - Saga (萨嘎 4,485m)
Driving: 380km, 7 hours

Today, we officially enter the Ali region, the Roof of the World, where the average elevation exceeds 4,500 meters. This vast and sparsely populated area offers a unique opportunity to witness rare wildlife, including Tibetan antelope, wild yak, wild donkey, argali, and the black-necked crane.

The region also boasts stunning and diverse high plateau landscapes. Along the way, we'll enjoy distant views of the Shishapangma mountain range and have the chance to visit Peiguacuo Lake, the largest lake in the Shigatse region, up close. In the evening, we'll rest at a comfortable hotel in Saga County.

Day5 Saga - Mayomu La Pass (马攸木拉山口 5,200m) - Lake Manasarovar (玛旁雍措) - Ghost Lake (鬼湖) - Darchen (塔钦 4,800m)
Driving: 500km, 8 hours

Traveling along the majestic Himalayan Range, we are greeted by breathtaking scenery at every turn. Our journey begins with a crossing of the Mayomu La Pass, situated at an elevation of 5,200 meters. We then approach the serene Lake Manasarovar—one of Tibet's three sacred lakes—revered as the "Western Jade Pool."

In the afternoon, we continue on to Mount Kailash, a mountain universally regarded as sacred and considered the spiritual center of the world by Tibet's Yungdrung Bon tradition, Hinduism, Tibetan Buddhism, and ancient Jainism. As evening falls, we arrive in Darchen, a small town nestled at the foot of Mount Kailash and the traditional starting point for the mountain's sacred circumambulation.

Day6 Darchen - Chugu Monastery (曲古寺) - Zhire Monastery (止热寺 5,100m)
Trekking: 22km, 300m ascent, 7 hours

We begin the sacred circumambulation from our hotel in Darchen. For the first 7 kilometers, a scenic shuttle bus takes us directly to the Prayer Flag Square, leaving only 15 kilometers to trek on foot. The square is adorned with mani stone piles and vibrant prayer flags, and from this point, the sacred Mount Kailash comes into view.

The trail then turns northward into the Lachu Valley, following the eastern bank of the river all the way to our lodging for the night—the Zhire Monastery Hotel. Situated at an elevation of approximately 5,100 meters, the hotel offers a remarkable experience: you can gaze directly upon Mount Kailash from the comfort of your bed.

Day7 Zhire Monastery - Sky Burial Site (天葬台) - Drolma La Pass (卓玛拉山口 5,630m) - Darchen (4,800m)
Trekking: 32km, 530m ascent, 830m decent, 7 hours

Today's trek is the most demanding of the entire journey, marked by both long distance and high elevation. We typically set out around 4 a.m., equipped with headlamps to guide us through the early darkness.

After passing the sky burial platform, we make the challenging ascent to Drolma La Pass, the highest point of the circumambulation, standing at 5,630 meters. From there, we begin a steep descent along a gravel path. On the south side of the pass, we are rewarded with a view of the emerald-colored Toji Lake (托吉措, Tuōjí Cuò), also known as the Lake of Compassion, situated at 5,608 meters.

After the descent, the trail leads into another valley, where we follow the river downstream, passing several monasteries along the way.

Eventually, we return to Darchen. Along the latter half of the route, small shops provide spots to rest and recharge. For those who find the final stretch too challenging, transportation is available for the last dozen kilometers back to town.

Day8 Darchen - Lungkar La Pass (隆嘎拉山垭口) - Zanda Earth Forest (札达土林) - Guge Kingdom (古格王朝) - Zanda (札达 3,600m)
Driving: 260km, 5 hours

We depart from Darchen towards Zanda, traveling north along the foothills of the Gangdise Mountain Range. After crossing Mount Aiyi, we enter the unique earth forest terrain surrounding Zanda—the Zanda Earth Forest.

The Zanda Earth Forest covers an area of hundreds of square kilometers, with the winding Xiangquan River flowing quietly through the canyons of the earth forest, making people feel as if they are in an ancient, primitive land.

After visiting the Zanda Earth Forest, we head to Zanda County Town to stay at a hotel.

Day9 Zanda - Payang (帕羊) - Gongzhu Lake (公珠错) - Saga (4,485m)
Driving: 700km, 10 hours

We depart from Zanda County, heading towards Payang, a quaint town in Zhongba County. The journey offers a glimpse into a wildlife paradise, where we may spot wild yaks, Tibetan antelope, Tibetan gazelles, Tibetan wild asses, and an abundance of other wildlife, all set against a backdrop of pristine lakes and endless grasslands.

Continuing on, we drive to Saga, where the landscape transforms into a mesmerizing desert expanse, providing a striking contrast to the vast, untouched beauty of the surrounding pastoral grasslands.

Day10 Saga - Lang Lake (浪措) - Shigatse (3,800m)
Driving: 450km, 7 hours

On the return journey, we pass through Ngari County in the Shigatse region, where we can see Lang Lake, which originates from snow mountains and ice peaks.

Here, the terrain opens up to reveal a serene and quiet environment, with lush grasslands that form an ideal natural pasture. From this tranquil setting near Lang Lake, we continue our journey toward Shigatse.

Day11 Shigatse - Gyantse (江孜) - Karola Glacier (卡若拉冰川) - Lake Yamdrok (羊湖) - Lhasa
Driving: 370km, 6 hours

Returning from Shigatse, we can see the Noijin Kangsang Snow Mountain (乃钦康桑雪山, Nǎiqīn Kāngsāng Xuěshān) and Karola Glacier, as well as Lake Yamdrok, one of the three holy lakes.

As the road extends endlessly before us, the vastness of the world comes rushing with the rolling of the wheels—sunshine, white clouds, blue sky, mountains, and ripe highland barley... The journey ends here, but vibrant energy begins to grow in our hearts.

Important Notes

- Best Season: May to October
- Suitable For: Healthy individuals aged 18-65 years with high-altitude trekking experience
- Potential Risks: 1. Two nights at elevations above 5,000 meters, which may increase the risk of altitude sickness.
    2. One day of strenuous high-altitude trekking covering 32 kilometers, demanding excellent physical fitness.
    3. Border permits are required.

1

33. Thani Tawon Trek
[他念他翁, Tā Niàn Tā Wēng]

8days
56km

Lijiang
[丽江, Lìjiāng]
Gathering City

11KM
Longest Single-Day Hike

900M
Maximum Daily Elevation Gain

4,970M
Highest Elevation Along the Route

★★★★★
Scenic Rating

★★★★⯪
Difficulty Level

Many people hearing "Thani Tawon" for the first time might not associate it with a mountain range, finding the name somewhat peculiar. However, in recent years, trekking routes through this range have become a new favorite among outdoor enthusiasts. Here, you'll encounter towering snow-capped peaks, vibrant seas of wildflowers, breathtaking starry skies, and lakes in an array of colors. It's a place of serene beauty, and perhaps it's best to visit soon, before it becomes overrun, to experience the tranquility that makes Thani Tawon so special.

The Thani Tawon Mountain Range (他念他翁山, Tā Niàn Tā Wēng Shān) forms part of the Hengduan Mountains and is located in the southeastern region of Tibet's Chamdo Prefecture, nestled between the Nu River (怒江, Nù Jiāng) and the Lancang River (澜沧江, Láncāng Jiāng). This narrow, elongated range is the second from west to east within the Hengduan Mountain system and represents the easternmost range in southeastern Tibet. Its central portion is commonly known as the Nu River Mountain Range, while the upper and lower sections continue to be referred to as the Thani Tawon Mountain Range.

Natural Features
The special geographical location and climatic conditions have created Thani Tawon's varied terrain and diverse plant species. Brilliant flower seas, the magnificent Damiyong Snow Mountain (大米勇雪山, Dàmǐyǒng Xuěshān), and numerous alpine lakes hidden in the valleys attract waves of outdoor enthusiasts brave enough to explore, who have developed trekking routes of varying difficulty and length.

Regardless of which route you take, Ruco Lake (揉措, Róu Cuò) at 4,700 meters is the biggest highlight of Thani Tawon, and almost all trekking routes are centered around it. It lies quietly among the mountains and stone peaks, appearing sapphire blue in the sunlight and deep blue on cloudy days, while the edges of the lake water appear slightly emerald green when viewed up close.

Beyond Roucuo, the most distinctive feature of the Thani Tawon region is the dense concentration of alpine lakes—countless in number, varied in color, and scattered like jewels across the landscape. These lakes serve as captivating highlights along the trekking routes, setting Thani Tawon apart from other destinations. Notable examples include Gyamco Lake (加米措, Jiāmǐ Cuò) and Gyico Lake (吉错, Jí Cuò). Remarkably, many of the lakes here remain unnamed and are unknown even to local residents. Yet these nameless lakes are no less breathtaking, each possessing its own unique beauty and character.

An excellent outdoor route should embody both the fluidity of water and the steadfastness of mountains. The mountains of Thani Tawon are steep and towering, with severe weathering on most mountain bodies, little surface vegetation, and steep slopes. They are mostly brown in color, with magnificent scenery similar to Patagonia in South America, and are visually stunning.

Besides snow mountains and lakes, the most impressive feature here is probably the endless flower seas in summer. The abundance and variety of flowers are unparalleled by most outdoor routes. The flower sea at Namcha Chullung Lake (南加曲隆, Nánjiā Qūlóng) is particularly spectacular—the saying "flowers in profusion dazzle the eyes" is no exaggeration!

The gentleness of flowers, the roughness of stones, the tranquility of lakes... In this challenging land that few have trodden, elements of contrasting styles are harmoniously interwoven, making it a true sanctuary in the hearts of many mountain lovers.

Cultural Significance

Averaging around 10 kilometers of walking per day, this high-altitude trek unfolds at a relaxed, steady pace. The route meanders through farm roads, mountain trails, gravel slopes, grasslands, streams, and lakes—offering ever-changing terrain and scenery that make the journey both vivid and rewarding. The trekking intensity is moderate, and most participants find they can recover quickly after a short rest at the campsite. Each campsite is thoughtfully located—nestled against the mountains and near water—featuring flat, spacious terrain that ensures a comfortable and enjoyable experience.

Along the Thani Tawon trekking route, nearly every campsite offers exceptional opportunities to photograph snow-capped mountains, starry skies, and mirror-like reflections. The campsite above Nanjiaqulongcuo lies on the southern side of Damiyong Snow Mountain. Surrounded by open terrain and encircled by peaks, it provides the best vantage point for capturing Damiyong in all its glory. The lakeside campsite at Wugequlongcuo (乌格曲隆错, Wūgé Qūlóng Cuò), situated at the foot of the mountain on Damiyong's western flank, offers close proximity to the peak. On calm days, the still waters of the lake reflect the snow mountain and starry sky in breathtaking detail. The Twin Lakes campsite (双湖营地, Shuāng Hú Yíngdì) is the ideal spot for photographing the Milky Way. At night, when the lake is still, the shimmering stars, snowy peaks, and the arching Milky Way reflected on the water create a truly awe-inspiring scene.

Notable Attractions

1 Damiyong Snow Mountain
[大米勇雪山, Dàmǐyǒng Xuěshān]

At an elevation of 6,324 meters, it is the main peak of the Thani Tawon Mountain Range. The mountain is majestic and covered in snow year-round. It is surrounded by a series of impressive snow-capped peaks ranging from 5,000 to 6,000 meters in height, lined up in striking formation. This dramatic scenery makes it the most captivating highlight of the entire trek.

2 Gyamco Lake
[加米措, Jiāmǐ Cuò]

Composed of three lakes of different sizes and colors, the lake water displays different colors depending on the light and season, sometimes peaceful and serene, sometimes glittering with ripples. In summer, a rare plateau plant—green poppy (绿绒蒿, Lǜróng Hāo)—often grows among the gravel by the lake.

3 Gyico Lake
[吉措, Jí Cuò]

Located in a mountain depression, the lake water is dark green. When the lake surface is calm, from a distance, its color looks like a huge dyeing vat.

In summer, the meadow by the lake is filled with purple and yellow flowers, full of vitality. From here, you can see a corner of the Damiyong Snow Mountain.

Itinerary

Day1 Gather in Lijiang (丽江 2,400m)

Day2 Lijiang - Shangri-La (香格里拉 3,300m) - Feilai Temple (飞来寺 3,450m) - Quzika (曲孜卡 2,350m)
Driving: 460km, 9.5 hours

In the morning, we depart from Lijiang by vehicle, passing through the picturesque Shangri-La before arriving in Benzilan (奔子栏, Bēnzǐlán) for lunch. In the afternoon, we cross the stunning Baima Snow Mountain (白马雪山, Báimǎ Xuě shān) and make our way to Feilai Temple. From there, we travel alongside the majestic Meili Snow Mountain (梅里雪山, Méilǐ Xuěshān) before heading north into Tibet, ultimately reaching Quzika, Tibet, where we'll spend the night at a local hotel.

Day3 Quzika - Lagang (拉岗 3,500m) - Tingtsa Lake (丁差措 3,850m) - Yizibeng (一字泵 4,400m)
Trekking: 7km, 900m ascent, 4 hours

After breakfast, we depart by vehicle, passing through the Yanjing Scenic Area (盐井景区, Yánjǐng Jǐngqū). The mountain road is rugged and bumpy, and we reach the starting point of the trek, Lagang Village, after more than an hour.

We traverse along a farm road for 2 kilometers, then begin to enter a mountain path, following the right side of a stream upward. The slope gradually steepens, and soon we can see Tingtsa Lake.

Afterward, we pass through a section of gravel slope path to reach Tsolai Pasture (措来牧场, Cuò Lái Mùchǎng). We continue along the river towards the waterfall for about 1 kilometer, arriving at the Yizibeng campsite at an elevation of 4,400 meters.

Day4 Yizibeng - Gyamco Lake (加米措 4,550m) - Gongla Pass (龚拉垭口 4,900m) - Qietan Pasture (切坛牧场 4,350m)
Trekking: 10km, 500m ascent/descent, 7 hours

We follow the cobblestone path along the riverbank and turn right onto the mountain road leading to Gyamco Lake. From there, we continue left toward Gongla Pass, which sits at an elevation of 4900 meters. As we ascend, the lush meadow gradually gives way to loose gravel.

At the pass, several prayer flags are strung across, and towering stone peaks rise on both sides. After crossing the pass, we traverse a gentle meadow known as Gugudang, but the trail soon becomes steep again. Continuing the descent, we eventually reach a flat and expansive meadow, the Qietan Camp, located at an elevation of 4350 meters.

Day5 Qietan - Danmaladingcuo (旦马拉丁措 4,200m) - Trifurcation (三岔口 4,050m) - Namcha Chullung (南加曲隆 4,400m)

Trekking: 10km, 400m ascent, 350m descent, 6 hours

We follow the river gently downward, passing through meadows and forests. In the middle, we pass a large lake—Danmaladingcuo. The lake water is clear and transparent, and the water surface is calm, perfect for photographing reflections.

After walking 5 kilometers to the trifurcation, we turn right into the primeval forest. We follow a gentle mountain path upward for more than an hour to reach a burned forest area, where the snow mountain begins to appear. We continue forward to the campsite above Namcha Chullung at an elevation of 4,400 meters. This is an excellent campsite for viewing Damiyong, with flat grassland, and in summer, a stunning flower sea.

Day6 Namcha Chullung - Lake 5 - Lake 6 - Nanjialagu Pass (南加拉古垭口 4,900m) - Wugequlongcuo (乌格曲隆措 4,600m)

Trekking: 7km, 500m ascent, 300m descent, 6 hours

We follow the valley upward. In summer, this area is filled with wildflowers throughout the valley; in autumn, it's colorful, with a blue sky, and accompanied by Damiyong mountian all the way. We continue forward towards Damiyong, passing through several alpine pastures, then climb up a gravel slope to the left to the edge of Lake 5. Lake 6 is adjacent to it, with emerald green water.

We continue upward along the gravel path to the Nanjialagu Pass at an elevation of 4,900 meters. From the pass, we can look back at Lakes 5 and 6, and looking forward, we can see Wugequlongcuo. We descend along the rocky mountain path, passing several small lakes, all the way to camp by the Wugequlongcuo lake-

side at an elevation of 4,600 meters. In good weather, we can photograph the golden mountain at sunset and the reflection of the snow mountain.

Day7 Wugequlongcuo - Zhenla Pass (真拉垭口 4,950m) - Lake 8 - Lake 9 - Twin Lakes Campsite (双湖营地 4,700m)

Trekking: 11km, 400m ascent, 300m descent, 6 hours

We follow the mountain path upward, gradually moving away from the lakes and snow mountains. We climb up a gravel slope to the Zhenla Pass at 4,950 meters.

Both sides are gravel path sections. From the pass, we can see the Damiyong Snow Mountain, Wugequlongcuo, and several lakes on the south side of the pass. We descend from the pass, passing Lakes 8 and 9, to reach the Twin Lakes campsite at an elevation of 4,700 meters.

Day8 Twin Lakes Campsite - Muduoguajin (木多瓜金) - Buqikekalong (布其克隆) - Lake 17 - Shuala Pass (耍拉垭口 4,970m) - Dibeng (地泵 4,350m) - Shaduo Village (沙多村) - Zogong County (左贡县 3,800m)

Trekking: 11km, 470m ascent, 820m descent, 6 hours

We descend from the broad meadow, passing through the Muduoguajin pasture before beginning to climb. We traverse gently along the mountain body to reach the Buqikelong meadow. Going further forward, the meadow turns into a gravel path, and on the lower left, we can see a emerald green lake—Lake 17. We slowly ascend along the gravel path to the steep wall before the Shuala Pass, repeatedly turning upward to reach the pass, where we can see Roucuo like a blue sapphire embedded in the mountains.

Afterward, we return to the Buqikekalong meadow and go down to the right to the Dibeng pasture. The trek ends here, and we take a vehicle through Shaduo Village out of the mountains to Zogong County, where the group disperses.

Important Notes

- ● Best Season: June to October
- ● Suitable For: Healthy individuals aged 18-65 years with high-altitude trekking and camping experience
- ● Potential Risks: 1. When trekking at high altitudes, be mindful of altitude sickness.
  2. Marmots may be encountered along the way, please don't disturbing them.
  3. The section near Roucuo at Shuala Pass is particularly dangerous, so extra caution is required when passing through.

34. Mount Everest East Slope Trek

[珠峰东坡, Zhūfēng Dōngpō] `12days` `67km`

Lhasa
[拉萨, Lāsà]
Gathering City

12KM
Longest Single-Day Hike

750M
Maximum Daily Elevation Gain

5,350M
Highest Elevation Along the Route

★★★★★
Scenic Rating

★★★★★
Difficulty Level

Credit
Image 1 | ©Liangshuang
Image 2 | ©Harrison
Image 3/4 | ©Majun

Mount Everest (珠穆朗玛峰, Zhūmùlǎngmǎ Fēng), with an elevation of 8,848.86 meters, is the ultimate dream of mountaineering enthusiasts. Some say that any way of approaching Everest is the ultimate expression of returning to nature. Although most people cannot spend a large amount of money and time to taste the experience of climbing to the top of the world, perhaps we can use another way to complete a trekking journey about Everest.

Mount Everest is a huge triangular pyramid with what people commonly call the South slope, North slope, and East slope. Each slope corresponds to a huge glacier and valley. The three valleys extend 30-50 kilometers in their respective directions, encompassing a relatively independent mountain area in the Himalayas and forming a super landscape group centered around Everest, which can be called the most concentrated area of extreme scenery in the world.

Among these three major regions, the Mount Everest East Slope trekking route in the Gama Valley (嘎玛沟, Gāmǎ Gōu) has the most little-known extreme scenery and is the most primitive and wild.

Natural Features

The Gama Valley is located in the core area of the Mount Everest Nature Reserve and is known as the "Most Beautiful Valley in the World" and one of the "Top Ten Landscapes in the World." The valley streches 55 kilometers long from east to west and 8 kilometers wide from north to south, with a total area of about 440 square kilometers. From the valley floor at an elevation of just 2,100 meters to Mount Everest at 8,848.86 meters, the relative height difference is over 6,000 meters.

As early as 1921, American and British explorers successively explored the Gama Valley, and they were all captivated by the dreamlike natural scenery here, praising the Gama Valley as the "Most Beautiful Valley in the World" and "One of the Top Ten Landscapes in the World." To this day, this beautiful valley still rests quietly in the embrace of Everest, enjoying the loftiness and pride of the pure snow land. It has long been isolated from the world, far from the hustle and bustle of the city, without external disturbances, and the only means of transportation is the yak.

It preserves the largest primeval forest in the Everest region and has a rich and spectacularly sized wild orchid valley. Several 8,000-meter snow mountains such as Everest, Lhotse (洛子, Luòzǐ), and Makalu (马卡鲁, Mǎkǎlú) stand on either side along the way. Rhododendrons bloom beneath the majestic snow mountains, and alpine lakes reflect the snow mountains like mirrors, creating breathtakingly beautiful scenes.

The Mount Everest East Slope trekking route traverses several high mountain passes, some exceeding 4,000 meters and even reaching over 5,000 meters in elevation. Along the way, trekkers journey through diverse environments—from lush primeval forests to rhododendron-covered transitional zones, and ultimately into glaciated permafrost regions. The East Slope of Everest offers visitors a breathtaking display of a three-dimensional ecosystem and a strikingly layered, ever-changing landscape.

Cultural Significance

Some say that trekking the East Slope of Everest is like enjoying a grand feast of 8,000-meter snow-capped peaks. The most captivating aspect of this route is the rare opportunity to view Mount Everest from the east, along with two other towering giants—Lhotse, the world's fourth-highest peak, and Makalu, the fifth-highest. Owing to differences in angle and distance, each of these mountains reveals a distinct character: Everest appears majestic, Lhotse graceful, and Makalu awe-inspiring.

Five kilometers north of Makalu, there is another awe-inspiring 7,000-meter peak—Chomolonzo (珠穆朗卓峰, Zhūmùlǎngzhuó Fēng). It is entirely within the Tibet Autonomous Region of China, with its main peak in the south at an elevation of 7,804 meters. Viewed from the northeast, Chomolonzo looks extremely like an eagle soaring with spread wings, hence it is also called the "Divine Bird Peak."

In addition to these high snow peaks, another striking landscape on the Mount Everest East Slope trekking route is the alpine lakes. Among the more famous ones are Cuoxue Renma (措学仁玛, Cuòxué Rénmǎ), Xiaowu Lake (晓乌措, Xiǎowū Cuò), Langmu Lake (朗姆措, Lǎngmǔ Cuò), and Cuoguo Lake (错果措, Cuòguǒ Cuò). Most of these lakes are good places to photograph reflections of snow mountains, with the two most classic locations being Xiaowu Lake and Cuoxue Renma.

Walking on the East Slope of Everest, besides the incredibly stunning snow mountains and lakes mentioned above, there are also colorful flowers and plants that fascinate people. With their delicate bodies, they face the violent climate of the snow mountains, blooming and falling in places rarely visited by humans, forming the coolest plant paradise in the world. Blue gentians, towering rheum, pale purple irises, pure white edelweiss, continuous rhododendrons... they bloom vigorously one after another in the barren soil.

On the way to the starting point of the Mount Everest East Slope trek, we will pass through two very famous cultural sites—Tashilhunpo Monastery (扎什伦布寺, Zhāshí Lúnbù Sì) and Sakya Monastery (萨迦寺, Sàjiā Sì), which are also worth visiting.

2

Notable Attractions

1 Lhotse
[洛子峰, Luòzǐ Fēng]

At an elevation of 8,516 meters, it means "South Peak" because it is located 3 kilometers south of Mount Everest.

Between the two peaks is a mountain depression, commonly known as the "South Col." In Tibetan, Lhotse is called "Dingjie Xiesangma," meaning "Beautiful Fairy" in Tebiten.

2 Xiaowu Lake
[晓乌措, Xiǎowū Cuò]

A beautiful alpine lake below the Xiaowu La Pass. Standing by the lake, you can see the massive reflection of Makalu on the surface of Xiaowu Lake. When the first ray of sunlight falls every morning, Makalu is illuminated by the sunlight.

Starting from a light golden-red color, Makalu seems to gradually put on a shining coat, with boundless light and unlimited scenery.

3 Tsho Shaparma Lakes
[措学仁玛, Cuòxué Rénmǎ]

Composed of six closely adjacent small lakes, it is also the most famous viewing platform on the Mount Everest East Slope trekking route. Under different lakes, different angles, and different weather conditions, the scenery presented is ever-changing and extremely rich.

Too many trekkers come here from afar just to witness its incomparable elegance. Every morning, the hymn of Himalayan ice and sunshine is performed punctually at Tsho Shaparma Lakes.

Sunlight falls sequentially from high to low on Everest, Lhotse, Makalu, Chomolonzo, and Chomolonzo Central Peak. A group of world-class high peaks successively receive the sun's glory from high to low, with peaks competing in beauty and all things reviving.

4 Makalu
[马卡鲁峰, Mǎkǎlú Fēng]

At an elevation of 8,463 meters, it is located in the middle section of the Himalayas, 24 kilometers from Mount Everest. The name "Makalu" comes from the Sanskrit "Maha-Kala," representing great evil, and is also an alias for Shiva, the supreme deity in Hinduism.

Her temperament is volatile, sometimes cold and ruthless, sometimes kind and benevolent.

5 Sakya Monastery
[萨迦寺, Sàjiā Sì]

Located at the foot of Benpo Mountain in Sakya County, Shigatse City, Tibet Autonomous Region, it is the main monastery of the Sakya sect of Tibetan Buddhism.

During the Northern Song Dynasty, Khön Könchok Gyalpo, a descendant of the noble Khön family of Tibet, funded the construction of this monastery, which now has a history of about a thousand years. The monastery houses precious scriptures, Yuan Dynasty mandala murals, ancient porcelain, and other cultural relics, and was listed as a national key cultural relics protection unit by the State Council in 1961, making it very much worth a visit.

Itinerary

Day1 Gather in Lhasa (拉萨 3,650m)

Day2 Lhasa - Shigatse (日喀则 3,800m)
Driving: 365km, 6 hours

Today we will pass by Lake Yamdrok (羊湖, Yánghú) and view Noijin Kangsang Snow Mountain (宁金抗沙雪山, Níngjīn Kàngshā Xuěshān) from a distance. After lunch in Langkazi (浪卡子, Làngkǎzǐ), we visit the Karola Glacier (卡诺拉冰川, Kǎnuòlā Bīngchuān), Manla Reservoir (满拉水库, Mǎnlā Shuǐkù), and view the ancient Gyantse Fortress (江孜古堡, Jiāngzī Gǔbǎo) from a distance.

Then, through the Nyangchu River Valley (年楚河谷地, Niánchǔ Hé Gǔdì), we arrive at Shigatse, with a local elevation of 3,800 meters.

Day3 Shigatse - Jiacuo La Pass (嘉措拉山口 5,248m) - Qudang Township (曲当乡 3,800m)
Driving: 370km, 8 hours

After departing from Shigatse, we cross the Jiacuo La Pass, where we can view the majestic form of five peaks above 8,000 meters, including

6 Tashilhunpo Monastery
[扎什伦布寺, Zhāshí Lúnbù Sì]

Located at the foot of Niseri Mountain in the south of Shigatse City, Tibet Autonomous Region, it is a Tibetan Buddhist Gelug sect temple and also the residence of successive Panchen Lamas. The temple was first built during the Ming Dynasty and has a history of more than 600 years. The entire monastery faces south with its back to the north, built against the mountain. The Buddhist palaces are staggered, integrating Buddhist architecture with traditional Tibetan architectural styles.

As early as 1961, Tashilhunpo Monastery was announced by the State Council as one of the first batch of national key cultural relics protection units, with extremely high observation and research value.

3

Mount Everest, from a distance. Then we enter the Mount Everest Nature Reserve and arrive at Qudang Township at an elevation of 3,800 meters in the afternoon.

Day4 Qudang Township (3,800m) - Youpa Village (优帕村) - Xiaowu Lake (晓乌措 4,700m)
Trekking: 10km, 750m ascent, 7 hours

In the morning, we drive to the starting point of the trek, Youpa Village, and then begin trekking. During the trekking, there are approximately three fairly large ascents as we continue up the valley to the Xiaowu Lake campsite at an elevation of 4,700 meters. Xiaowu Lake is an alpine lake below the Xiaowu La Pass. In good weather, reflections of Makalu and Chomolonzo can be seen by the lake.

Day5 Xiaowu Lake - Xiaowu La Pass (晓乌拉垭口 4,950m) - Zhuoxiang (卓湘 4,000m)
Trekking: 9km, 250m ascent, 950m decent, 7 hours

We rise early to see the golden sunrise on

Makalu and Chomolonzo by Xiaowu Lake, as well as their reflections. This is one of the best places to view Makalu during the entire journey.

After breakfast, we set out to cross the Xiaowu La Pass at an elevation of 4,950 meters. At the pass, we stop for a while to admire the massive forms of Makalu and Chomolonzo right before our eyes, then descend all the way through the Xueruo River Valley (雪若河谷, Xuěruò Hégǔ) to the Zhuoxiang campsite at the end of the valley.

Day6 Zhuoxiang - Tangxiang (汤湘 4,550m)
Trekking: 9km, 600m ascent, 7 hours

Today, after setting out, we first cross a primeval forest to reach the north side of the Gama Valley. Afterward, we will walk among the alpine meadows of the Himalayas.

After walking over a large slope, we descend to today's campsite, Tangxiang Pasture. This is one of the best photography spots of the trip, where you can directly face the 8,000- meter snow mountain group from your tent.

Day7 Tangxiang - E'ga (俄嘎 4,700m)
Trekking: 9km, 500m ascent, 350m decent, 7 hours

Tangxiang campsite is one of the best photography spots of the journey. In the morning, don't rush to pack up the campsite. Before the sun rises, under the pale pink sky, the three giant mountains stand silently before your eyes.

As the sun rises over the mountain peaks, the three snow peaks reflect a soft glow in the sunshine, captivating viewers. After breakfast, we set out, first descending to the bottom of the Gama Valley, crossing a small wooden bridge, then slowly ascending through shrubs and entering a section of jumbled rocks.

Beside the rocks, the traces of retreating glaciers are clearly visible. After passing through the rocky slope, we soon see the fairy-tale campsite surrounded by mountains—the E'ga campsite at an elevation of 4,700 meters. We camp by the stream here, sleeping beside the water.

Day8 E'ga - Baidang (白当 4,950m) - E'ga
Trekking: 6km, 250m ascent/decent, 4 hours

Today we don't change our campsite but make a light round trip to Baidang. With an open view at an elevation of 4,950 meters, Baidang allows you to feel the majesty of the world's highest peak up close. The adjacent Lhotse is equally spectacular, with both mountains within reach, incredibly awe-inspiring.

Day9 E'ga - Tsho Shaparma Lakes (措学仁玛 4,950m)
Trekking: 12km, 750m ascent, 500m decent, 9 hours

Today we return to near the previous Tangxiang campsite by the same route, then climb for about 3 hours from another direction to Tsho Shaparma Lakes at an elevation of 4,950 meters. Tsho Shaparma Lakes is the climax of the Mount Everest East Slope trek.

Here, you can see snow mountains such as Everest, Lhotse, Makalu, and Chomolonzo, and Tsho Shaparma Lakes is like a mirror where you can see reflections of the snow mountains.

Day10 Free Day at Tsho Shaparma Lakes

Staying one day at Tsho Shaparma Lakes is absolutely worth it. In the morning, we go to the lakeside to see the golden sunrise. When the first ray of sunlight shines on Everest, Lhotse, Makalu, and all the mountains and things gradually put on a charming golden hue, you can also see their brilliant reflections in the lake.

This moment might make you tear up! Even if you don't want to move, lying in your tent or sitting on the grass in a chair, the most extreme and stunning scenery of the East Slope of Everest is right before your eyes, surrounding you 360 degrees. In this incomparable five-star scenic campsite, doing nothing is also a great happiness!

Day11 Tsho Shaparma Lakes - Langma La Pass (朗玛拉垭口 5,350m) - Lunzhulin Village (轮朱林村 4,250m) - Qudang Township - Tingri (定日)
Trekking: 12km, 400m ascent, 1100m decent, 7 hours

From the campsite, we go straight up along the rocky uphill path, reaching the Langma La Pass at an elevation of 5,350 meters after three sections of climbing. This is the highest point of the journey.

Looking back at the path we came from, lakes are scattered and snow mountains stand tall. From here, we descend more than 1,100 meters to Lunzhulin Village, where we say goodbye to the East Slope of Everest completely. We then return to Tingri by vehicle, a drive of about 4 hours.

Day12 Tingri - Lhasa
Driving: 500km, 7 hours

4

Important Notes

● Best Season: May-June, September-October

● Suitable For: Healthy individuals aged 18-65 years with high-altitude trekking experience and camping experience

● Potential Risks: 1. High-altitude trekking carries the risk of altitude sickness.

2. The valley weather is unpredictable, so take precautions to stay warm and protect against the cold.

3. On the way to E'ga, there is a section of a steep traverse across rocky slopes—exercise caution for your safety.

35. Shishapangma Grand Circuit Trek
[希夏邦马大环线, Xīxiàbāngmǎ Dà Huánxiàn] **13days/78km**

Lhasa
[拉萨, Lāsà]
Gathering City

17KM
Longest Single-Day Hike

670M
Maximum Daily Elevation Gain

5,650M
Highest Elevation Along the Route

★★★★★
Scenic Rating

★★★★★
Difficulty Level

Credit
Image 1/3 | ©Shadow
Image 2 | ©Liangshuang

When discussing top-tier trekking routes in Tibet, the Greater Himalayas is a topic that cannot be missed. The massive and towering Himalayan range stretches across the border, with numerous 8,000-meter peaks lined up here. Their stunning natural scenery and the distinctive local customs and culture of Tibet will present you with a lesser-known Greater Himalayas.

If you plan to trek in Tibet, I strongly recommend the Shishapangma Grand Circuit trek, a top-tier trekking route, to admire the only 8,000-meter snow mountain entirely within China's territory, to touch the tenderness of the beautiful Gongco Lake (贡措, Gòngcuò), to comprehend the vastness and solitude of the Greater Himalayas, and to approach China's most beautiful ice tower forest by foot.

Natural Features

Shishapangma (希夏邦马, Xīxiàbāngmǎ), with an elevation of 8,027 meters, is the only 8,000-meter snow mountain completely within China's territory. It is located in Nyalam County (聂拉木县, Niè Lāmù Xiàn), Shigatse City, Tibet, situated in the middle section of the Himalayan range. Although its altitude of 8,027 meters is far lower than that of Mount Everest, it has caused even the world's best climbers to turn back. Its summit death rate is more than twice that of Everest, and it ranks sixth among the 14 peaks above 8,000 meters. Shishapangma not only attracts domestic and foreign mountaineers with its 8,000-meter height but also attracts many mountain enthusiasts to approach it in the form of trekking with its unique charm.

Currently, there are mainly two trekking routes related to Shishapangma, namely the Shishapangma Small Circuit and the Grand Circuit.

The Shishapangma Small Circuit connects the south and east slopes of Shishapangma, with mainly open and flat terrain along the way. The distance between the mountain peaks and people is within 10 kilometers, creating a strong sense of proximity and exposure. Especially on the road deep into the south slope, it is almost surrounded by snow mountains on three sides, allowing you to enjoy an ultimate feast of snow mountains. In addition to these magnificent peaks, you can also admire dozens of beautiful alpine lakes.

The Shishapangma Grand Circuit adds the Yebokang Jiale Glacier (野博康嘉勒冰川, Yěbókāng Jiālè Bīngchuān) on the north slope compared to the Small Circuit, allowing you to appreciate a group of seven to eight thousand-meter snow mountains from various angles, offering a visual enjoyment that is incomparable to other routes. The Yebokang Jiale Glacier is the biggest highlight along the way. The melting glacier has formed an ice tower forest that stretches for several kilometers, resembling an "ice crystal garden." This is truly a super snow mountain and glacier feast.

Before embarking on the trek to Shishapangma, it's hard to imagine that a route with an average elevation of 5,000 meters could be home to so many stunning, hidden lakes. From the vantage point of a drone, you can spot more than a dozen lakes, both named and unnamed. What a great route this is—simply breathtaking!

Before trekking Shishapangma, it's equally hard to imagine that in this frigid, thin-air

zone, you'd witness the serene coexistence of tranquil lakes and icy snow-capped mountains. The lake surfaces mirror the surrounding peaks, where mountains and water blend seamlessly, wind and clouds swirl together, and every upward or downward glance evokes a sense of awe. The vastness and solitude of the Greater Himalayas are fully expressed in the Shishapangma region—a place where only the most determined travelers dare to venture.

Cultural Significance

The scenery that can be seen in the Shishapangma mountain area is far more than just high mountains and lakes. The reason for choosing to trek here is also because of the super glacier on the north slope of Shishapangma that people look forward to on this Grand Circuit.

Beneath the 8,000-meter giant peak, after millions of years of accumulation, a huge glacier has formed, extending from an elevation of 5,300 meters to 5,800 meters. From a distance, it looks crystalline and bright, nestling against the massive body of Shishapangma, like a flowing tear. This is one of China's most beautiful glaciers—the Yebokang Jiale Glacier.

Shishapangma, ranking last among the 14 sets of 8,000-meter snow mountains, has always been overshadowed by the towering figures of other high peaks such as Mount Everest and Lhotse, with few travelers exploring it. Compared to the renowned Mount Everest East Slope trekking route, the Shishapangma Grand Circuit can be said to be unknown. But for outdoor enthusiasts who love the scenery of 8,000-meter snow mountains, this is absolutely a super snow mountain scenic highway. The towering 8,000-meter giant peaks, the scattered alpine lakes, and the magnificent and beautiful ice tower forest... all of these make it worth returning here repeatedly.

Notable Attractions

2

1 Yebokang Jiale Glacier
[野博康嘉勒冰川,
Yěbókāng Jiālè Bīngchuān]

This huge glacier extends from an elevation of 5,300 meters to 5,800 meters. It nestles against the massive body of Shishapangma. Ice wonders abound, from milky-white ice tower forests and mirror-like ice lakes to vibrant ice bridges.

Towering ice cliffs, reaching tens of meters in height, stretch on magnificently for thousands of meters, creating an awe-inspiring and endless landscape. Walking in this ice and snow world, you see crystal towers rising from the ground, all over 8-10 meters high. Sculpted by nature, they take on a thousand postures and forms. Being among them is like walking into a fairyland of jade palaces from mythology.

Itinerary

Day1 Gather in Lhasa (拉萨 3,650m)

Day2 Lhasa - Tingri (定日 4,300m)
Driving: 500km, 8 hours

Today's driving distance is relatively long. We depart from Lhasa and travel along National Highway 318, having lunch in Shigatse (日喀则, Rìkāzé), then crossing the Jiacuo La Pass (嘉措拉山口, Jiǎcuò Lā Shānkǒu) and arriving at Tingri for overnight stay.

Day3 Tingri - Nyalam County (聂拉木县 3,800m)
Driving: 220km, 4 hours

After breakfast, we set out, enjoying the super snow mountain group along the way—Mount Everest (珠穆朗玛, Zhūmùlǎngmǎ), Cho Oyu (卓奥友, Zhuó'àoyǒu), Gauri Sankar (格重康峰, Gé zhòngkāng Fēng), and Lapchi Kang (拉布吉康, Lābùjí Kāng).

Then we cross the Tong La Pass (通拉山口, Tōng Lā Shānkǒu), view the Shishapangma peak group from a distance, and arrive at Nyalam County Town for overnight stay.

Day4 Nyalam County - Trekking Starting Point (3,950m) - Xinde Campsite (欣德营地 4,620m)
Trekking: 10km, 670m ascent, 6 hours

From Nyalam, we drive to the starting point of the trek and meet up with the yak team. We proceed along the valley, and after crossing a small bridge, the elevation begins to rise. Along the way, we can see the beautiful Jialong Lake (嘉龙措, Jiālóng Cuò) and the handsome Lengbu Gang East Peak (冷布岗东峰, Lěngbù Gǎng Dōng Fēng).

We reach the Xinde campsite at an elevation of 4,620 meters in about 6 hours. Today marks the first day of trekking, so there's no need to rush. The main focus is on acclimating to the plateau and finding a comfortable rhythm for yourself.

Day5 Xinde Campsite - Jialong Lake (嘉龙措) - Zuzu Campsite (祖祖营地 4,950m)
Trekking: 5km, 330m ascent, 5 hours

Today we rise early to appreciate the golden sunrise on the Shishapangma peak group. Behind the Xinde campsite, there is a ridge where everyone can go early to wait for the beautiful moment when golden light illuminates the peaks.

Then we head to Jialong Lake to begin a super spectacular snow mountain trekking journey. In the afternoon, we reach the Zuzu campsite with an excellent view, which is closer to the snow mountains.

Day6 Zuzu Campsite - Jigabu Campsite (吉嘎布营地 4,850m)
Trekking: 6km, 5 hours

In the morning, we can photograph the golden sunrise at the campsite or trek to the slope behind the campsite to photograph the Shishapangma snow mountain.

For mountain lovers, the mountain's temperament is different every day. Only by perceiving the mountain up close do you discover that mountains also have personality. Today's route is relatively easy, basically downhill all the way. In the afternoon, we arrive at the upper Jigabu campsite.

Day7 Jigabu Campsite - Gongcuo Campsite (贡措营地 5,200m)
Trekking: 9km, 350m ascent, 6 hours

Today we trek to Gongcuo. We ascend gradually along the ridge line at high altitude. Along the way, we can see the most beautiful lake of the entire journey—Gongcuo Lake. In the afternoon, we reach the Gongcuo campsite at an elevation of 5,200 meters.

This is also a super viewing platform where we can photograph reflections of the Shishapangma peak group. You will discover that the huge mountains are actually so close to you.

Day8 Rest Day at Gongcuo Campsite

Today we rest at the Gongcuo campsite because with the blessing of the beautiful Gongcuo, this place is considered the best position to view the Shishapangma peak group in the entire circuit.

When the sun rises in the morning, it gradually paints the white snow mountains into a pale pink, then a blue-pink, and finally a brilliant golden color like flames. When the sun sets in the evening, the golden afterglow refracts a dreamlike light, making the originally cold mountains appear incredibly tender. At this moment, you can't help but marvel at the wonder and greatness of nature.

Day9 Gongcuo Campsite - Ere Village (俄热村 4,460m) - North Slope Base Camp (北坡大本营 5,050m)
Trekking: 14km, 7 hours

After breakfast, we depart from the campsite and trek along the beautiful Gongcuo, accompanied by snow mountains and lakes all the way. We climb a small slope to a pass. From the pass, we can look back at the Shishapangma peak group and the beautiful Gongcuo, then descend all the way to Ere Village. From there, we drive to the Shishapangma North Slope Base Camp.

Day10 North Slope Base Camp - Advance Camp (前进营地 5,500m)
Trekking: 17km, 450m ascent, 8 hours

Today we trek from the Shishapangma North Slope Base Camp at an elevation of 5,050 meters to the Advance Camp at an elevation of about 5,500 meters.

We can enjoy the magnificent sunrise of Shishapangma here, and then visit peaks on the north slope such as Gangben Qin (冈苯钦, Gāng běn Qín) and Molamenqing (莫拉门青, Mòlā ménqīng).

Day11 Advance Camp - Yebokang Jiale Glacier (野博康嘉勒冰川 5,650m) - Advance Camp
Trekking: 10km, 150m ascent, 6 hours

Today we depart from the Advance Camp and trek for about 3 hours to reach the Yebokang Jiale Glacier.

The threads on the ice towers are the annual rings of time, recording the changes here over the years. It's worth noting that this is currently one of the most beautiful accessible glaciers in China. Even just for appreciatin these slowly disappearing ice tower forests, this route is worth your visit!

Day12 Advance Camp - North Slope Base Camp - Tingri (4,300m)
Trekking: 17km, 5 hours

From the North Slope Advance Camp, we return to the Base Camp by the same route, then drive back to Tingri County.

Day13 Tingri - Lhasa
Driving: 500km, 8 hours

We depart from Tingri and return to Lhasa, successfully completing the Shishapangma Grand Circuit trek.

Important Notes
- Best Season: May-June, September-October
- Suitable For: Healthy individuals aged 18-65 years with high-altitude trekking and camping experience
- Potential Risks: The 8-day trek is mostly at altitudes above 5,000 meters, with the highest point reaching 5,650 meters, posing a risk of altitude sickness.

PART 3

NORTH
China Region

36. Taihang Mountains

[太行山, Tàiháng Shān]

7days

61km

Zhengzhou
[郑州, Zhèngzhōu]
Gathering City

18KM
Longest Single-Day Hike

800M
Maximum Daily Elevation Gain

1,700M
Highest Elevation Along the Route

★★★
Scenic Rating

★★
Difficulty Level

Credit
© All images in this piece
  by RK

The Taihang Mountains, together with the Greater Khingan Range, Wushan Mountains, and Xuefeng Mountains, form the natural boundary between China's second and third topographic steps. Spanning Hebei, Shanxi, and Henan provinces, the range extends over 800 kilometers from north to south. For ease of reference, people have divided it into eastern, western, and southern sections.

The Southern Taihang, which spans Henan and Shanxi provinces, is the section with the most quantity of scenic spots in the Taihang Mountain range and is renowned in outdoor community. It was once listed among "China's Top Ten Most Beautiful Canyons."

As the dividing line between the North China Plain and the Loess Plateau, the unique geological wonders formed by tectonic faults create a seamless blend of northern grandeur, with towering mountains and deep valleys, and southern elegance, with rolling clouds and flowing waters.

Natural Features
I once passed through Baodu Village in April, where the old pear trees at the village entrance were in full bloom, their white flowers resembling snow. Walking through the falling petals like rain into the small village of just a few households, amid the crowing of roosters and barking of dogs, it felt like

stepping back a thousand years...

I once walked through the lush, shady valleys in August, calming my restless heart amid the majestic mountains, making hotpot with clear river water and friends, and waking up early in Guoliang Village to watch a magnificent sunrise...

I once traversed golden fields in October, buying freshly picked pears from an elderly lady by the roadside using a long pole, borrowing rock sugar from a farmhouse in Baligou to cook wild hawthorn berries into a sweet and sour delight...

The Southern Taihang may lack a singularly spectacular perspective, but it does not lack any of the beauty one might expect. Unlike some classic routes that are challenging and risky, they offer more accessible and gentle paths, never disappointing with each visit.

Looking down, sheer cliffs are thousand-meter deep; looking up, mountain ridges stretch endlessly toward the horizon. Hiking here is a true delight, making this route a classic and a must-visit for mountain enthusiasts.

Along the route, majestic peaks, magnificent landscapes, waterfalls, and sheer cliffs abound. Baodu Village (抱犊村, Bàodú Cūn), Mawuzhai (马武寨, Mǎwǔzhài), Wangmangling (王莽岭, Wángmànglǐng), Shiziling (十字岭, Shízǐlǐng), Xiyagou (锡崖沟, Xīyágōu), Shuangdi (双底, Shuāngdǐ), Guoliang Village (郭亮村, Guōliàng Cūn)... these once obscure mountain villages have now become famous worldwide thanks to the continuous pilgrimages of generations of hiking enthusiasts.

This hiking route begins in Zhengzhou, the capital of Henan Province. As you leave Zhengzhou, with its roadsides adorned with fresh flowers, and head north, the scenery gradually shifts from towering buildings to the peaceful rural countryside.

Suddenly, a tall, textured wall comes into view—this marks the first sighting of the Southern Taihang Mountains. Taking a bus that winds upward from the entrance of Wanxianshan Scenic Area (万仙山景区, Wànxiān Shān Jǐngqū), you'll soon see the cliff-hanging road featured in travel magazines. It appears before you like a belt embedded in the rock layers, formed over billions of years, now an integral part of the mountain.

In 1972, Guoliang Village Chief Shen Mingkai (申明凯, Shēn Míngkǎi) and village party secretary Shen Mingxin (申明信, Shēn Míngxìn) led thirteen brave villagers to carve out a cliff-hanging road, 1,250 meters long, 6 meters wide, and 4 meters high, without any mechanical tools, in a deep valley with a maximum drop of over 1,000 meters. This five-year project was once hailed as the "Ninth Wonder of the World."

As night falls, the cliff-hanging road is lit up by warm yellow decorative lights, creating a romantic atmosphere when standing in the middle to take photos. Who could have imagined that, just years ago, this remote road in an isolated village would become a popular tourist attraction today?

Notable Attractions

1 Cliff-Hanging Road
[挂壁公路, Guàbì Gōnglù]

In 1972, led by thirteen pioneering heroes, local villagers spent five years carving a cliff-hanging road measuring 1,250 meters in length, 6 meters in width, and 4 meters in height, all without the use of any mechanical tools.

Located in a deep valley with a maximum drop of over 1,000 meters, this road was once hailed as the "Ninth Wonder of the World" and was recognized as one of the "18 Most Extraordinary Roads in the World," among other accolades.

2 Baodu Village
[抱犊村, Bàodú Cūn]

The only village in Shanxi Province without road access, hidden deep in a valley with only nine households. Though isolated, it boasts beautiful scenery, steep mountains, and simple folk customs, making it a 21st-century version of a hidden paradise. After being discovered by outdoor enthusiasts, this secret village quickly became an outdoor enthusiast's base camp, with colorful flags of various outdoor organizations hanging in the village. Stepping into this place, one might think they've entered the starting point of an outdoor sports event.

3 Guoliang Village
[郭亮村, Guōliàng Cūn]

This village is perched high on a cliff and was established during the late Eastern Han Dynasty, giving it a history of over two thousand years. Thanks to the widespread recognition of the hanging road, this ancient village has gained attention from the outside world. The Southern Taihang Mountains—the last untouched paradise of the North—have gradually become a sought-after destination for travelers. Nowadays, Guoliang Village is also recognized as "Number One Film and Television Village in China."

Itinerary

Day1 Gather in Zhengzhou (郑州)

Day2 Zhengzhou - Guoliang Village (郭亮村) - Heavenly Ladder (天梯) - Watchtower (炮楼) - Wanxianshan (万仙山)
Driving: 170km, 3 hours
Trekking: 10km, 4 hours

After breakfast, we drive to Wanxian Mountain Scenic Area and hike along the "Ninth Wonder of the World"—the Hanging Road, where we can personally witness the enduring spirit of the thirteen heroes. Standing on the viewing platform of the cliff-top folk yard, you'll be greeted by the breathtaking view of the crimson Taihang Canyon, towering 200 meters high, with the Hanging Road winding along its face.

From the fort, you'll catch a glimpse of Jiaoding Mountain (轿顶山, Jiào Dǐng Shān) in the distance, rising like a celestial palace atop cliffs hundreds of meters high.

The Sky Ladder was the only means of communication with the outside world used by the earlier generations of Guoliang residents. We will then stay overnight at a farmhouse in Wanxian Mountain.

Day3 Wanxianshan - Wangmangling (王莽岭) - Double Ridge Highlights - Zhanggou (张沟)
Trekking: 15km, 500m ascent/desent, 7 hours

After breakfast, we drive across the Henan-Shanxi provincial border to the foot of Wangmangling, the cloud-top of Taihang.

The scenic area is filled with thousands of peaks, countless valleys, strange rocks, and undulating mountains, creating a magnificent landscape. Then we will begin our trek from Wangmangling and finally arrive Shiziling, the highest peak of the Southern Taihang, with mountain goats accompanying us along the way.

After viewing the uniquely shaped stone forests and layer upon layer of cloud seas from the summit, we descend along the treacherous Ant Ladder to reach Zhanggou, where we stay overnight at a local farmhouse.

Day4 Zhanggou - Mawuzhai (马武寨) - Bao du Village (抱犊村) - Baligou (八里沟)
Trekking: 18km, 200m ascent, 800m desent, 8 hours

After breakfast, we drive to Mawuzhai and prepare for our hike. Descending through the valley, we'll be immersed in the breathtaking scenery of cliffside waterfalls. The Yixiantian (一线天, Yīxiàntiān, "One Line Sky") is as narrow as an alley, while the Qixingtan (七星潭, Qīxīngtán, "Seven Star Pool") is adorned with a series of cascading waterfalls, all set in an undeveloped, pristine natural landscape. By noon, we will arrive at Baodu Village, surrounded on three sides by mountains and on one side by a cliff, nestled harmoniously between the mountains and water.

After lunch, we'll walk through the forest atop the cliff, where the dense trees will occasionally part, offering fleeting moments of walking among the clouds. Finally, we'll reach the Baligou Scenic Area, where we'll stay overnight.

Day5 Baligou - Baquanxia (八泉峡) - Grand Canyon Hotel
Driving: 100km, 3 hours

We rise early to witness the splendor of Baligou Scenic Area, often referred to as the "Soul of Taihang, Spirit of China."

After breakfast, we head to the most famous attraction of the Taihang Mountains— Baquanxia Gorge. In this breathtaking area, winding paths circle towering peaks, while meandering waterways carve their way through serene

valleys, resembling the "Three Gorges" of the north.

Day6 Grand Canyon Hotel - Cat's Road (猫路) - Natural Bridge (天生桥) - Wanfosi (万佛寺) - Yingguxia (瑛姑峡) - Shibanyan Hotel (石板岩宾馆)
Trekking: 18km, 800m ascent, 8 hours

After breakfast, we begin to enter the depths of the Taihang Mountains, hiking the most classic route of the Western Taihang—the Cat's Road to Yingguxia Gorge traverse. The zigzagging stone steps, embedded in the cliff, lead upward. Following this narrow path, we will reach the Natural Bridge.

Afterward, we will pass through Wanfosi Temple and descend all the way to Yingguxia, renowned as the "Zhangjiajie of the North." This hidden gem remains largely untouched by tourists, preserving some of the most pristine and unspoiled landscapes in the region.We will then continue to Shibanyan hotel and stay overnight.

Day7 Shibanyan Hotel - Painters' Village (画家村) - Jingdi Village (郭底村) - Zhengzhou
Driving: 270km, 4 hours

After breakfast, we drive to Painters' Village, where the tranquil and serene mountain village atmosphere has attracted art students and teachers from art academies across the country for sketching. Then we drive to Jingdi Village, where stone-paved streets, stone houses, stone tables, stone benches, stone mills, and stone rollers integrate with the magnificent natural scenery, forming a unique natural and cultural landscape.

Finally, we visit the world wonder of Jingdi Cliff-Hanging Road before driving back to Zhengzhou.

Important Notes
● Best Season: April to November
● Suitable For: Healthy individuals aged 16-65 years
● Potential Risks: 1. The traverse from Wangmang Ridge to Shizi Ridge follows an unmarked wilderness route, so it's important to stay close to the group for safety.
2. Trails can become slippery on rainy days, so be sure to watch your steps!

37. Mount Wutai
[五台山, Wǔtái Shān]

Taiyuan
[太原, Tàiyuán]
Gathering City

20KM
Longest Single-Day Hike

800M
Maximum Daily Elevation Gain

3,061M
Highest Elevation Along the Route

★★★★½
Scenic Rating

★★★
Difficulty Level

Mount Wutai is not a single peak, but rather a "summer retreat" made up of five distinct peaks. Located in the northern part of the Taihang Mountains in Xinzhou City, Shanxi Province, the five peaks are as follows: East Peak Wanghai (望海峰, Wànghǎi Fēng) at 2,795 meters, South Peak Jinxiu (锦绣峰, Jǐnxiù Fēng) at 2,485 meters, West Peak Guayue (挂月峰, Guàyuè Fēng) at 2,773 meters, Central Peak Cuiyan (翠岩峰, Cuìyán Fēng) at 2,894 meters, and North Peak Yedou (叶斗峰, Yèdǒu Fēng) at 3,061 meters. The North Peak Yedou is the highest point in the North China region, earning it the title of "Greater Wutai," in contrast to "Lesser Wutai" in Hebei Province.

During the Ice Age, geological processes caused the mountain-top rocks to fragment, resulting in flat, platform-like peaks, which led to the name Wutai ("Five Platforms"). Due to its unique geographical location and relatively high elevation, Mount Wutai, despite being situated at a low latitude on the North China Plain, has climate characteristics similar to those of the Greater Khingan Range. Even during the height of summer, visitors experience a cool, highland atmosphere, making it a renowned summer retreat.

Cultural Significance
Mount Wutai is foremost among China's four great Buddhist mountains and the only Buddhist holy site not located in ancient India among the world's five major Buddhist sacred

places. In 2009, it was listed as a UNESCO World Cultural Heritage site. Throughout various dynasties, with new constructions and expansions, the number of temples centered around Taihuai Town (台怀镇, Táihuái Zhèn) once reached over 360, with more than 100 still preserved today. The five high peaks respectively enshrine the five manifestations of Manjusri Bodhisattva, also known as the Five Directional Manjusri: East Peak Wanghai Temple enshrines Intelligent Manjusri, South Peak Puji Temple enshrines Wise Manjusri, West Peak Falei Temple enshrines Lion's Roar Manjusri, North Peak Lingying Temple enshrines Immaculate Manjusri, and Central Peak Yanjiao Temple enshrines Child Manjusri.

"Pilgrimage to the Peaks," or making a pilgrimage to Greater Wutai, is an activity that has continued for over 1,600 years. Buddhist devotees, in search of life wisdom, travel great distances to Mount Wutai to worship the Five Directional Manjusri Bodhisattvas enshrined on the five highest peaks in North China. For devout Buddhist followers, Mount Wutai is Manjusri's domain, a sacred place for spiritual practice. With each step, they measure the earth, holding deep reverence for the Dharma and offering prayers for a blessed life, seeking inner peace and liberation.

Those who complete the Greater Wutai pilgrimage are not limited to religious figures. For outdoor enthusiasts, this pilgrimage is a journey of self-challenge. The five peaks are at high elevations, with complex terrain and changeable weather, requiring good physical fitness and perseverance, as well as the ability to overcome rugged mountain paths and harsh weather. While trekkers continuously push their physical limits, they also gain immense inner confidence.

Mount Wutai is equally stunning when it comes to its natural scenery. In the evening, the warm glow of the setting sun creates a striking division, with deepening hues above and the enchanting purple clouds of sunset below. Under the vast sky, mountains rise in layers, and alpine meadows are carpeted with seas of flowers. Even without delving into the profound religious culture of the temples, simply sitting quietly in the meadow, soaking in the beauty of the landscape, is enough to leave one in awe. On rainy days, walking through the forest, shrouded in clouds and mist, with a few cattle grazing peacefully in the woods, evokes a serene, almost ethereal atmosphere, like stepping into a misty forest.

Many who walk this route describe it as an "arduous journey." But what is it that draws so many people to this challenging path year after year? Perhaps it is because, despite the physical hardships, the soul finds peace, guided by a deep Buddhist affinity. The "hardship" transforms into exclamations of "well worth it" once the journey is complete. Mount Wutai is, after all, a sacred pilgrimage route for the Chinese people.

Notable Attractions

1 Xiantong Temple
[显通寺, Xiǎntōng Sì]

The largest and oldest among the many temples on Mount Wutai, it not only enjoys flourishing incense offerings and commands respect across the mountain but is also the most popular landmark for tourists.

It was originally known as the Dafulingying Temple, built by Emperor Ming of Han, Liu Zhuang, around the same time as the White Horse Temple in Luoyang, recognized as one of the earliest Buddhist temples in China in record.

2 Shuxiang Temple
[殊像寺, Shūxiàng Sì]

This temple houses the largest Bodhisattva statue in Manjusri's domain and was once a holy site where Qing emperors came to worship Mount Wutai.

3 Five Sage Temple
[五爷庙, Wǔyé Miào]

Almost every visitor to Mount Wutai, specifically those coming to burn incense, makes it a point to queue up at the Five Sage Temple to make their wishes. Despite its modest size and historical insignificance, it remains the most popular spot on the mountain. The "Five Sage" is the financial manager of the East Sea Dragon Palace, commonly known as the "God of Wealth." People entrust their wishes for favorable weather and prosperity to him.

Itinerary

Day1 Gather in Taiyuan (太原)

Day2 Taiyuan - Hongmenyan (鸿门岩) - East Peak (东台) - North Peak (北台 3,061m) - Zaoyu Chi (澡浴池)
Trekking: 18km, 800m ascent, 7 hours

After breakfast, we drive to Mount Wutai, a revered Buddhist holy site renowned for its blend of natural beauty and cultural heritage. Upon reaching Hongmenyan, we begin our pilgrimage along the Greater Wutai path.

Our first stop is East Peak Wanghai, one of the best vantage points for viewing the sea of clouds at Mount Wutai. From there, we continue our hike to North Peak Yedou, standing at 3,061 meters and often referred to as the "Roof of North China." After a brief rest at North Peak, we make our way to Zaoyu Chi, where we will spend the night in a temple.

Day3 Zaoyu Chi - Central Peak (中台) - West Peak (西台) - Lion's Den (狮子窝) - Taihuai Town (台怀镇)
Trekking: 20km, 380m ascent, 780m desent, 8 hours

Today, we head to Central Peak Cuiyan, where Yanjiao Temple, enshrouded in clouds and mist, is dedicated to Child Manjusri. The sight of the temple's glazed golden roof and the layered mountains in the distance creates a scene that is truly breathtaking.

Next, we make our way to West Peak Guayue, where Falei Temple, dedicated to Lion's Roar Manjusri, awaits. After offering our worship, we descend the mountain, accompanied by the soothing sounds of pine winds and Buddhist chants, and reach Lion's Den, a renowned site for great spiritual practice. Finally, we head to Taihuai Town to check in to a hotel for the night.

Day4 Taihuai Town - Jinge Temple (金阁寺) - South Peak (南台) - Buddha Mother Cave (佛母洞) - Taihuai Town
Trekking: 15km, 460m ascent, 1000m desent, 7 hours

Today, we make our way to the final peak, South Peak Jinxiu, where the path is lined with continuous shade and vibrant flowers. Upon reaching the summit, we will pay our respects to Wise Manjusri, enshrined in Puji Temple.

After taking a moment to rest, we descend South Peak and return to Taihuai Town for our accommodation, marking the completion of the Greater Wutai pilgrimage.

Day5 Taihuai Town - Mount Wutai Temple Cluster - Foguang Temple (佛光寺) - Taiyuan
Driving: 4 hours

After breakfast, we have free time to explore Taihuai Town and visit various notable spots on Mount Wutai. These include the Five Sage Temple, renowned for its popularity and efficacy; Tayuan Temple (塔院寺, Tǎyuàn Sì), home to Mount Wutai's iconic Great White Pagoda; Xiantong Temple, the largest and oldest temple on the mountain.

Shuxiang Temple, which houses the largest statue of Manjusri Bodhisattva; and Pusa Ding (菩萨顶, Púsà Dǐng), the largest Lamaist temple. At the designated time, we will gather and drive to Foguang Temple, known as the "Buddhist Light of Asia," before returning to Taiyuan.

Important Notes

- Best Season: April to October
- Suitable For: Healthy individuals aged 8-65 years
- Potential Risks: 1. The mountaintop is often windy, and the actual temperature difference can exceed 10°C, so be sure to keep warm.

  2. In winter, the weather can be harsh, with risks of hypothermia and frostbite, so extra caution is required!

38. Northern Shanxi Wild Great Wall

[晋北野长城, Jìnběi Yě Chángchéng] (5days) (28km)

Taiyuan
[太原, Tàiyuán]
Gathering City

20KM
Longest Single-Day Hike

500M
Maximum Daily Elevation Gain

1,700M
Highest Elevation Along the Route

★★★
Scenic Rating

★★
Difficulty Level

When tracing history of Shanxi Province, one can easily go back to legendary ancestral figures of early Chinese civilization such as Nüwa, Emperor Yan, Emperor Huang, Chiyou, Yao, Shun, and Yu. The legendary battle of the century—Emperor Huang versus Chiyou—is said to have taken place in Shanxi. The capitals of three generations of sage rulers—Yao, Shun, and Yu—were also built in Shanxi. Thousands of years later, Shanxi remains the ancestral home of many Chinese people.

Northern Shanxi is mountainous, located at the junction of the Loess Plateau and the Inner Mongolian Plateau. As an "border region" of ancient China, defensive fortifications like the Great Wall have existed there since ancient times.

Cultural Significance

The Great Wall is one of the most magnificent architectural wonders in the world and the most invaluable cultural heritage in human civilization, which is the pride of every Chinese people. For more than two thousand years, rulers of different dynasties and regions have built sections of the Great Wall. According to the National Cultural Heritage Administration, dynasties throughout history collectively constructed over 20,000 kilometers of the Great Wall, widely distributed across 15 northern provinces, spanning deserts, mountains, and plateaus of varying terrains.

The construction of the Great Wall in Shanxi began as early as the Warring States Period and continued through the Ming and Qing dynasties, encompassing almost all dynasties that built the Great Wall in Chinese history. Ancient Great Wall buildings in Shanxi are well-preserved, with remains of border walls, fortress towns, and military fortresses, with the Yanmenguan Great Wall being the most typical. Among the nine strategic passes of China, Yanmenguan ranks first. This single pass, Yanmenguan, has witnessed half of Chinese history. Located in northern Shanxi and the middle section of the whole Great Wall, Yanmenguan controls Central Plains to the south and the desert to the north, guarded by the magnificent and uninterrupted Great Wall. From Li Mu and Meng Tian to Xue Rengui, from Li Guang and Huo Qubing to the generals of Yang family, this place witnessed the bloody wars of thousands of troops and dynastic changes.

Regarding scenery, the magnificent views you'll see during the Wild Great Wall trek in this area might be out of your expectation. Adhering to northern mountains,where the change of seasons is distinct, the Great Wall also possesses four different scenes throughout the year. In spring, the area at the foot of the Great Wall comes alive, with a succession of flowers blooming in vibrant colors. In summer, the landscape stretches into a sea of lush greenery. In autumn, the mountains turn golden, with red maples and yellow leaves swirling like colorful butterflies around the majestic, enduring Wall, captivating all who visit. In winter, the snow-covered Great Wall resembles a silver serpent, standing proudly against the cold.

When trekking the Wild Great Wall, you'll encounter ancient walls, villages, towers, and military fortresses at every turn, each seamlessly integrated with the mountain ridges. As you tranversing through them, the Wild Great Wall of Northern Shanxi becomes a gateway to the past, transporting you back to the ancient times.

Time erases everything. The ancient fortresses and Great Wall scattered in northern Shanxi may continue to be desolate. However, there will always be outdoor enthusiasts willing to measure every inch of China's mountains and rivers with their own steps. Waking on the Shanxi Wild Great Wall, you can enjoy both the beautiful natural scenery on the mountains and cultural heritages.

Notable Attractions

1 Northern Shanxi Military Fortresses
[晋北军堡, Jìnběi Jūnbǎo]

Around the Longqing period of the Ming Dynasty, the conflicts between the Ming Dynasty and Mongolian Tartars finally subsided after many years. The northern Shanxi Great Wall area, once filled with fights and wars, became an important channel for Ming-Mongolian trade. During this period, former military fortresses gradually transformed into ordinary towns or villages, and many fortress walls were even hollowed out by locals to build cave dwellings.

The northern Shanxi military fortresses, together with the Great Wall, form a unique cultural landscape in the northern frontier. Today, there are still farmers cultivating the land here, continuing the rural culture from five hundred years ago.

2 Yanmenguan
[雁门关, Yànmén Guān]

The Yanmenguan Great Wall is located in northern Shanxi, controlling the Central Plains to the south and the desert to the north. This pass witnessed wars of thousands of troops and changes of dynasties.

Time erases everything, and the northern Shanxi Great Wall outside Yanmenguan silently watches the vicissitudes of three thousand years.

3 Guangwu Great Wall
[广武长城, Guǎngwǔ Chángchéng]

This section of the Great Wall has densely packed enemy towers with a complete and well-preserved military defense system.

Especially notable is a sawtooth-shaped section of the wall that is considered a spectacular sight. Despite hundreds of years of weathering, the area maintains its original appearance, presenting a magnificent sight stretched across the mountaintops.

4 Motianliang Great Wall
[摩天岭长城, Mótiānlǐng Chángchéng]

Known as the "Little Badaling," it is one of the highest Great Wall sections in the world. Here, remnants of Great Wall from the Han and Northern Qi dynasties still stand, while the Ming Dynasty Great Wall winds like a giant dragon.

5 Yellow River Shanxi-Shaanxi Grand Canyon
[黄河晋陕大峡谷, Huánghé Jìn-Shǎn Dà Xiágǔ]

Originally flowing east, the Yellow River encountered the Lüliang Mountains, which stretch from south to north, causing it to change course and flow southward.

After millions of years of erosion, it carved a huge, deep canyon in the Loess Plateau—the Yellow River Shanxi-Shaanxi Grand Canyon. In 2005, National Geographic of China magazine rated it as "One of China's Top Ten Most Beautiful Canyons."

6 Yungang Grottoes
[云冈石窟, Yúngāng Shíkū]

Located in the western suburbs of Datong City, it is a famous World Cultural Heritage site and one of China's four major grottoes. It began construction in the Eastern Han Dynasty and flourished during the Northern Wei, Liao, and Jin dynasties, extending through the Yuan, Ming, and Qing dynasties. The scattered caves and niches hide countless fascinating stories. The Buddha statues, flying apsaras, musical instruments, birds, animals, and flowers together create a unique Buddhist world, a paradise of art.

7 Nanchan Temple
[南禅寺, Nánchán Sì]

The oldest wooden structure in China.

Itinerary

Day1 Gather in Taiyuan (太原)

Day2 Taiyuan - Yanmenguan (雁门关) - Guangwu Wild Great Wall (广武野长城) - Youyu (右玉)
Driving: 340km, 5 hours

After breakfast, we will drive to Yanmenguan, known as the 'First Pass of China.' After exploring the site, we continue through Yanmenguan to reach the Guangwu Wild Great Wall beyond the pass—an important defensive stronghold once guarding the entrance to Yanmenguan.

The rugged, desolate military fortresses and winding sections of the Wild Great Wall have withstood the ravages of war and time, with most now lying in ruins. After the visit, we will drive to Youyu and check into the hotel.

Day3 Youyu - Wild Great Wall - Youyu
Driving: 70km, 1 hours
Trekking: 20km, 500m ascent, 7 hours

After breakfast, we head to a military fortress along the Great Wall to begin our Wild Great Wall trek. The scattered ruins of ancient fortresses create a striking first impression—magnificent, desolate, heroic, and weathered by time.

The yellowed fortresses and sections of rammed earth walls, worn by centuries of exposure, show signs of age, yet still exude a sense of majesty from a bygone era. As we walk along the border wall, we gaze toward the beacon towers, stretching one after another into the distance.

The winding wall seems to tell tales from a distant past. After completing the trek, we drive back to the Youyu hotel to rest.

Day4 Youyu - Wild Great Wall - Shahukou (杀虎口) - Youwei Ancient City (右卫古城) - Youyu
Driving: 70km, 1 hours
Trekking: 8km, 300m ascent, 8 hours

After breakfast, we drive to the starting point of our trek. Along the way, the vast landscape unfolds before us—wide, open land, a low sky, crumbling border walls, and elderly locals herding sheep and working the fields—forming a scene that is both desolate and subtly vibrant. We walk along a narrow country path, less than a meter wide, flanked by broken walls and deep gullies, with the western wind howling in our ears.

Following the Great Wall up to Hualin Mountain (桦林山, Huàlín Shān), we cross the Erfenguan River Valley (二分关河谷, Èrfēnguān Hégǔ) and rush through Shahukou, feeling the glory and aspirations of the Shanxi merchant guilds who once ventured west. Afterward, we drive to Youwei Ancient City. Following our visit, we return to the Youyu hotel to rest.

Day5 Youyu - Motianliang Great Wall (摩天岭长城) - Yungang Grottoes (云冈石窟) - Datong
Driving: 150km, 2.5 hours

After breakfast, we drive to the Yungang Grottoes in Datong, one of "China's Four Major Grottoes" and a UNESCO World Cultural Heritage site.

Here, we have the opportunity to personally witness the profound role Buddhism played in fostering ethnic integration during the Northern Wei dynasty. Following the visit, we drive to Datong for departure.

Important Notes
- Best Season: April to November
- Suitable For: Healthy individuals aged 6-65 years
- Potential Risks: 1. Some sections are steep.
  2. Be cautious of falling!

1

39. Ulan Butong
[乌兰布统, Wūlánbùtǒng]

6days
30km

Beijing
[北京, Běijīng]
Gathering City

13KM
Longest Single-Day Hike

250M
Maximum Daily Elevation Gain

1,482M
Highest Elevation Along the Route

★★★★☆
Scenic Rating

★★☆
Difficulty Level

If you're wondering where to find autumn at its finest, I would say it's probably in Inner Mongolia. There's a place where you'll witness the most vivid shades of fall. This is the "Hometown of Chinese Photography," and a sacred land for countless autumn admirers—Ulan Butong Grassland.

Compared to more popular tourist destinations like Xinjiang and Tibet, Inner Mongolia is often underestimated, despite being the third-largest region in China by land area. Our stereotypical image of Inner Mongolia usually consists only of yurts and vast grasslands, giving the impression that this land has little to offer beyond these two features. However, with a deeper understanding, you'll realize that its expansive territory has endowed it with diverse natural landscapes. From east to west, Inner Mongolia spans three major ecological zones: forests, grasslands, and deserts, each offering unique scenic beauty and recreational opportunities that rival those of Xinjiang and Tibet. The Ulanbutong Grassland, for example, is a quintessential representation of the region's grassland scenery.

Ulan Butong, meaning 'red mountain' in Mongolian, is located on the southern edge of Hexigten Banner (克什克腾旗, Kèshíkèténg Qí) in the Inner Mongolia Autonomous Region. It was once part of the Mulan Hunting Ground (木兰围场, Mùlán Wéichǎng), the imperial hunting park of the Qing Dynasty, where Emperor Kangxi famously led Qing troops in a major battle against Galdan. Three hundred years later, with the era of war horses long past, Ulanbutong has transformed into the most diverse grassland on the Bashang Plateau. Here, forests, deserts, lakes, and pastures coexist harmoniously, creating a landscape that is as breathtaking as an oil painting, with its uniquely varied topography

Located just 400 kilometers from China's capital, Beijing, Ulanbutong can be reached by car in about six hours. As you walk through the area, you'll see a blend of soft, gentle colors, with cattle, sheep, and camels scattered across the landscape, creating an atmosphere of untamed wildness, freedom, and romance.

Natural Features

Beyond the grassland scenery, the Hunshandake Sandy Land (浑善达克沙地, Húnshàndákè Shādì) and Xar Moron River (西拉木伦河, Xīlāmùlún Hé) are also highlights of this journey. Inner Mongolia's sandy lands have typically left negative impressions, but trekking through them allows you to experience a different kind of charm.

Savoring Mongolian cuisine is indispensable experience on this trip. While enjoying hearty drinks and meat, the khoomei (throat singing) and morin khuur (horsehead fiddle) music quietly enter your ears, an exotic and primitive tradition that captivates you. In the vast Ulanbutong, the nature of the Mongolian people has been nurtured by the soil and water of the grassland. They are sincere, kind, and overflowing with warmth. This trekking journey is undoubtedly a cultural feast about the nomadic people.

Leaving Inner Mongolia, there is a cultural landscape you can't miss on the return trip–the Jinshanling Great Wall (金山岭长城, Jīnshānlǐng Chángchéng). As described by National Geographic of China: the Jinshanling Great Wall has the most luxurious mountain skyline in the world, the most beautiful viewing platform, and the most profound historical ruins.

If you visit Ulanbutong in winter, you can also experience snow tubing and snow drifting. In winter, the surface of Duolun Lake (多伦湖, Duōlún Hú) is covered with thick ice and heavy snow, forming a natural ice rink. Fishermen, dressed in thick cotton clothes, wearing leather hats and gloves, conduct winter fishing on the ice, creating a spectacular scene!

Notable Attractions

1 Hunshandake Sandy Land
[浑善达克沙地, Húnshàndákè Shādì]

The term "Hunshandake" comes from Mongolian, meaning "yellow wild horse," and is one of China's four major sandy lands. Spruce trees, either standing alone or in clusters, dot the undulating dunes and expansive grasslands.

While trekking through it, the sky's color gradually changes from warm to cool tones. Staying in local yurts, trying your hand at archery and traditional ball games, or simply relaxing and gazing into the distance, all offers an ultimate enjoyment.

2 Xar Moron River
[西拉木伦河, Xīlāmùlún Hé]

This is the birthplace of the Khitan people, with the Mongolian name meaning "Yellow River." Known as the "mother river" of the Mongolian people, it stretches 380 kilometers with a basin covering over 30,000 square kilometers, ultimately flowing into the Liao River.

As we trek along its banks, we climb slopes, walk through sandy stretches, cross small rivers, herd cattle with local herders in the forest, and rest in the shade of towering trees – everything feels peaceful and serene.

3 Jinshanling Great Wall
[金山岭长城, Jīnshānlǐng Chángchéng]

Originally built in the first year of the Hongwu era of the Ming Dynasty and later continued and renovated by Qi Jiguang, the Jinshanling section of the Great Wall is one of the best-preserved stretches, with a history spanning over 400 years, winding majestically along the mountain. As you climb the Great Wall step by step, gently touching the ancient stones, every brick and tile seems to hold the warmth of history. Despite the passage of time, the Jinshanling Great Wall remains steadfast between the blue sky and green fields, its incomplete yet resolute form telling a story of change and grandeur.

Itinerary

Day1 Gather in Beijing Fengning (丰宁)
Driving: 300km, 4.5 hours

We will gather in Beijing this morning. we have arranged for airport/station pick-up, then we will drive to Fengning for accommodation.

Day2 Fengning - Colorful Forest - Ulan Butong Grassland - Ulanbutong
Driving: 200km, 3 hours
Trekking: 13km, 5 hours

After breakfast, we begin with a 3-kilometer forest trek, where we experience the exhilarating aerial glass plank road and visit a Manchu folk culture park nestled in the woods.

Next, we drive to Mulan Hunting Ground to embark on a 10-kilometer grassland trek, passing through scenic spots like General's Pond (将军泡子, Jiāngjūn Pàozi) and Hunshandake Sandy Land. Finally, we make our way to the Ulan Butong observation deck to witness the breathtaking sunset. We will spend the night at Ulanbutong hotel.

Day3 Ulan Butong - Summer Pasture Grassland - Fairy Lake (仙女湖) - Film Base – Ulan Butong
Driving: 40km, 1.5 hours

After breakfast, we board off-road vehicles and head to the Mongolian summer pasture grassland. From there, we begin our trek toward the desert, passing by blue lakes nestled between the sand and grass, a journey that takes about three hours. In the afternoon, we continue on to Fairy Lake to admire the autumn colors and capture photos at the famous film base. In the evening, we return to the hotel.

Day4 Ulan Butong - Xar Moron River Bank Trek - Mongolian Hot Pot - Horseback Riding - Ulan Butong
Driving: 20km, 0.5 hours
Trekking: 10km, 4 hours

After breakfast, we drive to the Xar Moron River for a trek along its banks. Then, we will enjoy a traditional Mongolian hot pot for lunch. In the afternoon, we visit a Mongolian horse farm, where we experience everything from theoretical instruction to leisurely horseback rides and exhilarating gallops across the grassland—an unforgettable "horseback journey" through a hidden realm. In the evening, we return to the hotel.

Day5 Ulan Butong - Chengde (承德) - Jinshanling Great Wall
Driving: 300km, 4 hours
Trekking: 7km, 3 hours

After breakfast, we drive to Chengde, where we will enjoy the traditional Manchu Eight Bowls (a set of special dishes) for lunch.

Afterward, we head to the Jinshanling Great Wall for a trek. In the evening, we stay at a hotel located at the foot of the Great Wall.

Day6 Jinshanling Great Wall - Beijing
Driving: 190km, 4 hours

Important Notes

● Best Season: June to October

● Suitable For: Healthy individuals aged 5-68 years

● Potential Risks: 1. The weather in autumn is unpredictable, with significant temperature differences between morning and evening.

2. Be sure to prepare for suitable clothes.

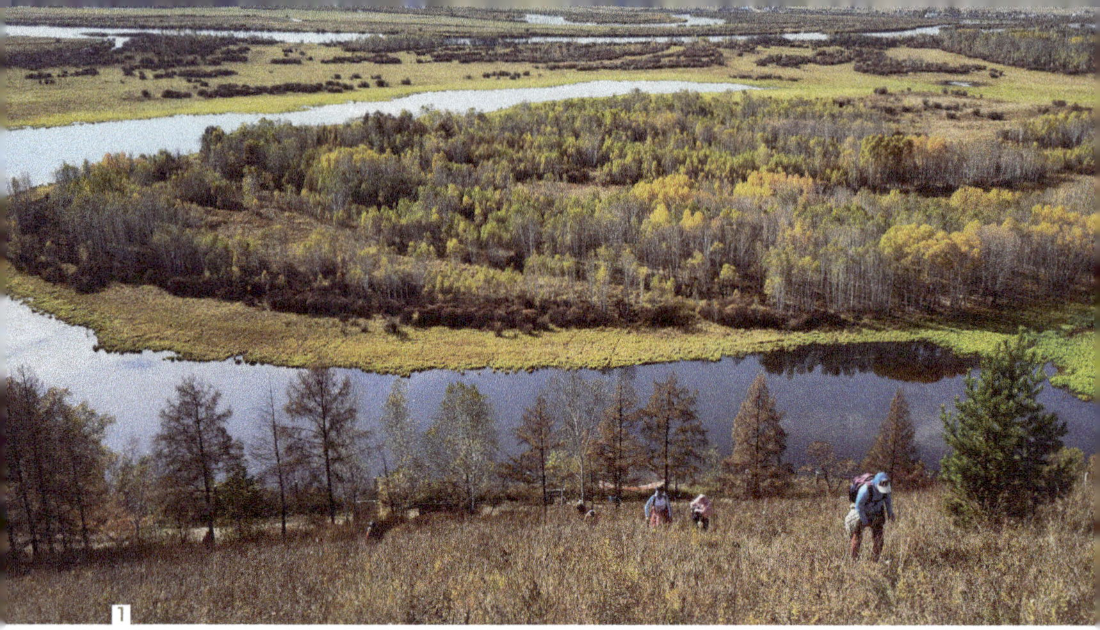

1

40. Hulunbeir Trek [呼伦贝尔徒步, Hūlúnbèi'ĕr Túbù]

7days

47km

Hailar
[海拉尔, Hăilā'ĕr]
Gathering City

20KM
Longest Single-Day Hike

250M
Maximum Daily Elevation Gain

850M
Highest Elevation Along the Route

★★★★☆
Scenic Rating

★★
Difficulty Level

Credit
Image 1/2 | ©Majun
Image 3 | ©Aheng
Image 4 | ©Kangaroo

Hulunbeir is located in the northeastern part of Inner Mongolia Autonomous Region. Its northwest border with Russia is defined by the Erguna River (额尔古纳河, È'ĕrgŭnà Hé), while its southwestern section shares a border with Mongolia. The combined border with Russia and Mongolia stretches over 1,700 kilometers.

Grasslands comprise only half of Hulunbeir's natural landscape; vast forests and wetlands are equally important features. Of its total area of 253,000 square kilometers, 120,000 square kilometers are forest, 80,000 square kilometers are natural grasslands, 30,000 square kilometers are wetlands, with over 3,000 rivers and more than 500 lakes. These impressive figures dispel the misconception that Hulunbeir offers only "monotonous scenery."

Natural Features

The Greater Khingan Range (大兴安岭, Dàxīng'ānlĭng) forest area is China's largest forest reserve. Deep within this region lies a rarely visited sanctuary–the homeland of the Evenki (鄂温克族, Èwēnkèzú) Aoluguya reindeer-herding tribe. The name "Evenki" means "people who live in the great forests," and they are the only ethnic group in China that still maintains a reindeer-herding culture. In the 17th century, the Evenki migrated from the shores of Lake Baikal to the depths of the Greater Khingan Range, where they have preserved their nomadic lifestyle centered around reindeer herding for generations.

The documentary "Remarkable Villages" offers an authentic and profound glimpse into their lives: women follow reindeer tracks through the deep forest daily, while men occasionally venture into the mountains to search for reindeer, sometimes disappearing for months. They live in conical dwellings called "cuoluozi" (撮罗子) made of birch bark and tent material. Although the remote mountains have brought them many hardships, this has not diminished their love and attachment to the land. Hiking through the primeval forests of Aoluguya, you'll regularly encounter rabbits and squirrels foraging for food, and you can gather wild blueberries and mushrooms along the way—an unforgettable experience during your trekking journey.

Also within Hulunbeir lies China's only Russian ethnic township—Enhe (恩和, Ēnhé). Walking through its streets, you'll frequently meet ethnic Russians with blonde hair, blue eyes, high cheekbones, and deep-set eyes. They are bold and romantic; despite having European features, they speak with authentic Northeastern Chinese accents, creating a sense of familiarity.

The journey takes you across grasslands and private ranches, into the Greater Khingan Range forests where you can gather moss to feed reindeer at the Aoluguya tribe; experience border folk customs and Russian-style architecture in the frontier town of Enhe and China's coldest city, Genhe (根河, Gēnhé); and enjoy pastoral hiking and horseback riding in Heishantou (黑山头, Hēishāntóu) amid the exotic atmosphere of Manzhouli (满洲里, Mǎnzhōulǐ). Though the trip lasts only a few days, the experiences are incredibly diverse.

Every May, after a long winter dormancy, wildflowers begin to bloom in competitive displays. Cattle and sheep dot the forests and meadows like scattered pearls across the green expanse, creating a landscape of endless emerald adorned with colorful flowers. In June, peonies bloom across the hillsides for a limited time; in July, golden canola flower fields spread from east to northwest; in August, waves of wheat undulate while vast sunflower fields shine brilliantly under the sun. By autumn, the land dons a golden mantle, with yellow birch trees blanketing the Greater Khingan Range forests, instantly transforming the area into an "autumn fairy tale." This perhaps is the wonder of the forest-grassland landscape—nature unfolds before your eyes in such a tangible way, with colors changing so dramatically between seasons, as if afraid you might overlook its presence. Hulunbeir is beautiful in all four seasons, and each one is not to be missed!

As this hiking route nears its end, you can visit the border city of Manzhouli to experience the unique cultures of China, Russia, and Mongolia. Manzhouli's streets are lined with various European-style buildings, with elaborate reliefs visible everywhere, creating a rich architectural atmosphere.

2

Notable Attractions

1 Arxan
[阿尔山, Ā'ěrshān]

Once rated by National Geographic as having "China's most beautiful autumn colors" and praised as the "Pearl of the Greater Khingan Range."

Its unique volcanic lava landscape features half forest-grassland and half volcanic hot springs. The Tianchi Lake (天池, Tiānchí) is surrounded by colorful forests, with golden fallen leaves floating on the water; Wusulangtze Lake (乌苏浪子湖, Wūsūlàngzǐ Hú) seamlessly connects with the sky, appearing and disappearing in the morning mist; the Unfrozen River glistens with golden waves, with verdant forests along both banks reflecting golden light, creating a dreamlike fairy-tale atmosphere where lakes mirror the golden autumn.

2 Enhe
[恩和, Ēnhé]

A small and beautiful Russian ethnic township located on the right bank of the Erguna River. The town is dominated by Russian-style log buildings that resemble elves' wooden houses hidden in the forest. Strolling through the town, you might encounter the melodious sound of an accordion from a street corner, or catch the occasional scent of baking bread wafting on the breeze.

Several thousand Russians and Chinese-Russian descendants live here, maintaining many Russian living habits, and their homes are heavily influenced by Siberian farmhouse architectural styles.

3 Hulun Lake
[呼伦湖, Hūlún Hú]

"The eagle Beir on the grassland fell in love with the beautiful and simple shepherdess Hulun. To stay together forever, they transformed into two magnificent pearls embedded in the vast grassland. Since then, this place has had the vast Hulun Lake and Beir Lake, and people have called the region Hulunbeir."

Itinerary

Day1 Gather in Hailar (海拉尔)

Day2 Hailar - Moji Gele River Grassland (莫日格勒河草原) - Erguna (额尔古纳)
Driving: 100km, 2 hours
Trekking: 10km, 5 hours

After breakfast, we drive to the iconic Moji Gele River, a hallmark of Hulunbeir. We'll trek 10 kilometers through the heart of the Moerdaoga River grasslands along its most scenic section, surrounded by herds of cattle and sheep, blooming flowers, and the river's winding meanders.

At the end of the day's journey, we'll climb the Moerdaoga River observation deck for a panoramic view of its magnificent scenery before arriving at the Starry Sky Ranch in the evening, where we'll sleep under the stars.

Day3 Erguna - Private Farm - Genhe (根河)
Driving: 180km, 3 hours
Trekking: 20km, 6 hours

After breakfast, we drive to the starting point of our trek. We'll hike through a private farm that sees few tourists, where canola fields, wildflowers, and wheat fields are interspersed with scattered birch forests, creating a breathtaking pastoral landscape that refreshes the soul.

After reaching the end of our trek, we drive to Genhe, China's coldest city, for overnight accommodation.

Day4 Genhe - Aoluguya Forest (敖鲁古雅森林) - Enhe (恩和)
Driving: 200km, 4 hours
Trekking: 7km, 2 hours

After breakfast, we drive to the starting point of the Aoluguya reindeer tribe trek. We'll hike through the primeval forests of the Greater Khingan Range, picking wild blueberries, mushrooms, and wildflowers.

At noon, we arrive at the Evenki hunters' tribe of Aoluguya, where we can interact with reindeer, chop wood, fetch water, and enjoy a forest picnic. Afterward, we drive to the Russian ethnic township of Enhe to stay in a guesthouse, enjoying limitless scenic views along the way.

Day5 Enhe - China-Russia Border - Qika (七卡) - Heishantou Horse Ranch (黑山头马场) - Grassland Yurt
Driving: 200km, 3 hours
Trekking: 10km, 3 hours

After breakfast, we drive to the starting point of our trek along the China-Russia border, enjoying pastoral scenery along the way.

After reaching the end of our trek, we drive to the Heishantou horse ranch for a one-hour horseback riding experience, galloping across the vast Hulunbeir grasslands. In the evening, we stay in a Mongolian yurt and participate in a bonfire party.

Day6 Grassland Yurt - Border - National Gate - Matryoshka Hotel (套娃酒店) - Manzhouli (满洲里)
Driving: 200km, 4 hours
Trekking: 10km, 3 hours

After breakfast, we depart by car to enjoy the scenery along the China-Russia border. This border road is known as China's Route 66, with the Erguna River running alongside it and cattle and sheep occasionally crossing the road.

At noon, we can enjoy a fish feast in Zhalainuoer (扎赉诺尔, Zhālàinuò'ěr), and in the afternoon, we'll visit the National Gate and Matryoshka Hotel in Manzhouli before checking into our hotel for free time.

Day7 Manzhouli - Barga Tribe (巴尔虎部落) - Hailar
Driving: 200km, 3 hours
Cultural Performance: 1.5 hours

After breakfast, we drive through grassland scenery to the Mongolian Memory Tribe, where we'll watch an authentic Mongolian cultural mini-Naadam performance (intangible cultural heritage). Experience milking cows, feeding lambs, and live like a true Mongolian.

At noon, enjoy grassland cuisine including hot pot with lamb. In the afternoon, the group disperses in Hailar.

Important Notes
● Best Season: June to October
● Suitable For: Healthy individuals aged 5-70 years
● Potential Risks: Be aware of sun protection and mosquito prevention.

PART 4
CENTRAL
China Region

41. West Hunan Hidden Road

6days

36km

[湘西秘境, Xiāngxī Mìjìng]

Changsha
[长沙, Chángshā]
Gathering City

12KM
Longest Single-Day Hike

550M
Maximum Daily Elevation Gain

850M
Highest Elevation Along the Route

★★★★
Scenic Rating

★★
Difficulty Level

Across the vast expanse of China, there are places that remain like hidden gems—understated yet brimming with an irresistible charm. Xiangxi, located in the northwestern mountainous region of Hunan Province, is one such enchanting destination. Its wealth of outdoor resources is more than enough to captivate the heart of every outdoor enthusiast.

Mentioning this place, many people might first recall the poetic border town depicted by Shen Congwen's writings, or the mysterious legends of "corpse drivers" and folk sorcery. However, the splendor of Xiangxi goes far beyond these features. This region possesses breathtaking outdoor resources waiting for those who truly appreciate them to unveil its mysterious veil.

Natural Features
Xiangxi is a region characterized by typical karst topography, where mountains of various shapes rise dramatically, and forested peaks are as sharp as swords. Natural stone bridges span across deep valleys, seemingly crafted effortlessly by nature. Clear streams wind through deep gorges, while sheer cliffs on either side appear to have been split by axes and

carved by knives. Caves are scattered throughout the landscape—entering them feels like stepping into a fantastical dream-world, with strange and beautiful formations at every turn. Narrow, deep rock crevices tower on both sides; looking up, the sky is just a thin line above. As you walk through these narrow passages, you breathe in rhythm with the earth's pulse, each step filled with the thrill of uncovering the unknown. The true allure of this place can only be understood through personal experience.

In addition to its breathtaking natural scenery, the cultural landscape of Xiangxi adds a unique dimension to the hiking experience. This is a multi-ethnic region, home to the Tujia (土家族, Tǔjiā Zú), Miao (苗族, Miáo Zú), and other minority groups who have lived here for generations, creating rich and distinct cultural traditions. Villages are beautifully scattered among the mountains and rivers, with traditional stilt houses (吊脚楼, diàojiǎolóu) and wisps of cooking smoke rising into the air, painting a peaceful and poetic picture of rural life.

Despite its abundant outdoor resources, Xiangxi has never promoted itself excessively. Unlike some well-known tourist destinations that are marked by heavy commercialization and overcrowding, here you can still experience a rare sense of tranquility and purity. You can roam freely across the vast wilderness, untouched by the usual hustle and bustle.

During the trek, you will pass through an expansive karst underground cave system, known as the "Lost Cave" (迷洞, Mí Dòng), a name derived from the legend that people once got lost within its labyrinthine passages. Inside the cave, you'll find underground rivers and a network of countless passages, with limestone formations creating stunning stalagmites, stone flowers, stalactites, and stone corals. Equipped

with helmets and headlamps, you'll embark on an extraordinary underground adventure, traversing an 800-meter-long river, until the first rays of daylight break through ahead, leading you from one magical world into another...

After experiencing various adventurous outdoor routes, a leisurely, relaxing journey would be the perfect way to round off your trip. In the winding valley, you'll see the Youshui River (酉水河, Yǒushuǐ Hé) winding like a slender snake through countless mountains and valleys. The Youshui River is the largest tributary of the Yuan River (沅江, Yuán Jiāng). Here, the honest and simpe Tujia people have crafted a unique culture through their long-standing traditions of production and daily life. Black-awning boats, bamboo poles, fishing nets, and the stilt houses along the riverbank all come together to form the tranquil rhythm of riverside living.

Sailing on the emerald Youshui River, you can take in the stunning mountains and crystal-clear waters, with towering peaks surrounding you. After about three hours on the water, you'll arrive at "Xiangxi's Famous Town"–Hibiscus Ancient Town (芙蓉镇, Fúróng Zhèn). Originally called Wang Village, it was renamed after the movie Hibiscus Town was filmed here. Surrounded by water on three sides, with a waterfall flowing through the town and cascading down its heart, it is an idyllic spot to relax and soak in the beautiful scenery.

Cultural Significance

Xiangxi is a place truly deserving of the title "hidden paradise"–unassuming, mysterious, and seldom visited, yet incredibly soothing for the soul. The outdoor routes here offer a variety of adventures, including stream trekking, cave exploration, and canyon crossing, all of which make it a treasure waiting to be discovered by more outdoor enthusiasts.

Notable Attractions

1 Jie Mu Stream
[借母溪, Jiè Mǔ Xī]

As the name suggests, this was once a place where impoverished people would "borrow mothers to bear children." It is said that many artifacts related to the "Niuhua culture" (狃花文化, Niǔ Huā Wénhuà), a tradition surrounding the practice of borrowing mothers to bear children, are still preserved here. The Jie Mu Stream National Nature Reserve protects rare primary and secondary forests.

Each season brings its own beauty—spring with blooming mountain flowers, summer with lush greenery, autumn with falling leaves, and winter with flying snow. Valleys crisscross the area, and crystal-clear streams wind through, while steep cliffs rise like natural screens, encircling a tranquil green valley. This serene landscape is home to rare animals and plants. Isolated from the outside world and little known to outsiders, this place remains rarely visited and is still inaccessible by car.

2 Binlang Valley
[槟榔谷, Bīnláng Gǔ]

Located in Luotaping Township, Yongding District, Zhangjiajie City, Hunan Province, it is an area rich in both Zhangjiajie landforms and karst topography. It is named for the unique rock formations in the area, which resemble betel nuts. It houses Central China's largest rock climbing base, and natural crevices comparable to those in Utah, USA.

It was allegedly a hiding place for Xiangxi bandits in legends. While Zhangjiajie World Geological Park receives millions of visitors from around the world each year, Binlang Valley has remained rarely visited for many years. Natural bridges, sinkholes, canyons, streams, crevices, caves, underground rivers... The rich landforms of Binlang Valley exceed imagination and are precisely the preferred destination for outdoor enthusiasts!

3 Zuolong Gorge
[坐龙峡, Zuò Lóng Xiá]

This 6.5-kilometer-long canyon features a maximum elevation difference of over 370 meters and is home to China's first special trail built deep within the gorge, nestled between towering cliffs. Equipped with iron chains for climbers to hold onto, the trail follows the mountain's natural contours.

At its widest, the trail spans less than 3 meters, and at its narrowest, there is barely enough room for one person to pass through. Walking along the mid-mountain trail, crossing the roaring stream below, and moving cautiously with bated breath offers an exhilarating yet safe experience.

Itinerary

Day1 Gather in Changsha (长沙)

Day2 Changsha - Jie Mu Stream (借母溪) - Jie Mu Stream Village (借母溪村)
Driving: 400km, 6 hours
Trekking: 6km, 350m ascent, 2 hours

After arriving at the starting point in the afternoon, we'll hike along Jie Mu Stream, its crystal-clear waters so pure that fish can be seen swimming. By evening, we'll reach the secluded Jie Mu Stream Village, where there is no cell phone signal.

As night falls, we can gather around, and the guesthouse owner will share stories about Yuanling's unique "Niuhua culture"—a traditional fertility custom.

Day3 Jie Mu Stream Village - Chen Jia Stream (陈家溪) - Youshui River Boat Ride (酉水行船) - Fenghuang Ancient Town (芙蓉镇)
Driving: 30km, 1 hour
Trekking: 12km, 4 hours
Boating: 3 hours

After breakfast, we'll trek through Chen Jia Stream. After lunch, we'll switch to a small vehicle to Fengtan Pier (凤滩码头, Fèng Tān Mǎtóu), then take a boat down the Youshui River for about 3 hours until we reach Hibiscus Ancient Town (芙蓉镇, Fúróng Zhèn) for overnight stay.

In the evening, we'll enjoy a night tour of the town.

Day4 Fenghuang Ancient Town - Zuolong Gorge (坐龙峡) - Wild Mountain Cave Exploration (野山洞探秘) - Yongshun (永顺)
Driving: 95km, 2 hours
Trekking: 6km, 5 hours

After breakfast, we'll head to Zuolong Gorge. We'll walk between the steep cliffs of the canyon, traversing wooden plank roads, jumping and crouching passages, stone paths, and iron ladders, experiencing the thrilling "China's First Special Trail."

We'll return to Hibiscus Ancient Town for lunch, then explore Wild Mountain Cave in the afternoon before heading to Yongshun for overnight accommodation.

Day5 Yongshun - Binglang Valley (槟榔谷) - Zhangjiajie (张家界)
Driving: 125km, 3 hours
Trekking: 7km, 4 hours

After breakfast, we'll drive to the outdoor paradise of Binglang Valley, and today is the highlight of our trekking journey. Today's itinerary combines cave exploration, canyon hiking, and rock climbing in one, giving you a comprehensive experience of outdoor fun.

The 800-meter Lost Cave exploration will be the most exciting and interesting part. After the activities, we'll drive to Zhangjiajie for overnight accommodation.

Day6 Zhangjiajie - Xingde Mountain (星德山) - Changsha
Driving: 370km, 6 hours
Trekking: 5km, 550m ascent, 3 hours

After breakfast, we'll head to Xingde Mountain to challenge a less-traveled hiking trail.

After descending, we'll drive back to Changsha where the trip concludes.

Important Notes

● Best Season: April to October
● Suitable For: Healthy individuals aged 8-65 years
● Potential Risks: The road is slippery when it rains, so please take care and stay safe.

1

42. Three Gorges Red Leaves

6days

33km

[三峡红叶, Sānxiá Hóngyè]

Yichang
[宜昌, Yíchāng]
Gathering City

11KM
Longest Single-Day Hike

400M
Maximum Daily Elevation Gain

1,370M
Highest Elevation Along the Route

★★★★⯪
Scenic Rating

★★
Difficulty Level

The Three Gorges has inspired countless literary tributes throughout history. Without visiting the Three Gorges, how could one truly understand Li Bai's poetic line "At dawn I bid farewell to Baidi amidst colorful clouds" or appreciate the exhilaration of "In a light boat, I've already passed thousands of mountains"?

The Yangtze Three Gorges is world-renowned for its "majestic, extraordinary, perilous, and beautiful" natural scenery. The red leaves of the Three Gorges form China's largest red-leaf area, boasting the most varieties and the longest viewing period. During autumn and winter, red becomes the dominant color of the Three Gorges. The round leaves of the Chinese sumac, scattered throughout the region, turn red after the first frost—the heavier the frost, the more intense the color—creating a viewing period that can last up to three months.

Stretching from Baidi City in Fengjie in the west to Yichang in the east, entering the Three Gorges is like stepping into a living scroll painting, where the red leaves set against the backdrop of mountains and waters create a breathtaking contrast.

Natural Features

Every autumn, countless visitors flock to the Three Gorges to witness the splendor of the red leaves. Walking through this vibrant landscape, they experience a striking contrast between the rugged grandeur of the gorges and the soft beauty of the autumn foliage. Intimate encounters with orange trees, red flowers, and crimson leaves captivate the senses, leaving visitors enchanted and reluctant to leave.

Why not embark on a light trek in the heart region of the Three Gorges? Experience the feast of red leaves covering the mountains through outdoor exploration, and immerse yourself in the rich Ba-Chu cultural heritage along the way.

The Three Gorges trek was once one of the most famous and classic hiking routes in China. While many believe its prominence waned due to the construction of the Three Gorges Dam, it now reveals its irresistible autumn charm in a new light. Here, the rugged gorges and the vibrant red leaves beautifully complement each other. As you trek, one side unveils the grandeur of the gorges, while the other offers the soft, serene essence of autumn, leaving visitors mesmerized and reluctant to leave.

During our trek, we will follow the Goddess Highway (神女天路, Shénnǚ Tiānlù), circling around the peak of Wu Gorge (巫峡, Wūxiá) and the western bank of Goddess Stream (神女溪, Shénnǚ Xī). Above Wu Gorge, mist drifts ethereally, with several classic viewing platforms scattered along the route. From these spots, you can watch Yangtze River cruise ships glide slowly below, while steep mountain slopes plunge sharply into the water. Patches of red leaves blanket the lush mountain walls, enveloping the surroundings in a vibrant autumn atmosphere.

Qutang Gorge (瞿塘峡, Qūtáng Xiá) has served as the gateway to the Three Gorges since the antient time. Within the gorge, the opposing White Salt Mountain (白盐山, Báiyán Shān) to the north and Red Armor Mountain (赤甲山, Chìjiǎ Shān) to the south form a naturally imposing gate called "Kuimen" (夔门, Kuímén). These two peaks are the highest in the Three Gorges and are known as the "Peaks of the Three Gorges." Nearby, a riverside walking path offers views of Qutang Gorge and Kuimen. The paths on both banks are connected by water, forming a classic hiking route that stretches for dozens of kilometers. This section of the trail is considered the most beautiful part of the Three Gorges red leaves route, with mountain paths entirely blanketed in red leaves, providing a stunning visual feast.

During the Three Gorges journey, there is also a cultural landmark you can't miss—the renowned Baidi City (白帝城, Báidì Chéng). Located on the northern bank of the Yangtze River at the entrance to Qutang Gorge, it is surrounded by water on all sides. Famous poets throughout Chinese history, such as Li Bai, Du Fu, Bai Juyi, Liu Yuxi, Su Shi, and Lu You, all visited Baidi City and Kuimen, leaving behind a vast collection of poems.

When trekking in the Three Gorges, in addition to the visual splendor of red leaves, you shouldn't miss the unique flavors of Wushan (巫山, Wūshān). The journey begins in Yichang, Hubei Province, from where we drive all the way to Chongqing. The trekking activities over the following days will focus around Wushan and Fengjie. Wushan grilled fish is regarded as the birthplace of all grilled fish recipes in China, and its flavor here is the most authentic, with a culinary tradition spanning over 1,700 years.

Another local specialty is the Zigui navel orange (秭归脐橙, Zǐguī qíchéng). These oranges are large, seedless, and have thin skin, vibrant color, a rich aroma, and a sweet flavor—once tasted, they're impossible to forget.

Notable Attractions

1 Qutang Gorge
[瞿塘峡, Qútáng Xiá]

Stretching from Baidi Mountain in Fengjie County to Daxi Township in Wushan County, this section spans 8 kilometers—though the shortest of the Three Gorges, it is the most awe-inspiring and steep. The banks rise in sheer, towering cliffs, with the mighty river surging through these narrow, jagged walls.

This dramatic stretch of water has earned the ancient praise:"Nothing is more dangerous than Jianmen Pass, nothing more majestic than Kuimen Gate."Here, the river narrows to a mere 100 meters wide, forming a sharp bend that accelerates the currents to a rapid, thunderous flow.

2 Wu Gorge
[巫峡, Wūxiá]

The beauty of Wushan lies in the majestic mountains that flank Wu Gorge, the serene tranquility along Goddess Stream, the untamed allure of the Lesser Three Gorges, and the striking contrast of towering gorges and peaceful lakes.

The scenery of Wushan's gorges is simply mesmerizing—one can't help but wish that the Goddess herself would visit their dreams tonight.

3 Wenfeng Pagoda
[文峰塔, Wénfēng Tǎ]

Located on Wenfeng Mountain, the structure was originally built to address the dangerous whirlpools created by the swift currents of the Sichuan River, which often engulfed passing boats, leading to property damage and loss of life. Therefore, a "Water-Calming Pagoda" was built to bless the safety of passing vessels.

Today, the once turbulent waters at the mouth of Wu Gorge have become gentle and peaceful, and the "Water-Calming Pagoda" has been renamed "Wenfeng Pagoda."

Itinerary

Day1 Gather in Yichang (宜昌)

Day2 Yichang - Wushan (巫山) - Wenfeng Taoist Temple (文峰观) - Wushan
Driving: 230km, 4 hours
Trekking: 6km, 4 hours

After breakfast, we depart from Yichang and drive to the Wenfeng Taoist Temple in Wushan for hiking. Standing at the summit, you can admire the spectacular view where the emerald river and red-leaved mountains illuminate each other magnificently. The red leaves follow the ridge lines, creating beautiful forms.

Looking down through the fiery red leaves at the Rainbow Bridge at the mouth of Wu Gorge, you'll appreciate how "a bridge connects the north and south, turning a natural barrier into a thorough-fare." In the evening, we check into a hotel in Wushan.

Day3 Wushan - Goddess Highway (神女天路) - Yaotai Flying Phoenix Peak (瑶台飞凤峰) - Wushan
Trekking: 8km, 5 hours

After breakfast, we drive to the Goddess Highway in Wushan and follow an extraordinarily scenic route, walking among the brilliant red foliage. The Goddess Highway is located at the top of Wu Gorge, facing Goddess Peak directly. The road here is flat and wide with no public vehicles, allowing you to take photographs while walking.

Along the way, we'll reach the Yaotai Flying Phoenix Peak observation deck to appreciate the magnificent scenery of Wu Gorge. In the evening, we take a boat back to our hotel in Wushan.

Day4 Wushan - Three Gorges Peak (三峡之巅) - Baidi City (白帝城)
Trekking: 11km, 1100m ascent, 6 hours

After breakfast, we take a boat to Wushan County, then drive to the Three Gorges Peak Scenic Area for hiking. Standing at the peak of the Three Gorges, we overlook the magnificent Yangtze River and the red leaves covering the mountains.

Afterward, we descend from the Three Gorges peak, following the Perilous Rock Bird Path (危石鸟道, Wēishí Niǎodào), Poetic Plank Road (诗意栈道, Shīyì Zhàndào), and Heavenly Sound Divine Path (天音神道, Tiānyīn Shéndào) down to Baidi City. We stay overnight in Baidi City.

Day5 Baidi City - White Salt Mountain (白盐山) - First Village of the Three Gorges (三峡第一村) - Yichang
Trekking: 8km, 5 hours

After breakfast, we head to the ancient town of Kuizhou (夔州, Kuízhōu). Upon reaching the pier, we board a boat that will take us to the starting point of our trek. We'll hike along the plank roads clinging to the steep cliffs of Kuimen, crossing White Salt Mountain and passing through the First Village of the Three Gorges, where we'll stop for a brief rest.

In the afternoon, we take a boat through the breathtaking Qutang Gorge. Once the day's activities come to an end, we drive back to Yichang.

Day6 Departure from Yichang

Important Notes
- Best Season: November to December
- Suitable For: Healthy individuals aged 8-65 years
- Potential Risks: Cliff sections, be cautious of falling.

43. Enshi Trek

[恩施徒步, Ēnshī Túbù]

6days
36km

Enshi
[恩施, Ēnshī]
Gathering City

10KM
Longest Single-Day Hike

600M
Maximum Daily Elevation Gain

1,600M
Highest Elevation Along the Route

★★★★☆
Scenic Rating

★★★
Difficulty Level

Near 30° North latitude, the Earth is home to numerous breathtaking wonders. For example, China's Qiantang River tidal bore, the Hanging Gardens of Babylon in Iraq, the Dead Sea in Jordan, the Bermuda Islands in the Caribbean, and even the ancient Mayan ruins—all of these remarkable landscapes lie along or near this latitude. When this mystical 30°North crosses through Hubei Province in China, nature creates a paradise, blending together sinkholes, underground rivers, fissures, grand canyons, and the legends of the Tujia people into one mesmerizing landscape. This paradise is Enshi (恩施, Ēnshī).

As the only ethnic minority autonomous prefecture in Hubei Province, Enshi is located at the intersection of Hubei, Hunan, and Chongqing. Despite being nestled between the two "furnace cities" of Wuhan and Chongqing, Enshi enjoys mild winters and cool summers, with forest coverage exceeding 70%. Surrounded by high mountains and deep valleys, this remote region is known for its simple folk customs and is celebrated as one of the most livable areas for people.

This small city isn't very large, covering just 2,995 square kilometers. The ceaselessly flowing Qingjiang River (清江, Qīng Jiāng) has carved out cliff faces as if cut by knives and axes. The unique cultural charm of this place has nurtured generations of Tujia people.

Natural Features

People often say that days spent in Enshi feel like floating in the sky—carefree and serene. Spring brings the scent of wild vegetables and fresh tea leaves; summer rains never lose their charm; deep autumn unveils the mesmerizing sight of red metasequoia trees, alongside local girls with equally rosy cheeks; and winter delights with cedar-smoked cured meats—all reflecting the simple, everyday beauty of life. The grandeur of the ancient Tujia town opens a gateway to history for future generations. Stilt houses (吊脚楼, diàojiǎolóu) are the iconic symbol of this region, while the bowl-breaking wine ceremony (摔碗酒, shuāi wǎn jiǔ) and the hand-waving dance (摆手舞, bǎishǒu wǔ) add a layer of enchanting mystery to the cultural fabric.

The charm of Enshi is worth exploring time and time again. Why not trek through this mysterious paradise along the 30th parallel north to witness the most authentic side of Enshi? Outdoor enthusiasts visiting Enshi must explore the Qingjiang Ancient Riverbed (清江古河床, Qīngjiāng Gǔhéchuáng). Though the hiking distance along the ancient riverbed isn't long, the journey is filled with thrilling and exciting. Afterward, one can visit the Enshi Grand Canyon (恩施大峡谷, Ēnshī Dàxiágǔ). There, geological features such as sinkholes, ground fissures, sheer cliffs, peak clusters, stone pillar groups, caves, and underground rivers can all be found, earning it the nickname "Natural Museum of Karst Landforms." Fifteen years ago, a joint Chinese-French expedition team came to Enshi and unexpectedly discovered this breathtakingly beautiful grand canyon among the towering mountains. National Geographic magazine described it as "a place that intoxicates even casual visitors." Here, you'll find the "Yunlong Ground Fissure" (云龙地缝, Yúnlóng Dìfèng), known as "Earth's most beautiful scar," and "Yizhuxiang" (一炷香, Yīzhùxiāng), rated by CNN as one of 40 most beautiful attraction in China. Famous architecture professor Zhang Lianggao once called it "the Colorado of the East"...

Cultural Significance

When visiting Enshi, besides experiencing its natural landscapes carved by divine craftsmanship, Tujia culture is a must-experience. If summarized in three elements, they would be: drinking, eating, and watching performances.

The replica ancient buildings and stilt houses in Enshi are truly distinctive. Every stone, brick, and wooden eave embodies a cultural symbol unique to the region. The streets are well-connected, lined with restaurants, teahouses, snack streets, and bars. Due to its proximity to Chongqing and Sichuan, the first defining feature of Enshi cuisine is its bold spiciness. The second characteristic, shaped by the concentration of various ethnic minorities such as the Tujia, Miao, and Dong peoples, is its authenticity, deeply rooted in the customs and traditions of these communities.

2

Enshi's outdoor routes are divided into the classic version and the "Hiking Festival" version. The classic route is a 5-day, 4-night loop that covers all the must-see scenic spots, with a total hiking distance of 24 kilometers. It's designed to be suitable for everyone, from 7-year-old children to 65- year-old seniors. The Hiking Festival route, on the other hand, takes visitors around the Grand Canyon, offering stunning views of the majestic karst landforms from unique angles, without entering the traditional Grand Canyon scenic area. We've specifically chosen two challenging hiking routes that are less crowded but offer breathtaking scenery. This route avoids large crowds, provides relief from the heat, showcases the natural beauty of the area, and offers an enriching cultural experience.

3

Notable Attractions

1 Qingjiang Ancient Riverbed

[清江古河床, Qīngjiāng Gǔhéchuáng]

Located in Lichuan City, Hubei, it is the remains left after the Qingjiang River, the mother river of Enshi, changed its course. Stretching 8 kilometers, it features typical karst topography. Within it, you'll find primitive forests, high mountain grasslands, thousand-meter cliffs, beautiful river valleys, dry riverbeds, as well as scree slopes and collapsed boulder formations.

There are unique landscapes like caves within caves, connected cave systems, mountains within caves, and caves within mountains, as if entering a prehistoric wilderness, allowing people to experience unique charm in a disorienting world.

As it remains undeveloped, the area still retains its relatively pristine natural features and is known as "Lichuan's most beautiful outdoor hiking route."

2 Luyuanping

[鹿院坪, Lùyuànpíng]

During the "Huguang Fills Sichuan" migration movement of the late Ming and early Qing dynasties, the Pei Kesong brothers from Changde, Hunan, moved to Xintian in Enshi. While searching for a place to plant Hunan rice, they were led to the foot of a cliff by a group of beautiful mountain deer and successfully planted rice and oil tea there. Their descendants later settled in there, multiplying and thriving. This traditional village, with its connection to "deer," is currently the only village in Enshi without road access. It is a real-life utopia, featuring stilt houses, waterfalls, terraced fields, and simple folk customs.

With an average elevation of 1,700 meters and a vertical drop of over 500 meters, about five square kilometers of flat land is surrounded by steep mountains on all sides, resembling a huge elongated "sinkholes" (天坑).

Itinerary

Day1 Gather in Enshi (恩施)

Day2 Enshi - Chao Dong Yan (朝东岩) - Grand Canyon - Mufu Ancient Town (沐扶古镇)
Driving: 90km, 2 hours
Trekking: 10km, 500m ascent, 6 hours

Today's highlight is the Chao Dong Yan trek. The route winds through numerous mountain paths and cliffside plank roads, offering breathtaking and dramatic scenery that makes the journey both exciting and thrilling. We will progress at a steady pace, prioritizing safety.

When navigating the more perilous sections, we will hold onto the iron chains, refrain from taking photos, and pass under the careful guidance and protection of our guide.

Day3 Mufu Ancient Town - Qingjiang Ancient Riverbed (清江古河床) - Mufu Ancient Town
Driving: 100km, 2 hours
Trekking: 10km, 700m ascent, 5 hours

Today, we head to the Qingjiang Ancient Riverbed for a hike, a location that has served as the backdrop for multiple TV dramas.

With its primitive caves, ancient villages, and impressive boulder formations, the area offers a sense of occasional disorientation and delightful surprises. It feels as though you're stepping through a portal in time.

Day4 Mufu Ancient Town - Dashandingchaotiansun (大山顶朝天笋)- Luyuanping (鹿院坪)
Driving: 35km, 1 hours
Trekking: 8km, 450m ascent, 5 hours

Today, we head to Dashanding for a hike, traversing canyons and pristine forests. Along the way, we'll encounter the unique Chaotiansun

(sky-reaching bamboo shoot) landscape formation. From the peak of Dashanding, we'll have a stunning view of the Enshi Grand Canyon and Chao Dong Yan in the distance.

After our hike, we'll drive to Luyuanping, a remote sinkhole village without road access, where we'll descend over 1,700 steps to reach this hidden gem.

Day5 Luyuanping (鹿院坪) - Xuanlu Ground Fissure (玄鹿地缝) - Hundred-Year-Old Bridge - Damiao Village (大庙村) - Enshi
Driving: 90km, 2 hours
Trekking: 8km, 600m ascent, 6 hours

Today we will trek through Luyuanping, a primitive village connected with "deer." We'll first thoroughly explore the exquisite beauty of "Xuanlu Ground Fissure," the four-tiered waterfall, "Water Curtain Cave," and other stunning sights.

Afterward, we'll embark on the most primitive outdoor hiking route here, climbing upward, passing through ground fissures, dense forests, ancient bridges, and more. After the trek, we'll drive back to Enshi.

Day6 Enshi - Dixingu (地心谷) - Enshi
Driving: 200km, 4 hours
Sightseeing: 3.5 hours

Today, our journey will be relatively relaxed and leisurely. After breakfast, we'll drive for 2 hours to Dixingu, a geological wonder formed 250 million years ago during the Triassic period, hidden between deep canyons and steep cliffs, known as "China's First Natural Barrier".

Around noon, we'll leave the scenic area for lunch, after which we'll return to Enshi, marking the successful conclusion of our trip.

Important Notes

- Best Season: June to October
- Suitable For: Healthy individuals aged 10-65 years
- Potential Risks: Some sections are cliff paths, those with a fear of heights should carefully consider participation. Please prioritize safety when passing through these areas.

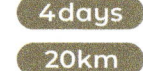

44. Shennongjia Trek
[神农架徒步, Shénnóngjià Túbù]

4days

20km

Yichang
[宜昌, Yíchāng]
Gathering City

8KM
Longest Single-Day Hike

400M
Maximum Daily Elevation Gain

2,597M
Highest Elevation Along the Route

★★★
Scenic Rating

★★★
Difficulty Level

Shennongjia (神农架, Shénnóngjià) is a true primeval forest bearing historical traces of the ancient Shennong travels. Its main peak, "Shennong Peak" (神农顶, Shénnóng Dǐng), stands at 3,105.4 meters high and is traditionally known as the "Roof of Central China." Its unique geographical environment and location have made it a refuge for many plant and animal species, helping them survive the Quaternary glaciation period.

Shennongjia was recognized as a Global Geopark in 2013, and in July 2016, it was officially inscribed on the World Heritage List, becoming the only UNESCO "Triple Crown" heritage site in China. The UNESCO World Heritage Committee praised it: "Hubei Shennongjia preserves the largest primeval forest in central China and is one of the three regions with the richest biodiversity in China; it possesses the world's most complete vertical natural spectrum, providing habitat for numerous rare animals and plants, and is the original habitat for widely introduced horticultural species around the world."

Natural Features
Legend says that Shennong (the Yan Emperor) came here to collect medicinal herbs, and despite his great powers, he could not climb the steep cliffs. So he built 36 ladders to finally reach the peak surrounded by towering cliffs. Since then,

this place has been called "Shennongjia" (meaning "Shennong's Ladders"). With its well-preserved subtropical forest ecosystem, extremely rare species, and multiple unique landscape features, Shennongjia is also known as the "Mysterious Green Kingdom of Central China."

In addition to the legend of Shennong, its mysterious character is also attributed to the "Wild Man" legend. What is the "Wild Man"? Does such a species really exist in this world? The so-called "Wild Man" is a folk name for an unknown animal in the forests of Shennongjia and many other regions. Legend has it that people have seen "Wild Men" in the deep forests of Shennongjia—tall beings that resemble humans but are not human, who can walk upright but cannot straighten their backs like humans.

While spring in most parts of China typically begins in February and ends around the Qingming Festival, spring in Shennongjia arrives leisurely in May. The alpine rhododendrons of Shennongjia represent the most concentrated rhododendron resource in central China, with the most primitive rhododendron populations and native rhododendron forests. There are 35 species of rhododendrons, earning it the title "Home of Alpine Rhododendrons."

Within the 3,253-square-kilometer area of Shennongjia, there are countless traversing routes. The Laojun Mountain (老君山, Lǎojūn Shān) small loop is one of the most classic routes with the most beautiful scenery. We will trek 3 days, totally 21 kilometers to reach the summits of Laojun Mountain with two nights of camping. This is a genuine traverse through an uninhabited area that has never been developed. The trekking route involves the core of the Shennongjia Nature Reserve. The surrounding areas see very few human visitors, and progress is only possible under

the guidance of local guides, making it a rare outdoor experience.

The primeval forest of Laojun Mountain is located northeast of Shennongjia's main peak and is named after the legend that the ancient Taoist deity Taishang Laojun once practiced alchemy here. Laojun Mountain stands at 2,936 meters high. From its summit to its base, ten prominent mountain ridges descend like plunging dragons, with nine winding streams flowing between the ridges like silver belts. On both sides of the ridges, ancient trees grow densely, medicinal herbs spread out, wild fruits hang abundantly, and wild animals occasionally appear.

In autumn, small streams converge in the vast golden forest. Entering the forest, you'll step on thick, soft meadows, traverse between mountains, and wind along alpine meadows, as the most mysterious beautiful scenery of Shennongjia gradually unfolds before you. Upon reaching the summit of Laojun Mountain, you'll see layers of peaks rolling with flowing clouds. Open your arms and fully enjoy this moment!

2

Itinerary

Day1 Gather in Yichang (宜昌)

Day2 Yichang - Muyu (木鱼) - Caiqi Protection Station (彩旗保护站) - Yunpan Forest Station (云盘护林站) - Camp1
Driving: 180km, 6 hours
Trekking: 6km, 400m ascent, 300m descent, 3 hours

After breakfast, we depart from Yichang, and arrive at Muyu Town in about 4 hours. We then switch to small vehicles to enter the mountains, reaching the starting point of our trek in about 2 hours. Then, we officially begin our mysterious journey through this uninhabited area! We climb upward to reach Camp 1, then pass through City Wall Rock (城墙岩, Chéngqiáng Yán) to summit Laojun Mountain (altitude 3,000m). After a brief rest at the summit, we descend and return to Camp 1, where our guides will have prepared dinner for us.

After having dinner, everyone can play small games on the large meadow and fall asleep under the starry sky.

Day3 Camp 1 - Laojun Fortress (老君寨) - Cijian Pass (刺剑垭) - Laojun Cave (老君洞) - Camp 2 (1,600 m)
Trekking: 9km, 300m ascent, 650m descent, 7 hours

Weather permitting, we'll rise early to capture the breathtaking sunrise. Shennong Peak, the roof of Central China, stands majestically opposite. After breakfast, we pack up and head out.

Today's trek won't involve much elevation gain, and we'll spend most of the time walking through alpine meadows.

Along the way, we may catch glimpses of wildlife—antelope, tufted deer, and wild boars leave traces in the terrain.

We'll climb to the summit of Laojun Fortress, reaching an altitude of approximately 2,900 meters, before beginning our descent. The route takes us through some of the most pristine forests in the region, eventually leading us to Camp 2, where we'll set up camp for the night.

Day4 Camp 2 - Turtle Gorge (乌龟峡) - Black Water River (黑水河) - Caiqi Protection Station (彩旗保护站) - Yichang
Trekking: 6km, 320m descent, 3 hours
Driving: 180km, 4 hours

After breakfast, we depart on schedule, following the Black Water River (named for its dark waters that flow deep in the gorge, never seeing daylight, creating the eerie sensation of nighttime even in daylight). We trek downstream to the river's base before beginning the ascent to Snake Head Ridge (蛇头岭, Shétóu Lǐng).

From there, we cross the mountain range to reach the Caiqi Protection Station within the reserve. Finally, we drive back to Muyu, transfer to a bus, and make our way back to Yichang, bringing our unforgettable journey to a close.

Important Notes

- Best Season: April to November
- Suitable For: Healthy individuals aged 10-65 years
- Potential Risks: 1. The climate in Shennongjia can be unpredictable, so it's important to pack waterproof and warm clothing.
  2. Be cautious of slippery paths, especially when it rains.

PART 5

NORTHEAST

China Region

45. Autumn Scenaries of Changbai Mountains

19km/7days [长白山秋色,Chángbái shān qiūsè]

Changchun
[长春, Chángchūn]
Gathering City

8KM
Longest Single-Day Hike

300M
Maximum Daily Elevation Gain

2,600M
Highest Elevation Along the Route

★★★★★
Scenic Rating

★★
Difficulty Level

Credit
Image 1 | ©Majun
Image 2 | ©Kangaroo
Image 3 | ©RK

Changbai Mountain (长白山, Chángbái Shān), as renowned as the Five Great Mountains of China, stands as the premier mountain in Northeastern China. It is also the region's most iconic scenic destination and serves as the natural border between China and North Korea. The main peak reaches an altitude of 2,691 meters.

The Tianchi Lake (天池, Tiān Chí), also known as "Heavenly Lake," takes the mountain's center stage. Majestic and pristine, it is surrounded by sixteen peaks arranged in a formation that resembles stars encircling the moon. With white clouds reflected in its azure blue waters and the clear sky above, the scene creates a breathtaking harmony that captivates all who behold it.

The Tianchi Lake is the highest volcanic crater lake in the world. Due to its high latitude and the elevation of surrounding mountains, the lake remains covered by ice and snow for nearly nine months of the year. From July to mid-October, spring, summer, and autumn seem to alternate at the speed of light, as if time has been accelerated in this place.

The autumn sceneries are not to be missed. Changbai Mountain is divided into four slopes—North, South, West, and East—with the North, South, and West slopes belonging to China and the East slope within the territory of North Korea. Tianchi Lake is visible from the North, South, and West slopes. In autumn, beneath clear skies and scattered clouds, the mountains unfold a vibrant tapestry of colors, while the sapphire lake sparkles like a crystal, its surface dazzling in the sunlight.Throughout the journey, visitors are greeted by sturdy pine trees, roaring waterfalls, steep gorges, and cinstently shifting landscape with each step.

The journey to Tianchi Lake is an exhilarating adventure in itself, with reaching the summit to behold the lake requiring a touch of good fortune. While it's often said that "nine out of ten days are cloudy," even in rainy weather, the clouds often miraculously part for a few moments, offering visitors a fleeting glimpse of the lake. The views from the North, South, and West slopes each present a unique and captivating perspective of the landscape.

On the North Slope, in addition to the coveted view of Tianchi Lake at the summit, visitors can explore four other renowned attractions: a rich variety of scenic beauty offered by vertical climate zones, hot springs rich in hydrogen sulfide and various microelements, the majestic Changbai Mountain Waterfall, and Tianchi Lake, where many people believe mythical creatures lie hidden. Visitors can also appreciate the elegance of Beauty Pine trees, the magnificence of the Underground Forest, the tranquility of Small Tianchi, and the serenity of Green Deep Pool Waterfull (绿渊潭, Lǜ Yuān Tán), among other pristine natural landscapes.

The South Slope of Tianchi Lake was the last untouched ares of Changbai Mountain until August 6, 2018, when it was officially opened to the public. Its landscape remains largely pristine, offering broader views, but it also features a more fragile ecosystem. Therefore, the South Slope is open only from July to October each year, with a daily limit of 1,000 tickets available by advance reservation, making it a rare privilege to witness. Vehicles can drive directly to the summit of Crown Peak, which is only 314 meters above the lake's surface. From the summit, visitors can have a bird's-eye view of crescent-shaped lake. On clear days, the entire panorama of Tianchi Lake unfolds, unobstructed by any surrounding peaks. In the distance, visitors can also spot the No. 4 border marker between China and North Korea, along with border guards. Besides Tianchi Lake, the "Erman's birch Double Waterfalls" (岳桦双瀑, Yuè Huà Shuāng Pù) is another must-see attraction. The secondary waterfall, nestled amidst dense Erman's birch forests, offers a tranquil and serene atmosphere, presenting a spectacular view when the forests are ablaze with autumn colors.

The North Slope offers classic and varied views， while the South Slope provides pristine landscapes with limites access. However, the West Slope provides perhaps the best perspective of Tianchi Lake. From the West Slope, Tianchi Lake appears vast and radiant, with the surrounding mountain slopes seeming more gradual, as if gently shaped by the tranquil waters of the lake.

2

Itinerary

Day1 Gather in Changchun (长春)

Day2 Changchun - Canyon Stream - Erdao-baihe Town (二道白河镇)
Driving: 6 hours | Trekking: 4km, 3 hours

After breakfast, we will depart from Changchun City by vehicle and head towards Changbai Mountain. We will begin our adventure with stream trekking through the stunning Pumice Forest Canyon (长白山浮石林峡谷, Chángbái Shān Fú Shí Lín Xiá Gǔ).

Afterward, we will continue to Erdaobaihe Town, renowned as the "Home of Beauty Pine."

Day3 Erdaobaihe Town - Changbai Mountain North Slope Scenic Area (长白山北景区) - Erdaobaihe Town
Driving: 70km, 1 hour

After breakfast, we will depart by vehicle for the North Slope Scenic Area of Changbai Mountain. Upon arrival, we will transfer to environmentally friendly shuttle buses to explore Tianchi Lake (长白山天池, Chángbái Shān Tiān Chí), Changbai Waterfall (长白瀑布, Chángbái Pùbù), Green Deep Pool (绿渊潭, Lǜ Yuān Tán), Small Tianchi Lake (小天池, Xiǎo Tiān Chí), and Underground Forest (地下森林, Dì Xià Sēn Lín) in sequence.

After the tour, we will return to Erdaobaihe Town by bus.

Day4 Erdaobaihe Town - Primeval Forest - Donggang Town (东岗镇)
Driving: 180km, 3 hours
Trekking: 5km, 300m ascent, 4 hours

After breakfast, we will depart by vehicle for the pristine Changbai Mountain Forest. We will start the day with a hike to Red Stone Peak (红石峰, Hóng Shí Fēng), surrounded by vast stretches of maples, offering a breathtaking panorama. Following the hike, we will enjoy an exhilarating rafting experience on the Changbai Mountain rivers.

Later, we will follow a "Lao Ba Tou" (local ginseng master) for a deep dive into the forest, where we'll learn about the customs of ginseng harvesting, the worship of mountain gods, and the techniques involved in collecting this precious root. We will even have the chance to try harvesting it ourselves.

Day5 Donggang Town - Changbai Mountain South or West Slope Scenic Area (长白山南/西景区) - China-North Korea Border Yalu River (鸭绿江) - Changbai County (长白县)
Driving: 130km, 3 hours

After breakfast, we will head to the southern slope of Changbai Mountain. If it's closed, we go to the western slope instead. In the afternoon, we will take a leisurely stroll along the country border of the Yalu River, enjoying distant views of North Korea across the water.

We will spend the night in Changbai County, located in the southeastern part of Jilin Province.

Day6 Changbai County - Alpine Meadow - Linjiang City (临江市)/Baishan City (白山市)
Driving: 180km, 3 hours
Trekking: 5km, 2 hours

After breakfast, we will drive to the trailhead of the alpine medaow and begin our ascent along a winding mountain path. While ascending the mountain, you can observe the meandering Yalu River flowing westward like a blue ribbon. The panoramic view extends across the border into North Korea, allowing you to appreciate the landscape of a neighboring country.

On the alpine meadows, cattle and sheep graze leisurely beneath the vast blue sky, while the autumn colors of the highland prairie create a scene as vibrant and serene as the Garden of Eden.

Day7 Linjiang City/Baishan City - Lao Tudingzi Mountain (老秃顶子山) - Changchun
Driving: 300km, 5 hours
Trekking: 5km, 4 hours

Today, we will embark on a hike through the pristine Lao Tudingzi Mountain forest, a remote and rarely visited region where towering peaks and dense forests create a breathtaking autumn landscape.

From the main summit of Lao Tudingzi Mountain, panoramic views unfold, with Changbai Mountain range stretching far into the horizon. After our hike, we will return to Changchun City by vehicle.

tips: If Lao Tudingzi Mountain is temporarily closed, we will hike in the nearby Red Leaf Valley (红叶谷, Hóng Yè Gǔ) instead.

Important Notes

- Best Season: September to October
- Suitable For: Healthy individuals aged 7-65 years
- Potential Risks: Weather conditions at Tianchi Lake is changeable, please prepare appropriate clothing for cold temperatures

1

46. Snowy Forest and Plains

[冬季林海雪原,Dōngjì lín hǎi xuě yuán]

`6days`
`38km`

Harbin
[哈尔滨, Hā'ěrbīn]
Gathering City

15KM
Longest Single-Day Hike

800M
Maximum Daily Elevation Gain

1,696M
Highest Elevation Along the Route

★★★★★
Scenic Rating

★★
Difficulty Level

As is well known, Northeast China boasts the largest forest area and the most concentrated woodland regions in the country. The mountains are adorned with rolling, dense forests that stretch from the foreground to the horizon. Autumn here is fleeting, and by October, the region transitions into a long winter, with vast forests and landscapes blanketed in snow, creating "Snowy Forest and Plains" (林海雪原, Lín Hǎi Xuě Yuán).

The Greater Khingan Mountains (大兴安岭, Dà Xīng'ān Lǐng), Lesser Khingan Mountains (小兴安岭, Xiǎo Xīng'ān Lǐng), Changbai Mountains (长白山, Chángbái Shān), and even Kanas (喀纳斯, Kā Nà Sī) across China's borders could all be considered part of the "Snowy Forest and Plains." This raises the question—where, exactly, can the Snowy Forest and Plains be found? Perhaps the answer lies in the classic Chinese novel <Snowy Forest and Plains>(《林海雪原》, Lín Hǎi Xuě Yuán) and the modern Beijing opera <Taking Tiger Mountain by Strategy> (《智取威虎山》, Zhì Qǔ Wēi Hǔ Shān).

In the winter of 1946, a small detachment from the Northeast Democratic United Army, led by regimental staff officer Shao Jianbo, ventured deep into the snowy forests and plains on a mission to eliminate a bandit group. Yang Zirong (杨子荣, Yáng Zǐróng), an intelligence hero, led his troops across forests and snowy plains, fighting the "Sitting Tiger" (座山雕, Zuò Shān Diāo) bandits of Tiger Mountain with remarkable wit and courage. The bandit suppression story depicted in the classic novel

"Snowy Forest and Plains" took place in Hailin City (海林市, Hǎi Lín Shì), Mudanjiang Prefecture, southeastern Heilongjiang Province. In the film adaptation <Taking Tiger Mountain by Strategy> directed by Xu Ke, the story of capturing "Sitting Tiger" also takes place in this region. Located on the southern slope of the Zhang Guangcai Range (张广才岭, Zhāng Guǎng Cái Lǐng), which is part of the Changbai Mountain range, this area has an average elevation higher than that of the surrounding regions.

Since October, cold fronts from Siberia in the north and warm, moist air currents from the Sea of Japan in the south frequently converge in this region, creating distinct mountain microclimates and leading to heavy snowfall. The winters here are exceptionally long, with the snow season lasting up to half the year. The snow is incredibly thick and fluffy, layering like cream atop a cake base. Due to its mountainous terrain, the region is often described as having "90% of its beauty in the mountains, 5% in the water, and 5% in the fields."

Qu Bo, the author of <Snowy Forest and Plains>, once said in an interview: "Standing atop a mountain and gazing down at the forest below, when the wind blows, the trees undulate like ocean waves–that's where the term 'Lin Hai' (referring to the vast forest) comes from; the snow blankets the endless plains–that's where 'Xue Yuan' (referring to the snowy plains) originates." And so, the name <Snowy Forest and Plains> was born.

The vast forests and snowy plains of Northeast China bear witness to the heroic legends of a detachment of the People's Liberation Army, who fought blood-soaked battles and strategically dismantled bandit strongholds.

Place names, such as Jiapi Gou (夹皮沟, Jiā Pí Gōu) and Wuhelou (五合楼, Wǔ Hé Lóu), as well as characters like Sitting Tiger and Xu Damabang, all from Heilongjiang province, became widely known to people through these stories.

Notable Attractions

1 Tiger Mountain
[威虎山, Wēi Hǔ Shān]

Nestled among the steep mountains of Hailin City in Mudanjiang Prefecture, Tiger Mountain features the typical rugged landscape of Northeast China. The Hailin mountain area, with its heavy snowfall and dense forests covering over 90% of the land, was once a notorious stronghold for bandits.

The route to eliminate these bandits is steeped in heroic legends. Stretching from a railway in the west to the headquarters of Jiapi Gou Forest Farm in the east, this was the only route in and out of the lair of 'Sitting Tiger,' whose grandfather and father were both infamous bandits. Yang Zirong, the intelligence hero, once infiltrated into the bandits' lair alone and captured 'Sitting Tiger' alive. Remnants of the battle still endure, including the Tiger Hall (威虎厅, Wēi Hǔ Tīng)

2 Phoenix Mountain
[凤凰山, Fèng Huáng Shān]

Phoenix Mountain, located in Wuchang City (五常市, Wǔ Cháng Shì), which is renowned for poducing premium rice, rises to an elevation of 1,696 meters, making it the highest peak in Heilongjiang Province.

As the highest summit of the Zhang Guangcai Range, it boasts vibrant Lapland rosebay in spring, serene and winding valleys with waterfalls in summer, brilliant crimson leaves in autumn, and dreamlike snow-covered landscapes in winter.

3 Rime Ridge
[雾凇岭, Wù Sōng Lǐng]

Rime Ridge, also known as 'Winnowing Basket Lowland' (簸箕崴子, Bò Ji Wǎi Zi), derives its name from the winnowing basket shape of its terrain. 'Bò Qí' refers to the winnowing basket, while 'Waizi' is a Northeast dialect term for a low-lying area between two mountains, similar to a lowland.

This dialectical name vividly captures the features of the region, offering a distinctly Northeast flavor that is both unique and intriguing to visitors. The area's distinctive mountain terrain and humid climate contribute to an annual snowfall that exceeds 170 days, making it one of the snowiest regions in China.

Itinerary

Day1 Gather in Harbin (哈尔滨)

Day2 Harbin - Longjiang Main Peak (龙江主峰) - Northeast Folk Village (东北民俗村)
Driving: 5 hours | Trekking: 2km, 1 hours

After breakfast, we will drive to the Longjiang Main Peak to experience hiking through a snow-covered valley, giving you a first taste of trekking in the high mountains. You'll be captivated by the small streams blanketed in white snow, ice waterfalls cascading down cliffs, and rime frost stretching along the path.

Afterward, we'll head to the Northeast Folk Village, where you can try your hand at paper-cutting, enjoy frozen pears, and have fun with ice sleds and sledges on the frozen surface.

Day3 Northeast Folk Village - Longjiang Main Peak Phoenix Mountain(龙江主峰凤凰山 1,696m) - Dongsheng Snow Valley (东升雪谷)
Driving:3 hours
Trekking: 6km, 300m ascent, 3 hours

Today we will climb Phoenix Mountain, namely the Longjiang Main Peak, as we trekking through vast forest and snow-covered plains, with snow depths reaching up to one meter.

Along the route, hidden frozen springs lie tucked away, with icicles and cedars all around, creating the feeling of being in a magnificent winter wonderland.

After the hike, we'll travel by vehicle to Dongsheng Snow Valley, where we can dress in traditional local costumes, learn about the customs, and make dumplings together. Then, we'll light a bonfire and enjoy warm Chinese liquor beneath the twinkling starry sky.

Day4 Dongsheng Snow Valley - Yangcao Mountain (羊草山) - China Snow Village (中国雪乡)
Trekking: 15km, 800m ascent, 6 hours

This is a classic outdoor route, crossing from Snow Valley to Snow Village, as we hike through vast forests and snow-covered plains.

In the afternoon, we'll explore the Snow Village, and in the evening, you can join the parade and the lively dance party.

Day5 China Snow Village - Jingpo Lake (镜泊湖) Hiking on the Blue Ice- South Jingpo Lake - Hailin City (海林市)/Mudanjiang Prefecture (牡丹江市)
Driving: 4.5 hours | Trekking: 8km, 3 hours

Jingpo Lake is China's largest volcanic lava barrier lake, stretching 45 kilometers from north to south, and is famously known as the "Hundred-Mile-Long Lake."

In winter, the lake's surface freezes, creating one of China's most stunning blue ice landscapes. We'll embark on an 8-kilometer hike across its surface, with a chance to witness winter fishing, if we're lucky. Afterward, we will travel to either Hailin City or Mudanjiang Prefecture in southeastern Heilongjiang Province, where we will stay overnight.

Day6 Hailin City/Mudanjiang Prefecture - Yang Zirong Memorial Hall (杨子荣纪念馆) - Tiger Mountain (威虎山) - Yabuli Ski Resort (亚布力滑雪场)
Driving: 4.5 hours | Trekking: 7km, 3 hours

The Yang Zirong Memorial Hall marks the site where the heroic story of his fight against bandits took place.

At the hall, we'll relive the scenes of Yang Zirong, who disguised himself as a bandit, engaging in a battle of wits and courage with Sitting Tiger and his eight famous followers, known as the "Eight Golden Warriors." After the hike, we will head to Yabuli Ski Resort for an overnight stay.

Day7 Yabuli Ski Resort - New Sports Committee Ski Field- Harbin City
Driving: 3.5 hours | Skiing: 3 hours

Yabuli Ski Resort is renowned in China and is a paradise for ski enthusiasts from around the world. Whether you're a beginner or an experienced skier, you can enjoy an exhilarating snow adventure on slopes suited to all skill levels.

In the afternoon, we will conclude our journey and return to Harbin City by vehicle.

Important Notes
● Best Season: December to February of the following year
● Suitable For: Healthy individuals aged 8-65 years
● Potential Risks: Extremely cold weather,please ensure you have appropriate clothing to stay warm.

PART 6

SOUTH

China Region

47. Li River Trek

[漓江徒步, Lí Jiāng Túbù]

6days
54km

Guilin
[桂林, Guìlín]
Gathering City

16KM
Longest Single-Day Hike

600M
Maximum Daily Elevation Gain

1,100M
Highest Elevation Along the Route

★★★
Scenic Rating

★★
Difficulty Level

Credit
© All images in this piece
by RK

Speaking of Guilin, almost everyone knows it. Its significance for Chinese people is evident from the age-old saying "the landscape of Guilin is the finest under heaven" (桂林山水甲天下, Guìlín shānshuǐ jiǎ tiānxià). Even if you haven't been there, it feels familiar, as if embedded in your genetic memory.

More than two thousand years ago, the Qin Dynasty established Guilin Prefecture, which governed most area of Guangxi in present day. Starting from the Lingqu Canal, digged during the Han Dynasty, and going through Hepu to the sea, there was the bustling Maritime Silk Road, where vessels sailed in and out from all directions. Bordering Guangdong to the east and Yunnan to the west, Guangxi has long been overshadowed by these two popular tourist destinations, often lacking recognition of its own. In fact, considering its climate, topography, and cultural resources, Guangxi is a hidden gem. Unlike the harsh borderlands of Ningxia, Qinghai, and Jiangxi, or the more inland provinces, Guangxi lies at low latitudes, with the Tropic of Cancer crossing its central region. Endowed with a subtropical monsoon climate, the area enjoys a comfortable and pleasant environment, with average annual temperatures ranging from 17.5℃ to 23.5℃. Spring and summer bring abundant rainfall and sunshine, while autumn and winter are dry and warm, making it a highly desirable winter retreat.

Natural Features

As one of the best tourist cities in China recommended by the World Tourism Organization, Guilin has hosted nearly 200 heads of state and dignitaries. As one of China's representative destination, its reputation truly resonates worldwide. However, just as that household slogan feels outdated, Guilin has struggled to stand out among popular tourist destinations in recent years. Perhaps because of its decades- long fame, it seems as though everyone has already visited, leaving little that feels fresh or new. As a well-established destination, it has even become stereotypically regarded as "too commercialized and overdeveloped, having lost its original charm" due to its widespread recognition. But is that really the case? Has Guilin lost its appeal? Is it still worth visiting?

The answer is certainly YES. On the Li River, gentle waters flow through the city and around mountains, with continuous karst peaks winding along both banks. The water's surface reflects a beautiful ink painting scroll, slowly unfolding and flowing in front of your eyes. In the distance, mountain shadows appear faintly, as if delicately sketched in diluted ink. Nearby, the water's surface shimmers with ripples, so clear that the bottom is visible. The mountains and waters embrace one another, while the sounds of fishermen singing from their boats fill the air in the evening, amidst cloud reflections and glistening waves. This is the ultimate feast of breathtaking landscapes. The sounds of flowing water, mountain birds, and gentle breezes rustling through leaves intertwine, giving people an unprecedented sense of tranquility. It is almost synonymous with Chinese landscape and pastoral scenery, a poetic and classical moonlight in the hearts of Chinese people. Even after seeing many mountains and rivers, Guangxi's landscape can still bring the most primitive emotion from the depths of your heart.

Beyond that poetic sense, comfort and leisure are the most direct feelings Guilin gives people. There, one can feel infinitely close to the tranquility and peace of pure nature, as if time has stopped flowing. Walking on small paths between rice fields, fresh greenery carries hopes of harvest; looking up, karst peaks cluster together, light and shadows interplay on the river's surface, and people living here are nourished with inner abundance. The grandfather cutting hair beneath the large tree on the old street, the grandmother resting peacefully against the door with a fan, swallows neatly lined up on the electrical wires, a sky ablaze with the soft hues of the sunset at dusk, and an array of delicious, affordable food—these images transport one back to that summer in their twenties.

However, for outdoor enthusiasts, it is a pity if they don't venture into the mountains for wilderness exploration.

Trekking along the Li River is one of the best ways to experience the breathtaking beauty of Guilin's landscape. From Nine Horses Fresco Hill (九马画山, Jiǔmǎ Huàshān) to Yangdi (杨堤, Yángdī), the journey takes you through mountain trails, riverside paths, and riverbanks. Spending two days immersed in the Li River's most exquisite scenery feels like strolling through a living ink painting.

If the Li River and terraced fields are Guilin's visiting cards, then caves are secret gardens hidden underground. Stepping into a cave feels like crossing into another world. Seventy percent of China's karst landforms are located in Guangxi, and half of Guangxi's karst landforms are concentrated in the Guilin-Yangshuo area. Thus, Guilin has mountains everywhere, and every mountain has caves.

Entering the 1,150-meter-long Luotian Cave (罗田溶洞, Luótián Róngdòng), with its vast interior spanning over 50,000 square meters, offers a unique experience compared to developed scenic areas filled with artificial neon lights. This cave is little known, and thus more primitive and vibrant—exactly the kind of wild charm outdoor enthusiasts prefer most. Stone pillars, stalagmites, draperies, and flowers... stepping inside feels like entering a natural underground palace where millions of years of geological changes have showed silent stories.

Arriving in Yangshuo (阳朔, Yángshuò), visitors can not only enjoy the tranquility of the mountains and waters but also experience the thrill of ferrata climbing. The region's unique karst topography offers ideal conditions for rock climbing, with its steep and diverse rock faces drawing climbing enthusiasts from around the world.

Ferrata is a type of iron cable path fixed on rock faces that allows even non-professional climbers to experience the joy of climbing in safety. Under professional coaching guidance, after putting on safety equipment, you climb step by step along iron cables and pedals fixed on cliff edges, with each step bringing a sense of achievement.

Standing at a height, surrounded by layers of mountains, with the Li River, mountain ranges, and pastoral scenery stretching out before you, this experience is unmatched by any ground-level sightseeing. In that moment, all fatigue melts away, and all fear seems to vanish, as if the world has come to a standstill, leaving only you and the landscape, silently communicating with each other.

Additionally, at Nanyu Sinkholes (南圩天坑, Nánwéi Tiānkēng), you can experience the thrill of "cave traversing" and listen to the sounds of underground rivers. Here, caves, sinkholes, rocks, and subterranean rivers intertwine, preserving their pristine, untouched state. Outside the cave, dense trees line the path, allowing you to journey through a lush landscape of flora. This hidden paradise offers a perfect escape from holiday crowds, inviting you to embrace the serenity of nature.

In Guilin city and throughout Guangxi province, outdoor adventures await beyond your imagination. Each exploration offers a new way to rediscover this magical land. Whether you're seeking thrilling adventures or simply enjoying the tranquil beauty of nature, Guangxi is sure to surprise you with its hidden wonders.

Itinerary

Day1 Gather in Guilin (桂林)

Day2 Guilin - Longsheng Dazhai Village (龙胜大寨) - Xiaozhai (小寨) - Dazhai
Driving: 110km, 2.5 hours
Trekking: 10km, 400m ascent/desent, 5 hours

After breakfast, we drive to the Longji Rice Terraces Scenic Area in Longsheng. Upon arrival, we transfer to shuttle buses that will take us to Dazhai Village, which was named "UNWTO Best Tourism Village" in 2022. For lunch, we'll sample oil tea and traditional dishes of the Yao ethnic minority.

Afterward, we'll begin our hike. Weather permitting, we'll enjoy a stunning sunset over the terraced fields from "Golden Buddha Peak." In the evening, we'll have dinner in Dazhai, tasting local specialties such as "medicinal chicken" and other regional delicacies.

Day3 Longji Dazhai - Nanwei Tiankeng Cave Traversing (南圩天坑穿岩) - Dawei Ancient Town (大圩古镇)
Driving: 140km, 3 hours
Trekking: 9km, 150m ascent/desent, 5 hours

After breakfast, we drive to Nanwei and begin our hike. We'll enter the mouth of the underground river, venture into the sinkhole, and climb to the entrance of the "cave passage."

As we explore the caves and underground rivers, we'll reach the summit to enjoy breathtaking views of the "Xitang" reservoir, where karst peaks are mirrored in the water. After the hike, we'll drive to Dawei Ancient Town to check into our hotel, where you'll have time to relax, watch the sunset, and explore at your leisure.

Day4 Dawei Ancient Town - Yangdi Xianei Village (杨堤下内村) - Li River Trek - Xingping Ancient Town (兴坪古镇)
Trekking: 16km, 8 hours
Driving: 65km, 1.5 hours

After breakfast, we drive south to Yangdi Xianei Village to begin our Li River trek. At noon, we'll enjoy a simple meal at a farmhouse in Quanjiazhou (全家洲, Quánjiāzhōu).

Afterward, we'll continue hiking to our endpoint at Nine Horses Fresco Hill. In the evening, we'll stay at a guesthouse in Xingping Ancient Town. Early the next morning, if you wish, you can hike up the popular Xianggong Mountain (相公山, Xiànggōng Shān) to witness the stunning Li River sunrise.

Day5 Xingping Ancient Town - Luotian Cave Traversing (罗田溶洞) - Xingping Ancient Town
Trekking: 8km, 180m ascent/desent, 5 hours

After breakfast, we begin hiking—traversing Luotian Cave. This is a primitive natural cave where we'll explore stalactites and other natural rock formations.

After cave exploration, we hike down the mountain and drive back to our guesthouse. You can visit Xingping's famous scenic spot (the background scene on the 20 yuan RMB note) or explore Xingping Ancient Town on your own. In the evening, we'll enjoy special Li River cuisine prepared by a private chef.

Day6 Xingping Ancient Town - Via Ferrata - Bamboo Rafting - Guilin
Driving: 120km, 2.5 hours
Rafting: 50 min | Ferrata: 2 hours

After breakfast, we drive to Yangshuo, China's rock climbing mecca, to experience the thrill of ferrata, "dancing on the rock face." Around noon, we'll enjoy lunch together at Gongnong Bridge (工农桥, Gōngnóng Qiáo).

Afterward, we'll head to the dock to board bamboo rafts and drift down the scenic section of the Yulong River (遇龙河, Yùlóng Hé). Finally, we'll transfer you to the train station or airport for your departure.

Important Notes
- Best Season: Year-round
- Suitable For: Healthy individuals aged 8-65 years
- Potential Risks: Be cautious of slippery roads when it rains and take care to avoid falling.

1

48. Guangdong-Hong Kong-Macau Four-City Traverse

28km/7days [粤港澳四城穿越, Yuè-Gǎng-Ào Sì Chéng Chuānyuè]

Shenzhen
[深圳, Shēnzhèn]
Gathering City

12KM
Longest Single-Day Hike

450M
Maximum Daily Elevation Gain

554M
Highest Elevation Along the Route

★★★★⯪
Scenic Rating

★★
Difficulty Level

Away from the concrete jungle, setting aside packed schedules, we always yearn for a quiet haven amid our busy urban lives. The Guangdong-Hong Kong-Macau four-city traverse hiking route is an excellent choice that seamlessly connects cities with nature. Here you are close to international metropolises, bright lights, and prosperity. Beyond the office buildings lies expansive, secluded countryside and the azure sea. This route offers a different way to explore the Greater Bay Area. Rather than focusing on urban prosperity and bustle, we choose to immerse in mountains and seas, discovering urban natural aesthetics through outdoor activities.

In its early development, Hong Kong wisely preserved nearly three-quarters of its natural countryside, avoiding excessive urbanization. Over time, while the city has become known for its densely packed skyscrapers, large expanses of natural countryside have been preserved and transformed into world-class country parks and hiking trails, maintaining rich biodiversity. This abundant countryside gives Hong Kong a unique blend of urban and natural aesthetics, offering a much-needed escape for residents living in the city's confined spaces.

Natural Features

Before entering Hong Kong, we'll first hike an entry-level coastal route–the Shenzhen Dong and Xi Chong coastal trail (深圳东西冲海岸线, Shēnzhèn Dōngxī Chōng Hǎi'àn Xiàn). It has been selected by *China National Geographic magazine* as one of the most beautiful coastlines in China and is one of China's most classic coastal hiking routes. Located at the southernmost tip of Dapeng Peninsula (大鹏半岛, Dàpéng Bàndǎo) in Shenzhen, it's about 80 kilometers from the city center. Dong Chong and Xi Chong, also known as Dongyong Beach (东涌海滩, Dōngchōng Hǎitān) and Xiyong Beach (西涌海滩, Xīchōng Hǎitān), serve as the starting and ending points of the hiking route, respectively.

The total length is about 6 kilometers, including a coastal section of about 4 kilometers, taking 5-6 hours to complete. The route follows mountains and coasts, with few beaches but many reefs, offering views of coastal erosion landforms such as rocks, caves, and pillars. The scenery is beautiful, and the sea breeze is refreshing.

After leaving the Shenzhen Dong and Xi Chong coastal trail, we'll enter Hong Kong. The MacLehose Trail (麦理浩径, Màilǐhào Jìng), the earliest long-distance hiking trail in Hong Kong, has a 44-year history. Named after Sir Murray MacLehose, the former Governor of Hong Kong, it is one of the 20 best hiking trails in the world according to National Geographic magazine.

The MacLehose Trail is 100 kilometers long, starting from Pak Tam Chung (北潭涌, Běitán Yǒng) in Sai Kung and crossing the New Territories from east to west, ending in Tuen Mun (屯门, Túnmén). The trail is divided into ten sections, each ranging from 5 to 16 kilometers, with various scenery along the way. Section 2 is the most beautiful and is the first choice for visitors to know country parks of Hong Kong.

The MacLehose Trail crosses 8 of 24 country parks in Hong Kong and traverses more than 20 peaks, including the 420-meter-high Buffalo's Ear Rock (牛耳石山, Niú'ěr Shí Shān), the 702-meter-high Ma On Shan (马鞍山, Mǎ'ān Shān), the 649-meter-high Grassy Hill (草山, Cǎo Shān), and the 957-meter-high Tai Mo Shan (大帽山, Dàmào Shān). While preserving the natural, pristine landscape, this route also offers basic needs to hikers, with trail markers along the way, rest areas at each section, and even multiple stores providing supplies.

Hong Kong has 263 outlying islands, each with its own unique character and landscape. Cheung Chau (长洲岛, Chángzhōu Dǎo), which still preserves its fishing port character, is a holiday destination for Hong Kong locals to escape the hustle and bustle.

Cheung Chau is located in the southwestern waters of Hong Kong Island and got its name from its long, strip-like shape. It is the hometown of Lee Lai Shan, the gold medalist in sailing at the 1996 Atlanta Olympics, and also the hometown of the classic animated character "McDull" (麦兜, Màidōu). Most people who come to Cheung Chau spend their time eating seafood, enjoying the sea breeze, and drinking coffee in the bustling area near the pier. But if you walk to the eastern side of the island, you'll discover a hiking trail with stunning sea views that very few people know about, where you can be rewarded with unexpectedly magnificent ocean views.

Since we're visiting Hong Kong, this international metropolis, it's essential to explore the urban streets and experience its vibrant prosperity, in addition to hiking. If shopping is on your agenda, Tsim Sha Tsui (尖沙咀, Jiānshāzuǐ) is a must-visit shopping paradise. With malls like Harbor City (海港城, Hǎigǎng Chéng), Mira Mall (美丽华商场, Měilìhuá Shāngchǎng), and the DFS

Global Duty-Free Center, your shopping desires will be fully satisfied. For those interested in celebrity culture, a stroll along the Avenue of Stars (星光大道, Xīngguāng Dàdào) is highly recommended. And if you're seeking breathtaking night views, Victoria Peak (太平山, Tàipíng Shān) is undoubtedly the best choice.

After completing the Hong Kong itinerary, we'll head to Zhuhai (珠海, Zhūhǎi) and Macau (澳门, Àomén), and of course, we'll cross the famous Hong Kong-Zhuhai-Macau Bridge.

Cultural Significance

The Hong Kong-Zhuhai-Macau Bridge is also one of the highlights of this journey. This bridge-tunnel project, connecting Hong Kong, Zhuhai, and Macau, is located in the Lingdingyang area of Guangdong Province and is the southern section of the ring expressway of Pearl River Delta region. We'll take the Hong Kong-Zhuhai-Macau Bridge bus from Hong Kong to Zhuhai, experiencing this historic engineering marvel up close.

Born from the sea, Zhuhai is a city naturally imbued with a romantic charm. With its hundreds of islands and rows of coconut trees lining the coastal boulevard, the gently swaying waters create an atmosphere of tranquility–beautiful and romantic to the extreme.

Afterward, we'll cross into Macau from Zhuhai, where we can visit the hidden gem of a country park–Taipa Grande (大潭山, Dàtán Shān). From the hilltop of Taipa Grande, you'll enjoy panoramic views, offering a stunning perspective of Macau's beautiful landscape. In addition, Macau's old town area, the Ruins of St. Paul's (大三巴, Dàsānbā), and the fortress are also very worth visiting.

Notable Attractions

1 Tsim Sha Tsui
[尖沙咀, Jiānshāzuǐ]

Hong Kong is a shopping paradise, featuring Harbor City, Mira Mall, the DFS Global Duty-Free Center, and more, catering to a wide range of shopping needs across various categories and price points.

Whether you're hunting for great deals or simply strolling along the Avenue of Stars, you can place your hand on the handprints of Hong Kong celebrities along the railings, connecting with the stars of a bygone era.

2 Victoria Peak
[太平山, Tàipíng Shān]

Located in the northwest of Hong Kong Island, Victoria Peak is one of the city's most iconic landmarks. Standing at 373 meters, the peak offers stunning views of Hong Kong Island and the Kowloon Peninsula on either side of Victoria Harbour.

The area is also home to the residences of dignitaries and celebrities. At dusk, the sunset casts a golden glow over the city, dressing it in a new light. After sunset, the lights of Victoria Harbour dazzle, offering a breathtaking view of Hong Kong's transformation into a glittering international metropolis.

3 Ruins of St. Paul's
[大三巴, Dàsānbā]

Macau's landmark historical site, where you can feel the beauty of Baroque architecture and history.

2

Itinerary

Day1 Gather in Shenzhen (深圳)

Day2 Shenzhen - Dongxi Chong Coastal Traverse (东西冲穿越) - Shenzhen
Driving: 170km, 4 hours
Trekking: 7km, 5 hours

After breakfast, we drive to DongyongVillage on Shenzhen's Dapeng Peninsula and begin hiking "the most beautiful coastal route in Shenzhen," the Dongxi Chong Coastal Traverse.

The route mainly consists of dirt paths and stone paths, with some sections requiring climbing with hands and feet, offering an excellent experience and allowing you to enjoy the views of Shenzhen's coastline along the way. We'll have lunch on the trail, and in the afternoon, we'll drive back to downtown Shenzhen.

Day3 Shenzhen - Cross the Border to Hong Kong - Sai Kung Pier (西贡码头) - Wong Shek Pier (黄石码头) - Camp
Transit: 3 hours

We gather at the hotel at 8 AM and depart, crossing into Hong Kong via Futian Port (福田口岸, Fútián Kǒu'àn). From there, we'll take a bus to Sai Kung, where we'll enjoy fresh seafood and purchase supplies at Sai Kung Pier around noon.

Afterward, we'll head to Wong Shek Pier and take a boat to our island camping site.

Day4 Camp - MacLehose Trail Section 2 (麦理浩径第二段) - Hong Kong Urban Hotel
Transit: 4 hours
Trekking: 9km, 400m ascent, 5 hours

After breakfast, we'll board a boat to the starting point of our hike and begin trekking the most scenic section of the MacLehose Trail, Section 2. We'll pass through Ham Tin Wan (咸田湾, Xián Tián Wān) and Sai Wan (西湾, Xī Wān). Along the way, there are shops where trekkers can purchase any necessary supplies. Once the hike is complete, we'll take a bus back to our hotel. The evening will be free for you to explore at your leisure.

Day5 Hotel - Cheung Chau Island Trek (长洲岛徒步) - Victoria Peak (太平山顶) - Hotel
Trekking: 12km, 4 hours

After breakfast, we'll take transportation to Central Pier No. 5 (中环 5 号码头, Zhōnghuán 5 Hào Mǎtóu) to catch a ferry to Cheung Chau Island for a hike, enjoying the scenic beauty of the outlying islands. We'll have lunch on the island before returning to Central by ferry in the afternoon.

With the guide's assistance, we'll then hike a peaceful path up to Victoria Peak, where we'll witness the breathtaking transition from sunset to nightfall and enjoy the stunning night view of Victoria Harbour—one of the three most beautiful night views in the world. After descending, we'll return to the hotel or enjoy free time to explore.

Day6 Hotel - Free Time - Hong Kong-Zhuhai-Macau Bridge (港珠澳大桥) - Zhuhai (珠海)
Transit: 2 hours

The morning is free for your own activities. At noon, we'll gather at the hotel and take a bus across the Hong Kong-Zhuhai-Macau Bridge to Zhuhai, where we'll check into our hotel.

After dinner, you'll have free time to explore. We recommend a visit to Lovers' Road (情侣路, Qínglǚ Lù) or the iconic Grand Lisboa (大贝壳, Dà Bèiké).

Day7 Zhuhai - Macau City Walk - Zhuhai

After breakfast, we'll gather at the hotel, and then walk to the Gongbei Port (拱北口岸, Gǒngběi Kǒu'àn). In Macau, we'll take a bus to the starting point of our hike and begin our one-day City Walk.

At noon, we'll taste local cuisine at a Macau food street, and in the afternoon, we'll return to Zhuhai where the group will disperse.

Important Notes

- Best Season: October to May of the following year
- Suitable For: Healthy individuals aged 7-65 years
- Potential Risks: Some sections of the Dong and Xi Chong hike are steep, please be cautious.

49. Hong Kong Four Trails Traverse

[香港四径连穿, Xiānggǎng Sì Jìng Lián Chuān] `53km/6days`

Shenzhen
[深圳, Shēnzhèn]
Gathering City

15KM
Longest Single-Day Hike

900M
Maximum Daily Elevation Gain

869M
Highest Elevation Along the Route

★★★★⯪
Scenic Rating

★★★
Difficulty Level

Credit
Image 1/2 | ©Ningle
Image 3/4 | ©Xiaohai

Hong Kong, world-renowned for its vibrant urban charm, still preserves three-quarters of its land as undeveloped, with 70% of the area covered in forests. With numerous offshore fishing villages and scenic hiking trails, it remains a highly regarded destination for outdoor enthusiasts, both in China and abroad.

You might wonder: what is all that undeveloped land used for? The answer is simple—it's preserved to prevent excessive development and maintain these areas as natural countryside.

For example, in eastern Hong Kong, stretching from the northeastern New Territories to Sai Kung (西贡, Xīgòng), you'll find volcanic rocks formed by eruptions 16,000 years ago, now recognized by UNESCO as a Global Geopark. This area showcases typical island landscapes, where the waves and mountains merge seamlessly, offering uninterrupted views of the horizon where the sea meets the sky.

Natural Features

Due to its proximity to the ocean, the elevation rises abruptly from sea level, giving the mountains impressive stature despite their relatively modest absolute elevation, creating a sense of steep magnificence. The well-conserved land over the past century has also protected the animals inhabiting it, providing hikers with delightful surprises along the way.

Hong Kong's abundant mountain resources attract countless outdoor enthusiasts. Many visitors come specifically for hiking, drawn by the four classic main trails that form the backbone of the city's entire trail system. These trails span a total of 298 kilometers, crossing beaches, rugged coastlines, dense forests, and undulating mountain ranges that reach nearly a thousand meters in height.

Cultural Significance

If you're looking to fully experience the essence of Hong Kong's wilderness and natural beauty in a single visit, the Hong Kong Four Trails Traverse is your ideal choice.

This route features prime sections of Hong Kong's four major hiking trails, spanning 6 days and 5 nights. With 5 hiking sections totaling 53 kilometers and a cumulative elevation gain of over 3,000 meters, it's designed for outdoor enthusiasts with some experience.

Each day's hike covers about 10 kilometers, with a well-paced itinerary that ensures a great experience. Along the way, you'll be treated to the breathtaking mountain and sea views of Hong Kong's four iconic trails, all in one journey!

Notable Attractions

1 Lantau Trail
[凤凰径, Fènghuáng Jìng]

The Lantau Trail, which starts and ends at Mui Wo (梅窝, Méiwō) on Lantau Island (大屿山, Dàyǔshān), was officially opened in 1984. Located on Hong Kong's largest island, the trail is named after Lantau Peak, the highest point on the island. Spanning 70 kilometers, the Lantau Trail is divided into twelve sections, beginning in Mui Wo on the easternmost part of Lantau Island and looping around the island in a counterclockwise direction.

2 MacLehose Trail
[麦理浩径, Màilǐhào Jìng]

As Hong Kong's earliest long-distance trail, it now has been opened for 44 years. Named after the then-Governor of Hong Kong, Sir Murray MacLehose, it is one of the world's 20 best hiking trails as selected by *National Geographic magazine*.

The MacLehose Trail stretches 100 kilometers, starting at Pak Tam Chung (北潭涌, Běitán Yǒng) in Sai Kung and crossing the New Territories from east to west, ending in Tuen Mun (屯门, Túnmén). The trail is divided into ten sections, ranging from 5 to 16 kilometers each, offering diverse scenery along the way. Section 2 is considered the most beautiful and is the top choice for visitors looking to experience Hong Kong's country parks.

The MacLehose Trail crosses 8 of Hong Kong's 24 country parks and traverses more than 20 peaks, including the 420-meter-high Buffalo's Ear Rock (牛耳石山, Niú'ěr Shí Shān), the 702-meter-high Ma On Shan (马鞍山, Mǎ'ān Shān), the 649-meter-high Grassy Hill (草山, Cǎo Shān), and the 957-meter-high Tai Mo Shan (大帽山, Dàmào Shān). While preserving its natural, pristine landscape, this route also offers basic needs to trekkers, with trail markers along the way, rest areas at each section, and even multiple stores providing supplies.

2

3 Wilson Trail
[卫奕信径, Wèiyìxìn Jìng]

The Wilson Trail, stretching 78 kilometers from Stanley (赤柱, Chìzhù) on Hong Kong Island to Nam Chung (南涌, Nán Chōng) in the New Territories, is Hong Kong's second-longest trail after the MacLehose Trail. Officially opened in 1996 and named after Hong Kong's 27th Governor, Sir David Wilson, it is divided into ten sections, mainly distributed in the east-central area of New Territories, crossing eight country parks.

Along the way, there are relaxing sections suitable for families with elderly and young members, as well as very steep climbing paths. There are ancient trails that delve deep into forests and undulating mountain ranges, offering rich and varied scenery.

4 Hong Kong Trail
[港岛径, Gǎngdǎo Jìng]

The Hong Kong Trail, running 45 kilometers from Victoria Peak (太平山顶, Tàipíng Shāndǐng) to Big Wave Bay (石澳大浪湾, Shí'ào Dàlàng Wān), was officially opened in 1985. The Hong Kong Trail is 45 kilometers long, divided into eight sections. The longest section is less than 10 kilometers, while the shortest is 4.5 kilometers, with no camping sites along the entire route. The Hong Kong Trail is much easier compared to the MacLehose and Wilson Trails.

It doesn't have the elevation of Tai Mo Shan or the steepness of Lantau Peak (凤凰山, Fènghuáng Shān). Winding through forests and stone houses, it offers experiences of both urban prosperity and countryside tranquility. Section 8 of the Hong Kong Trail is quite famous, requiring only about 4 hours to complete, and is often the first choice for many foreign visitors hiking in Hong Kong.

It has been selected by the travel guide *Lonely Planet* as one of "Hong Kong's Best Hiking Routes" and is also one of the "Five Beginner Hiking Routes on Hong Kong Island" recommended by CNN Travel.

Itinerary

Day1 Gather in Shenzhen (深圳)

Day2 Shenzhen - Cross the Border to Hong Kong - MacLehose Trail Section 1 (麦理浩径一段) - Beach Camping
Trekking: 15km, 7 hours

After breakfast, we gather and depart for Hong Kong. We take transportation to the starting point of the MacLehose Trail, enjoying the scenery of High Island Reservoir (万宜水库, Wànyí Shuǐkù). Along the way, we pass Broken Island (破边洲, Pòbiān Zhōu).

After lunch, we continue forward, passing Long Ke Wan (浪茄湾, Làngjiā Wān), crossing Sai Wan Shan (西湾山, Xīwān Shān), and arriving at our beach campsite in the evening.

Day3 Beach Camp - MacLehose Trail Section 2 (麦理浩径二段) - Sai Kung Pier (西贡码头) - New Territories Hotel
Trekking: 9km, 600m ascent, 4 hours

After breakfast at the campsite, we gather and depart. Today we'll walk through Sai Wan (西湾, Xīwān) and Ham Tin Wan (咸田湾, Xiántián Wān), two of the beautiful "Four Bays of Tai Long" (大浪四湾, Dàlàng Sìwān), with distant views of Sharp Peak (蚺蛇尖, Ránshé Jiān), Hong Kong's most dangerous peak.

Then we pass through the ancient village of Chek Keng (赤径, Chìjìng), arriving at Pak Tam Au (北潭凹, Běitán Āo), the endpoint of Section 2 of the MacLehose Trail, by noon. We'll take transportation to Sai Kung Pier for a seafood feast, then take transportation to our hotel in the New Territories.

Day4 New Territories Hotel - Wilson Trail Section 9 Pat Sin Leng (卫奕信径9段八仙岭) - New Territories Hotel
Trekking: 12km, 900m ascent, 7 hours

Today we'll hike the prime section of Hong Kong's second-longest trail, the Wilson Trail—Pat Sin Leng (八仙岭, Bāxiān Lǐng). From the ridge, we can see the "Eight Immortals Crossing the Sea" (八仙过海, Bāxiān Guòhǎi) and look across the sea to Shenzhen.

This is an adventure filled with natural greenery and magnificent views. With the sunset, we'll reach the endpoint at Tai Mei Tuk (大美督, Dàměidū) around 5 PM, then return to our hotel in the New Territories by vehicle.

Day5 New Territories Hotel - Hong Kong Trail Section 8 Dragon's Back Hike (港岛径8段龙脊徒步) - Shek O (石澳) - Hong Kong Island Hotel
Trekking: 8km, 450m ascent, 4 hours

Today we'll hike Section 8 of the Hong Kong Trail, the Dragon's Back segment, which has been rated by *TIME* magazine as Asia's best urban hiking trail. We'll climb to the top of Shek O Peak (打烂埕顶山, Dǎlàn Chéng Dǐng Shān).

The ridge path undulates like the back of a flying dragon. After the hike, we'll take transportation to Shek O Village (石澳村, Shí'ào Cūn), and after our visit, we'll travel to our hotel on Hong Kong Island.

Day6 Hong Kong Island Hotel - Central Pier (中环码头 - Mui Wo (梅窝) - Lantau Trail Sunset Peak (凤凰径大东山) - Urban Area
Trekking: 9km, 780m ascent, 4 hours

After breakfast, we gather and take transportation and a ferry to hike Sunset Peak (大东山, Dàdōng Shān), a popular spot nicknamed "Eason Chan Mountain" (referring to the famous Hong Kong singer). This is the most beautiful Section 2 of Hong Kong's third-longest trail, the Lantau Trail.

Looking out, the golden sea of silver grass against the mountain-top stone houses creates a uniquely charming landscape. In the afternoon, we return to the hotel where the group will disperse.

Important Notes

- Best Season: October to May of the following year
- Suitable For: Healthy individuals aged 12-65 years
- Potential Risks: Trails can be muddy during the rainy season, be cautious of slippery surfaces.

50. MacLehose Trail 100km

6days
100km

[麦理浩径百公里, Màilǐhào Jìng Bǎi Gōnglǐ]

Shenzhen
[深圳, Shēnzhèn]
Gathering City

22.5KM
Longest Single-Day Hike

1,380M
Maximum Daily Elevation Gain

957M
Highest Elevation Along the Route

★★★★
Scenic Rating

★★★⯪
Difficulty Level

When it comes to densely populated areas in China, many might first think of Hong Kong. However, Hong Kong's high population density isn't due to a lack of land, but rather the result of its many mountains. Hong Kong residents value these mountains, choosing to live in compact spaces rather than encroach on the pristine wilderness. The dazzling lights on both sides of Victoria Harbour illuminate the never-sleeping "Asian Financial Center" and "Shopping Paradise," but the bustling, shoulder-to-shoulder crowds of Kowloon and Hong Kong Island make up only one-fourth of the city. Paradoxically, this land—worth its weight in gold—is also home to interconnected mountains, seas, shoals, dense forests, and peaks. The countryside, which makes up three-fourths of Hong Kong's total area, represents the lesser-seen side of the city.

Today, Hong Kong has 24 country parks and over 100 hiking trails, ranking first in Asia. Among these, the MacLehose Trail (麦理浩径, Màilǐhào Jìng) is Hong Kong's first 100-kilometer long-distance trail. It is both Hong Kong's first hiking trail and its longest, officially opened in 1979 and named after Sir Murray MacLehose, the Governor of Hong Kong. Crossing mountains and seas, it has been rated by National Geographic as one of the world's 20 best hiking trails.

Natural Features

The MacLehose Trail is 100 kilometers long, starting from Pak Tam Chung (北潭涌, Běitán chōng) in Sai Kung (西贡, Xīgòng) and traversing the New Territories from east to west, ending in Tuen Mun (屯门, Túnmén). Many Hong Kong trail running and mountain racing events are also held on the MacLehose Trail. This route is divided into ten sections, each ranging from 5 to 16 kilometers.

Section	Trail	Distance
1	Pak Tam Chung – Long Ke (浪茄)	10.6km
2	Long Ke – Pak Tam Au (北潭凹)	13.5km
3	Pak Tam Au – Kei Ling Ha (企岭下)	10.2km
4	Kei Ling Ha – Gilwell Campsite (基维尔营地)	12.7km
5	Gilwell Campsite – Tai Po Road (大埔公路)	10.6km
6	Tai Po Road – Shing Mun Reservoir (城门水塘)	4.6km
7	Shing Mun Reservoir – Lead Mine Pass (铅矿坳)	6.2km
8	Lead Mine Pass – Tsuen Kam Highway (荃锦公路)	9.7km
9	Tsuen Kam Highway – Tin Fu Tsai (田夫仔)	6.3km
10	Tin Fu Tsai – Tuen Mun (屯门)	15.6km

The MacLehose Trail crosses 8 of Hong Kong's 24 country parks and traverses more than 20 peaks, including the 420m-high Buffalo's Ear Rock (牛耳石山, Niú'ěr Shí Shān), the 702m-high Ma On Shan (马鞍山, Mǎ'ān Shān), the 649m-high Grassy Hill (草山, Cǎo Shān), and the 957m-high Tai Mo Shan (大帽山, Dàmào Shān). While preserving its natural, pristine landscape, this route also offers basic needs to trekkers, with trail markers along the way, rest areas at each section, and even multiple stores providing supplies.

Following the markers, you'll encounter mountain paths, stone steps, and well-preserved ancient trails. Different types of paths wind between the many hills of western Sai Kung. Completing the entire trail is undoubtedly arduous, but the path blends perfectly with nature, full of charm, and offers a comprehensive experience of Hong Kong's hiking culture.

Itinerary

Day1 Gather in Shenzhen (深圳)

Day2 Shenzhen - Cross the Border to Hong Kong - MacLehose Trail Sections 1 & 2 - Sai Wan Campsite (西湾营地)
Trekking: 16km, 600m ascent, 5 hours

We will gather in Shenzhen and depart for Hong Kong, where we will take transportation to the starting point of the MacLehose Trail—Pak Tam Chung.

Our hike will cover Section 1 and the first half of Section 2 of the trail. We'll first pass by the stunning High Island Reservoir (万宜水库, Wànyí Shuǐkù) and then make our way to Long Ke Wan (浪茄湾, Làngjiā Wān). Finally, we'll reach Sai Wan Campsite, where we'll set up camp and enjoy the breathtaking, unobstructed sea view.

Day3 Sai Wan Campsite - MacLehose Trail Sections 2 & 3 - Shui Long Wo (水浪窝) - Sha Tin Hotel (沙田酒店)
Trekking: 19km, 900m ascent, 7 hours

We continue along Section 2, which is considered the prime section of the MacLehose Trail due to its stunning scenery. Entering Section 3, you'll need to climb several high mountains in western Sai Kung, with views of Chek Keng Hau (赤径口, Chìjìng Kǒu), Sai Kung Sea, Tsam Chuk Wan (斩竹湾, Zhǎnzhú Wān), and Kei Ling Ha Sea, as well as distant views of Sharp Peak (蚺蛇尖, Ránshé Jiān) and Ma On Shan.

Today, you only need to hike to the endpoint of Section 3, Shui Long Wo Campsite, making it relatively easy.

Day4 Sha Tin Hotel - Kei Ling Ha - MacLehose Trail Sections 4 & 5 - Tai Po Road - Sha Tin Hotel
Trekking: 22.5km, 1140m ascent, 8 hours

Today, you'll tackle Sections 4 and 5 of the MacLehose Trail, making it the most challenging day of the trip due to the long distance, significant elevation gain, tight schedule, and demanding terrain.

We'll start as early as possible, continuously climbing mountain paths and stone steps to reach the southern ridge of Ma On Shan. After this, the terrain becomes more gradual as the trail winds between hills.

Upon entering Section 5, there's a steep uphill segment, during which you'll be treated to views of iconic peaks such as Tate's Cairn (大老山, Dàlǎo Shān), Kowloon Peak (飞鹅山, Fēi'é Shān), Lion Rock (狮子山, Shīzi Shān), and Beacon Hill (笔架山, Bǐjià Shān). From the Beacon Hill viewing platform, you can enjoy a panoramic view of Hong Kong.

The endpoint of today's hike is Tai Po Road, at the end of Section 5. However, there are no legal campsites in this section, so after reaching the endpoint, we will take transportation to the Sha Tin Hotel for the night.

Day5 Sha Tin Hotel - Tai Po Road - MacLehose Trail Sections 6, 7 & 8 - Tsuen Kam Highway - Sha Tin Hotel
Trekking: 20.5km, 1380m ascent, 8 hours

Today, you'll tackle Sections 6, 7, and 8 of the MacLehose Trail. Although the distance is slightly shorter than yesterday, the cumulative elevation gain exceeds 1,300 meters, making it another physically demanding day. We will begin by taking transportation to yesterday's endpoint and then continue hiking Section 6. This section mostly consists of road paths, with monkeys often seen along the way—be sure not to provoke them.

In Section 7, you'll pass Needle Hill (针山, Zhēn Shān) and Grassy Hill, where some parts of the trail run along exposed ridges without tree cover, making it easy to get sunburned, so be sure to take precautions.

Finally, in Section 8, you'll reach the summit of Tai Mo Shan, Hong Kong's highest peak, standing at 957 meters above sea level.

After taking in the views, the trail becomes a long downhill stretch, leading to the end of Section 8. From there, we'll take transportation to the Sha Tin Hotel for the night.

Day6 Sha Tin Hotel - Tsuen Kam Highway - MacLehose Trail Sections 9 & 10 - Trail End - Tuen Mun
Trekking: 22km, 250m ascent, 7 hours

Today marks the final day of hiking, with the trail primarily consisting of paved cement roads, making it a relatively easy walk. Along the way, you'll be able to enjoy the beautiful scenery of Hong Kong's "Thousand Island Lake"—the Tai Lam Chung Reservoir (大榄涌水塘, Dàlàn chōng Shuǐtáng)—and the striking views of Castle Peak (青山, Qīng Shān). The trail will lead you to the endpoint of the MacLehose Trail in Tuen Mun, where the group will disperse.

Tuen Mun is conveniently located just 15 kilometers from the Shenzhen Bay Port, with direct franchise buses available for easy transportation back.

Important Notes

- Best Season: October to May of the following year. (During the summer months, the heat can be intense, so please exercise caution when planning your trip)
- Suitable For: Healthy individuals aged 18-65 with some outdoor hiking and camping experience
- Potential Risks: 1. During your hike and camping, you may encounter wildlife such as wild boars, monkeys, and others.
2. Please exercise caution and avoid any close contact,to prevent disturbances, do not store food inside your tent, as wild boars may be attracted to it.

徒步帮 TUBUBANG

Bring the world to you

Tububang, One of China's leading outdoor media communities and expedition specialists. We deliver global adventures, outdoor culture storytelling, gear retail, professional training, and brand partnerships. Your one-stop solution for premium outdoor experiences worldwide.

In 2014, founder Mr. Ma Jun (known online as "行摄匆匆"), launched the Trekking in China WeChat official account, which now has over 1600,000 followers. Our multi-platform network covers WeChat Channels, Douyin, Rednote, Bilibili, YouTube, Tiktok and Instagram, producing text, images, videos and live content. Total followers across all platforms now over 1 million.

Since 2017, We established strategic partnerships with 50+ global organizations and crafted 150+ iconic trekking routes (over 100 in China). Over the past 8 years, we've hosted more than 50,000 participant visits across all expeditions.

Our company currently has more than 50 full-time employees and over 100 part-time team leaders, with offices in Shenzhen and Chengdu. The team is characterized by its youthful demographics, professional expertise, and high comprehensive capabilities, while core members possess extensive practical experience in the outdoor industry.

Our office

Chengdu Office
⚲ B238,Huacai Road n.158,Debi Chuanbao Yiyuan,Jinjiang Distrct, Chengdu,Sichuan

Shenzhen Office
⚲ B02-A,27th floor,Allianz Build,Jintian road,Futian Distrct, Shenzhen,Guangdong

Homepage

www.tububang-outdoors.com

「Trekking In China」
WeChat Official Account

「Tububang Travel」
WeChat Mini Program

Find us

小红书   GlobalTrekkingTravel

Instagram   tububangoutdoors

YouTube   TrekkinginChina

TikTok   TrekkinginChina

徒步帮 / 徒步中国 / 带你徒步世界

Inbound Contact

Margherita 菲菲
📞 +86 133 4290 0679
💬 tububang01
🟢 +86 158 6910 3963
✉ tububang_intl@163.com

Frieda 阿衡
📞 +86 176 0286 4923
💬 Friedaforward7234
🟢 +86 176 0286 4923
✉ tububang@gmail.com

The following page contains promotional content provided by Tububang, a commercial outdoor expedition service. The information is for informational and branding purposes only and does not constitute editorial endorsement.